P9-AOZ-230

STARTERS

STARTERS

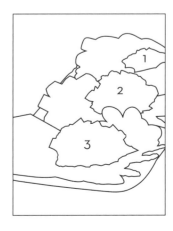

Pictured on reverse:

1. Baba Ganoush, page 4
2. Hot Crab Dip, page 7
3. Artichoke Spinach Dip, page 5

Curried Almonds

A nice curry flavour makes for very good nibbles.

Natural almonds with brown skin (325 mL, 1 1/3 cups)	1/2 lb	225 g
Hard margarine (or butter)	1 tbsp	15 mL
Salt	1/4 tsp	1 mL
Curry powder	1 1/2 tsp	7 mL

1. Place all 4 ingredients in 3.5 L (3 1/2 quart) slow cooker.

2. Cook on High to melt margarine. Stir well. Cover.

3. Cook on Low for about 2 hours. Stir.

4. Turn heat to High. Cook, uncovered, for about 1 hour, stirring halfway through. Spread on tray to cool. Makes 325 mL (1 1/3 cups).

SALTED ALMONDS:
Simply omit curry powder.

30 mL (2 tbsp): 544 Kilojoules (130 Calories); 11.7 g Total Fat; 76 mg Sodium; 4 g Protein; 4 g Carbohydrate

Sugar and Spice Pecans

These sweet, toasted treats won't stay in the dish for long.

Pecan halves	4 cups	1 L
Butter	1/3 cup	75 mL
Brown sugar, packed	1/2 cup	125 mL
Ground cinnamon	1 1/2 tsp	7 mL
Ground allspice	1/4 tsp	1 mL

1. Put pecans into 3.5 to 4 L (3 1/2 to 4 quart) slow cooker.

2. Stir butter and sugar in small saucepan on Medium until butter is melted. Stir. Pour over pecans. Stir until coated. Cook, covered, on High for 30 minutes. Stir. Reduce heat to Low. Cook, covered, for about 2 hours, stirring every 30 minutes, until pecans are glazed and golden.

3. Combine cinnamon and allspice in small cup. Sprinkle over nuts. Stir. Spread evenly on ungreased baking tray (sheet) to cool. Makes about 1 L (4 cups).

60 mL (1/4 cup): 1034 Kilojoules (247 Calories); 23.2 g Total Fat; 30 mg Sodium; 3 g Protein; 11 g Carbohydrate

Snack Mix

An easy way to whip up a bowl of very addictive munchies.

Hard margarine (or butter)	1/4 cup	60 mL
Seasoning salt	1 1/2 tsp	7 mL
Garlic powder	1/4 tsp	1 mL
Onion powder	3/4 tsp	4 mL
Celery salt	1/4 tsp	1 mL
Grated Parmesan cheese	1 tbsp	15 mL
Pretzel sticks	1 1/2 cups	375 mL
Salted peanuts	1 1/2 cups	375 mL
'O'-shaped toasted oat cereal	2 cups	500 mL
Whole wheat cereal squares	2 cups	500 mL

1. Combine first 6 ingredients in 5 L (5 quart) slow cooker. Cook on High to melt margarine. Turn heat to Low.

2. Add remaining 4 ingredients. Stir well. Cover. Cook for 3 1/2 hours. Remove cover. Stir. Cook for about 30 minutes, stirring once or twice. Makes 1.75 L (7 cups).

125 mL (1/2 cup): 812 Kilojoules (194 Calories); 12.5g Total Fat; 537 mg Sodium; 6g Protein; 17g Carbohydrate

Pacific Pecans

Dark coloured nuts with good spicy flavour.

Hard margarine (or butter)	2 tbsp	30 mL
Soy sauce	1 tbsp	15 mL
Salt	1/2 tsp	2 mL
Garlic powder	1/4 tsp	1 mL
Onion powder	1/4 tsp	1 mL
Cayenne pepper	1/8 tsp	0.5 mL
Pecan halves	2 cups	500 mL

1. Stir first 6 ingredients in 3.5 L (3 1/2 quart) slow cooker. Cook on High to melt margarine.

2. Add pecans. Stir well. Reduce heat to Low. Cover. Cook for 1 1/2 hours, stirring halfway through. Turn heat to High. Remove cover. Cook for 20 minutes, stirring twice. Spread on tray to cool. Makes 500 mL (2 cups).

30 mL (2 tbsp): 444 Kilojoules (106 Calories); 10.8 g Total Fat; 161 mg Sodium; 1 g Protein; 3 g Carbohydrate

Chilli Snack Mix

This crunchy treat balances sweet and spicy flavours,
and is great for all ages. It will disappear fast when snack time arrives!

'O'-shaped toasted oat cereal	2 cups	500 mL
Small pretzels	2 cups	500 mL
Butter (or hard margarine), melted	1/4 cup	60 mL
Chilli seasoning mix, stir before measuring	2 tbsp	30 mL
Trail mix	2 cups	500 mL

1. Combine first 4 ingredients in 3.5 to 4 L (3 1/2 to 4 quart) slow cooker. Cook, covered, on High for 30 minutes. Stir. Cook, covered, on Low for 1 to 1 1/2 hours, stirring every 20 minutes, until crisp and golden. Spread on ungreased baking tray (sheet) to cool. Transfer to large bowl.

2. Add trail mix. Stir. Makes about 1.5 L (6 cups).

75 mL (1/3 cup): 557 Kilojoules (133 Calories); 7.9 g Total Fat; 174 mg Sodium; 3 g Protein; 14 g Carbohydrate

Cajun-Spiced Nuts

The spicy heat of Cajun seasoning pairs well with the
roasted crunch of this flavourful, nutty snack.

Raw cashews	1 1/2 cups	375 mL
Whole natural almonds	1 1/2 cups	375 mL
Pecan halves	1 cup	250 mL
Butter (or hard margarine), melted	1/4 cup	60 mL
Cajun seasoning	2 tbsp	30 mL

Combine all 5 ingredients and a sprinkle of salt in 3.5 to 4 L (3 1/2 to 4 quart) slow cooker. Cook, covered, on Low for 2 hours. Stir well. Cook, covered, on High for about 1 hour, stirring occasionally, until nuts are browned. Spread on ungreased baking tray (sheet) to cool and crisp. Makes about 1 L (4 cups).

60 mL (1/4 cup): 909 Kilojoules (217 Calories); 19.8 g Total Fat; 262 mg Sodium; 5 g Protein; 8 g Carbohydrate

Nacho Cheese Fondue

Serve with cubed bread or corn (nacho) chips straight from the slow cooker on the lowest setting, or transfer to a serving bowl.

Processed cheese spread	2 cups	500 mL	Finely chopped red pepper (capsicum)	1/2 cup	125 mL	
Finely chopped roasted red capsicum in cream cheese (roasted red pepper cream cheese)	1 cup	250 mL	Can of diced green chillies	4 oz	113 g	
Salsa	1 cup	250 mL				

Combine all 5 ingredients in 3.5 to 4 L (3 1/2 to 4 quart) slow cooker. Cook, covered, on Low for 2 to 3 hours or on High for 1 to 1 1/2 hours until heated through. Makes about 1.25 L (5 cups).

60 mL (1/4 cup): 444 Kilojoules (106 Calories); 8.4 g Total Fat; 291 mg Sodium; 4 g Protein; 4 g Carbohydrate

Baba Ganoush

Cooking up this exotic favourite doesn't get any easier than with the slow cooker. Try it hot or cold and serve with fresh pita or pita chips.

Chopped, peeled Asian eggplant (aubergine)	5 cups	1.25 L
Garlic cloves, minced	2	2
Ground cumin	1 tsp	5 mL
Olive oil, divided	3 tbsp	50 mL
Lemon juice	1 tbsp	15 mL

1. Combine first 3 ingredients, 30 mL (2 tbsp) olive oil, 60 mL (1/4 cup) water and a generous sprinkle of salt and pepper in 3.5 to 4 L (3 1/2 to 4 quart) slow cooker. Cook, covered, on Low for 4 to 6 hours or on High for 2 to 3 hours, stirring once at halftime, until soft and fragrant.

2. Transfer to blender or food processor. Add lemon juice and remaining olive oil. Process until smooth (see Safety Tip). Makes about 425 mL (1 3/4 cups).

Pictured between pages 16 & 17 and before page 1.

SAFETY TIP: Follow blender manufacturer's instructions for processing hot liquids.

75 mL (1/3 cup): 368 Kilojoules (88 Calories); 7.9 g Total Fat; 214 mg Sodium; 1 g Protein; 5 g Carbohydrate

Artichoke Spinach Dip

Lovely wine and pesto flavours give this rich dip a real bistro feel –
it tastes fabulous served with fresh baguette slices.

Jar of marinated artichoke hearts, drained and chopped	12 oz	340 g
Herb and garlic cream cheese	1 cup	250 mL
Dry (or alcohol-free) white wine	1/2 cup	125 mL
Coarsely chopped fresh spinach leaves, lightly packed	4 cups	1 L
Basil pesto	1/4 cup	60 mL

1. Combine first 3 ingredients and a sprinkle of pepper in 3.5 to 4 L (3 1/2 to 4 quart) slow cooker. Cook, covered, on Low for 4 to 5 hours or on High for 2 to 2 1/2 hours. Stir until smooth.

2. Add spinach and pesto. Stir. Makes about 625 mL (2 1/2 cups).

Pictured between pages 16 & 17 and before page 1.

60 mL (1/4 cup): 473 Kilojoules (113 Calories); 8.8 g Total Fat; 256 mg Sodium; 3 g Protein; 4 g Carbohydrate

White Bean and Garlic Spread

For garlic lovers! Spread over crostini slices or melba toast.
One clove can be left out if you prefer a milder garlic flavour.

Dried cannellini (navy) beans	1 1/2 cups	375 mL
Italian seasoning	2 tbsp	30 mL
Large lemon	1	1
Olive oil	2 tbsp	30 mL
Garlic cloves, minced (or 1/2 tsp, 2 mL, powder)	2	2

1. Put beans into medium bowl. Add water until 5 cm (2 inches) above beans. Let stand overnight (see Tip, page 55). Drain. Rinse beans. Drain. Transfer to 3.5 to 4 L (3 1/2 to 4 quart) slow cooker.

2. Add Italian seasoning and 750 mL (3 cups) water. Cook, covered, on High for 3 1/2 to 4 hours until beans are tender (see Note). Drain, reserving 60 mL (1/4 cup) cooking liquid. Transfer beans and liquid to food processor.

3. Grate 5 mL (1 tsp) lemon zest into bean mixture. Squeeze in 30 mL (2 tbsp) lemon juice. Add olive oil, garlic and a generous sprinkle of salt and pepper. Carefully process until smooth (see Safety Tip). Makes about 875 mL (3 1/2 cups).

SAFETY TIP: Follow blender manufacturer's instructions for processing hot liquids.

NOTE: Cooking this spread on Low is not recommended, as it may not fully cook the beans.

75 mL (1/3 cup): 281 Kilojoules (67 Calories); 2.8 g Total Fat; 279 mg Sodium; 3 g Protein; 8 g Carbohydrate

Mexi Dip

When you dip down with a sturdy chip or spoon, you get different layers. This wrecks many a diet. Serve with corn (nacho) chips.

Light cream cheese, 250 g (8 oz) each, softened	2	2
Canned flakes of ham, with liquid, or shredded canned ham with liquid, mashed together	6.5 oz	184 g
Grated Cheddar cheese	3 cups	750 mL
Medium or hot salsa	1/2 cup	125 mL
Canned chopped green chillies, drained	4 oz	114 g
Chilli powder	1/2-1 tsp	2-5 mL

1. Mash cream cheese with fork in bowl. Spread in bottom of 3.5 L (3 1/2 quart) slow cooker.

2. Sprinkle ham evenly over top. Sprinkle with Cheddar cheese.

3. Stir salsa and green chillies together. Spoon over top.

4. Sprinkle with chilli powder. Cover. Cook on Low for 2 to 2 1/2 hours until quite warm. Do not stir. Makes 1 L (4 1/4 cups).

15 mL (1 tbsp): 176 Kilojoules (42 Calories); 3.4 g Total Fat; 173 mg Sodium; 2 g Protein; 1 g Carbohydrate

Refried Bean Dip

A smooth bean mixture with cheese and spring (green) onion. Serve with corn (nacho) chips and vegetables.

Refried beans (less than 1% fat)	14 oz	398 mL
Grated medium or sharp Cheddar cheese	1 cup	250 mL
Chopped spring (green) onion or scallion	1/4 cup	60 mL
Chilli powder	1 tsp	5 mL

Put beans, cheese, spring (green) onion and chilli powder into 3.5 L (3 1/2 quart) slow cooker. Stir. Cover. Cook on Low for 1 1/2 hours, stirring every 20 minutes, until melted and quite warm. Makes 500 mL (2 cups).

15 mL (1 tbsp): 121 Kilojoules (29 Calories); 1.3 g Total Fat; 77 mg Sodium; 2 g Protein; 3 g Carbohydrate

Hot Crab Dip

This tomato-topped, cheesy crab dip will be a hit at any gathering. Scoop up tasty mouthfuls with toasted baguette rounds, pita crisps or crackers.

Cream cheese, softened	1 1/2 cups	375 mL
Cans of crabmeat (170 g, 6 oz, each), drained, cartilage removed, flaked	2	2
Grated Asiago (or Parmesan) cheese	1 cup	250 mL
Diced, seeded Roma (plum) tomato	1 cup	250 mL
Finely chopped spring (green) onion	2 tbsp	30 mL

1. Combine first 3 ingredients in 3.5 to 4 L (3 1/2 to 4 quart) slow cooker. Cook, covered, on Low for about 2 hours or on High for about 1 hour, stirring twice, until heated through. Transfer to serving dish.

2. Combine tomato, onion and a sprinkle of salt in small bowl. Spoon over crab mixture. Makes about 875 mL (3 1/2 cups).

Pictured between pages 16 & 17 and before page 1.

60 mL (1/4 cup): 603 Kilojoules (144 Calories); 7.5 g Total Fat; 286 mg Sodium; 9 g Protein; 2 g Carbohydrate

Cheese Fondue

Cook fondue on Low to avoid cheese going stringy. At home, dip broccoli florets or cauliflower florets (cooked tender but crisp), or warmed frankfurt chunks into sauce.

Cheese spread (Cheddar cheese soup)	1 1/4 cups	315 mL
Grated Cheddar (Monterey Jack) cheese	1 cup	250 mL
Grated Parmesan cheese	2 tbsp	30 mL
Chopped chives	2 tbsp	30 mL
Garlic powder	1/8 tsp	0.5 mL
Cayenne pepper	1/8 tsp	0.5 mL
White wine (or alcohol-free wine or milk)	1/4 cup	60 mL

Place all ingredients in 3.5 L (3 1/2 quart) slow cooker. Stir well. Cover. Cook on Low for 2 to 2 1/2 hours until quite warm. Makes 425 mL (1 3/4 cups).

30 mL (2 tbsp) fondue: 263.8 Kilojoules (63 Calories); 4.4 g Total Fat; 215 mg Sodium; 3 g Protein; 2 g Carbohydrate

Beef Dip

Lean over bowls of dipping sauce, dunk and enjoy.

Boneless beef chuck (or blade) roast	2 1/2 lbs	1.1 kg
Boiling water		
Beef stock (bouillon) powder	4 tsp	20 mL
Onion powder	1/2 tsp	2 mL
Salt	1/2 tsp	2 mL
Pepper	1/8 tsp	0.5 mL
Hamburger buns, split (buttered, optional)	10	10

1. Place roast in 3.5 L (3 1/2 quart) slow cooker. Add boiling water until halfway up sides of roast. Cover. Cook on Low for 7 to 9 hours or on High for 3 1/2 to 4 1/2 hours. Remove roast. Strain beef juice into a heatproof container. Skim off any fat. Add hot water to beef juice, if needed, to make 750 mL (3 cups).

2. Add stock (bouillon) powder, onion powder, salt and pepper. Stir.

3. Slice beef thinly. Insert slices into each bun. Serve with a small bowl of beef juice for dipping. Makes 10 buns and 750 mL (3 cups) beef juice.

1 bun with 75 mL (1/3 cup) beef juice: 1062.6 Kilojoules (253 Calories); 8.3 g Total Fat; 636 mg Sodium; 19 g Protein; 24 g Carbohydrate

Spinach Dip

Mild and tasty, this is Popeye's favourite. Serve with chunks of bread or chips (crisps).

Light cream cheese, softened	8 oz	250 g
Light salad dressing (or mayonnaise)	1/2 cup	125 mL
Lemon juice	2 tsp	10 mL
Salt	1/2 tsp	2 mL
Garlic powder	1/8 tsp	0.5 mL
Worcestershire sauce	1/2 tsp	2 mL
Chopped spring (green) onion or scallion	1/2 cup	125 mL
Frozen chopped spinach, thawed and squeezed dry	10 oz	300 g

1. Mash first 7 ingredients together with fork in bowl.

2. Add spinach. Stir. Turn into 3.5 L (3 1/2 quart) slow cooker. Cover. Cook on Low for 1 1/2 hours, stirring every 30 minutes, until quite warm. Makes generous 500 mL (2 cups).

15 mL (1 tbsp): 121 Kilojoules (29 Calories); 2.2 g Total Fat; 149 mg Sodium; 1 g Protein; 1 g Carbohydrate

Clam Dip

A lovely subtle dip. Serve with crackers, chips (crisps) or chunks of bread.

Light cream cheese, softened	8 oz	250 g
Light sour cream	1/4 cup	60 mL
Worcestershire sauce	1 tbsp	15 mL
Grated onion	1 tbsp	15 mL
Lemon juice	1 tbsp	15 mL
Salt	1/2 tsp	2 mL
Garlic powder	1/8 tsp	0.5 mL
Canned or fresh clams, drained, minced	5 oz	142 g

1. Combine first 7 ingredients in bowl. Mix until well blended.

2. Add clams. Mix. Turn into 3.5 L (3 1/2 quart) slow cooker. Cover. Cook on Low for 1 3/4 hours, stirring occasionally, until quite warm. Makes 500 mL (2 cups).

15 mL (1 tbsp): 88 Kilojoules (21 Calories); 1.4 g Total Fat; 121 mg Sodium; 2 g Protein; 1 g Carbohydrate

Beefy Chip Dip

Thick, meaty and cheesy. Add more chilli powder to suit
your taste. Serve with corn (nacho) chips.

Lean beef mince (ground beef)	1 lb	454 g	Chilli powder	1/2 tsp	2 mL
			Onion powder	1/2 tsp	2 mL
Grated Cheddar cheese (340 g, 3/4 lb)	3 cups	750 mL			
Worcestershire sauce	2 tsp	10 mL			
Canned chopped green chillies	4 oz	114 g			
Medium or hot salsa	1 cup	250 mL			

1. Scramble-fry beef mince (ground beef) in non-stick frying pan (skillet) until no longer pink. Drain. Use fork to mash and break up beef. Turn into 3.5 L (3 1/2 quart) slow cooker.

2. Add next 6 ingredients. Stir. Cover. Cook on Low for 1 3/4 to 2 hours, stirring occasionally, until quite warm. Makes 1 L (4 cups).

15 mL (1 tbsp): 138 Kilojoules (33 Calories); 2.2 g Total Fat; 103 mg Sodium; 3 g Protein; 1 g Carbohydrate

Artichoke Dip

This cream-coloured dip has the delicious flavours of Parmesan
cheese and artichokes. Serve with chunks of bread.

Light cream cheese, softened	4 oz	125 g	Jars marinated artichoke hearts 170 g (6 oz) each, drained and chopped	2	2
Salad dressing (or mayonnaise)	1/2 cup	125 mL			
Light sour cream	1/4 cup	60 mL			
Grated Parmesan cheese	1/2 cup	125 mL			
Garlic powder	1/4 tsp	1 mL			
Onion powder	1/4 tsp	1 mL			
Chopped spring (green) onion or scallion	1 tbsp	15 mL			

1. Beat cream cheese, salad dressing and sour cream together in bowl until smooth. Stir in Parmesan cheese, garlic powder, onion powder and spring (green) onion.

2. Add artichokes. Turn into 3.5 L (3 1/2 quart) slow cooker. Cover. Cook on Low for about 2 hours, stirring occasionally, until quite warm. Makes 500 mL (2 cups).

15 mL (1 tbsp): 130 Kilojoules (31 Calories); 2.2 g Total Fat; 119 mg Sodium; 1 g Protein; 2 g Carbohydrate

Chilli Con Queso

This south-of-the-border classic is great served with corn (nacho) chips.

Processed cheese, cubed	1 lb	454 g
Canned chopped green chillies	4 oz	114 g
Medium or hot salsa	1 1/4 cups	300 mL

Combine cheese, green chillies and salsa in 3.5 L (3 1/2 quart) slow cooker. Stir. Cover. Cook on Low for 1 1/2 hours, stirring occasionally, until quite warm. Makes a generous 750 mL (3 cups).

15 mL (1 tbsp): 142 Kilojoules (34 Calories); 2.2 g Total Fat; 258 mg Sodium; 2 g Protein; 2 g Carbohydrate

Spicy Black-Eyed Pea Dip

Perfect for dipping fresh vegetables or corn (nacho) chips.
Serve warm from the slow cooker, as it will thicken as it cools.

Cans of black-eyed peas (or cannellini /navy beans) (540 g, 19 oz, each),rinsed and drained	2	2
Processed cheese block, chopped	16 oz	450 g
Hot chunky salsa	1 cup	250 mL

Taco seasoning mix, stir before measuring	1 tbsp	15 mL
Canned sliced jalapeño chillies, finely chopped	2 tsp	10 mL

Combine all 5 ingredients in 3.5 to 4 L (3 1/2 to 4 quart) slow cooker. Cook, covered, on Low for 2 to 3 hours or on High for 1 to 1 1/2 hours, stirring twice, until heated through. Break up mixture with potato masher. Makes about 1.25 L (5 cups).

60 mL (1/4 cup): 419 Kilojoules (100 Calories); 4.8 g Total Fat; 703 mg Sodium; 6 g Protein; 10 g Carbohydrate

Brown Quick Bread

A porous scone-like (biscuit-like) pre-mealtime or coffee-break treat.

Wholemeal (wheat) flour	2 cups	500 mL
Plain (all-purpose) flour	1 cup	250 mL
Baking powder	1 tbsp	15 mL
Salt	1 tsp	5 mL
Treacle (molasses)	2 tbsp	30 mL
Cooking oil	2 tbsp	30 mL
Water	1 1/3 cups	325 mL

1. Combine first 4 ingredients in bowl. Stir.

2. Add treacle (molasses), cooking oil and water. Mix until moistened. Turn into greased 5 L (5 quart) slow cooker. Place 5 paper towels between top of slow cooker and lid. Put wooden match or an object 3 mm (1/8 inch) thick between paper towels and edge of slow cooker to allow some steam to escape. Do not lift lid for the first 1 3/4 hours cooking time. Cook on High for about 2 hours. Loosen sides with knife, taking care not to scratch the slow cooker's liner. Turn out onto rack to cool. Cuts into 14 wedges.

1 wedge: 511 Kilojoules (122 Calories); 2.4 g Total Fat; 200 mg Sodium; 3 g Protein; 22 g Carbohydrate

Tomato Herb Bread

This flavourful loaf gets its colour from the tomato purée (tomato sauce).

White (granulated) sugar	1 tsp	5 mL
Warm water	1/3 cup	75 mL
Active dry yeast	1 tbsp	15 mL
Plain (all-purpose) flour	2 cups	500 mL
White (granulated) sugar	1 tbsp	15 mL
Finely minced onion	1/4 cup	60 mL
Lukewarm tomato purée (tomato sauce), plus water to make 250 mL (1 cup)	7.5 oz	213 mL
Grated sharp Cheddar cheese	1/4 cup	60 mL
Salt	1 tsp	5 mL
Pepper	1/4 tsp	1 mL
Dried oregano	1/2 tsp	2 mL
Plain (all-purpose) flour	1 cup	250 mL

1. Stir first amount of sugar into warm water in large warmed bowl. Sprinkle yeast over top. Let stand for 10 minutes. Stir to dissolve yeast.

2. Add next 8 ingredients. Beat on Low to moisten. Beat on High for 2 minutes.

3. Work in second amount of flour. Turn into greased 3.5 L (3 1/2 quart) slow cooker. Smooth top with wet spoon or hand. Place 5 paper towels between top of slow cooker and lid. Put wooden match or an object 3 mm (1/8 inch) thick between paper towels and edge of slow cooker to allow a bit of steam to escape. Do not lift lid for the first 2 hours cooking time. Cook on High for about 2 1/2 hours. Loosen sides with knife taking care not to scratch the slow cooker's liner. Turn out onto rack to cool. Cuts into 14 slices.

1 slice: 519 Kilojoules (124 Calories); 1 g Total Fat; 303 mg Sodium; 4 g Protein; 25 g Carbohydrate

Pumpernickel Bread

Dark coloured, aromatic and so good. There's no pre-rising to this.

White (granulated) sugar	1 tsp	5 mL
Warm water	1 1/3 cups	325 mL
Active dry yeast	1 tbsp	15 mL
Plain (all-purpose) flour	1 cup	250 mL
Rye flour	1 cup	250 mL
Treacle (molasses)	2 tbsp	30 mL
Cooking oil	2 tbsp	30 mL
Cocoa	2 tbsp	30 mL
Salt	1 tsp	5 mL
Caraway seed (optional)	2 tsp	10 mL
Rye flour	1 cup	250 mL

1. Stir sugar into warm water in large bowl. Sprinkle yeast over top. Let stand for 10 minutes. Stir to dissolve yeast.

2. Add next 7 ingredients. Beat on Low to moisten. Beat on High for 2 minutes.

3. Stir in second amount of rye flour. Grease bottom of 3.5 L (3 1/2 quart) slow cooker. Turn dough into cooker. Lay 5 paper towels between top of slow cooker and lid. Put wooden match or an object 3 mm (1/8 inch) thick between paper towels and edge of slow cooker to allow a bit of steam to escape.
Do not lift lid for the first 1 3/4 hours cooking time. Cook on High for about 2 hours. Loosen sides with knife, taking care not to scratch the slow cooker's liner. Turn out onto rack to cool. Cuts into 14 slices.

1 slice: 494 Kilojoules (118 Calories); 2.4 g Total Fat; 196 mg Sodium; 3 g Protein; 22 g Carbohydrate

White Bread

This bread has a touch more porous texture with the same homemade aroma and flavour as regular bread.

White (granulated) sugar	2 tsp	10 mL
Warm water	1 1/4 cups	300 mL
Active dry yeast	1 tbsp	15 mL
Plain (all-purpose) flour	2 cups	500 mL
White (granulated) sugar	2 tbsp	30 mL
Cooking oil	2 tbsp	30 mL
Salt	1 tsp	5 mL
Plain (all-purpose) flour	1 cup	250 mL

1. Stir first amount of sugar and warm water together in large bowl. Sprinkle with yeast. Let stand for 10 minutes. Stir to dissolve yeast.

2. Add first amount of flour, second amount of sugar, cooking oil and salt. Beat on Low to moisten. Beat on High for 2 minutes.

3. Knead in second amount of flour until a stiff dough forms. Grease bottom of 3.5 L (3 1/2 quart) slow cooker. Turn dough into slow cooker. Lay 5 paper towels between top of slow cooker and lid. Put wooden match or an object 3 mm (1/8 inch) thick between paper towels and edge of slow cooker to allow a bit of steam to escape. Do not lift lid for the first 1 3/4 hours cooking time. Cook on High for about 2 hours. Loosen sides with knife, taking care not to scratch the slow cooker's liner. Turn out onto rack to cool. Cuts into 16 slices.

1 slice: 481 Kilojoules (115 Calories); 2 g Total Fat; 170 mg Sodium; 3 g Protein; 21 g Carbohydrate

Cranberry Loaf

Lots of flavour and moist colourful slices make an interesting appetiser.

Large egg	1	1
Orange juice	2/3 cup	150 mL
Hard margarine (or butter), melted	2 tbsp	30 mL
White (granulated) sugar	1 cup	250 mL
Salt	1 tsp	5 mL
Vanilla essence	1/2 tsp	2 mL
Plain (all-purpose) flour	2 cups	500 mL
Baking powder	1 1/2 tsp	7 mL
Coarsely chopped fresh (or frozen, thawed, or canned in natural juice, drained) cranberries	1 cup	250 mL

1. Beat egg in bowl. Add next 5 ingredients. Beat until smooth.

2. Add flour and baking powder. Stir just to moisten.

3. Add cranberries. Stir lightly. Turn into greased 22 x 12 x 7.5 cm (9 x 5 x 3 inch) loaf pan. Set pan on wire trivet in 5 L (5 quart) oval slow cooker. Place 5 paper towels between top of slow cooker and lid. Put wooden match or an object 3 mm (1/8 inch) thick between paper towels and edge of slow cooker to allow a bit of steam to escape. Do not lift lid for at least 2 hours. Cook on High for about 2 1/2 hours until wooden pick inserted in centre comes out clean. Remove pan from slow cooker. Let stand for 20 minutes. Loosen sides with knife. Turn out onto rack to cool. Cuts into 18 slices.

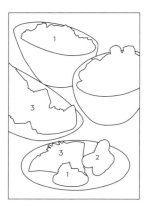

1. Red-Peppered Chorizo, page 23
2. Smokin' Smokies, page 27
3. Pork and Guacamole Tostadas, page 26

1 slice: 511 Kilojoules (122 Calories); 1.8 g Total Fat; 171 mg Sodium; 2 g Protein; 25 g Carbohydrate

Date Loaf

A large moist loaf. Spread with butter – delicious!

Boiling water	2/3 cup	150 mL
Bicarbonate soda (baking soda)	1 tsp	5 mL
Chopped dates	1 cup	250 mL
Large egg, fork-beaten	1	1
White (granulated) sugar	2/3 cup	150 mL
Hard margarine (or butter), melted	2 tbsp	30 mL
Vanilla essence	1/2 tsp	2 mL
Salt	1/4 tsp	1 mL
Plain (all-purpose) flour	1 2/3 cups	400 mL
Chopped walnuts	1/2 cup	125 mL

1. Pour boiling water over bicarbonate soda (baking soda) in bowl. Stir. Add dates. Stir. Let stand until cool.

2. Combine egg, sugar, margarine, vanilla and salt in separate bowl. Beat. Add date mixture. Stir.

3. Add flour and walnuts. Stir. Turn into greased 22 x 12 x 7.5 cm (9 x 5 x 3 inch) loaf pan. Place pan on wire trivet in 5 L (5 quart) oval slow cooker. Place 5 paper towels between top of slow cooker and lid. Put wooden match or an object 3 mm (1/8 inch) thick between paper towels and edge of slow cooker to allow a bit of steam to escape. Do not lift lid for the first 2 hours cooking time. Cook on High for about 2 3/4 hours until wooden pick inserted in centre comes out clean. Remove pan to rack. Let stand for 20 minutes. Loosen sides with knife. Turn out onto rack to cool. Cuts into 18 slices.

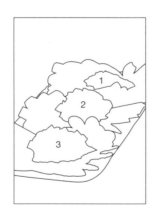

1. Baba Ganoush, page 4
2. Hot Crab Dip, page 7
3. Artichoke Spinach Dip, page 5

1 slice: 578 Kilojoules (138 Calories); 4 g Total Fat; 134 mg Sodium; 2 g Protein; 24 g Carbohydrate

Banana Bread

Makes a large dark loaf with good flavour. Serve plain or buttered.

Hard margarine (or butter), softened	6 tbsp	100 mL
White (granulated) sugar	2/3 cup	150 mL
Large egg	1	1
Mashed banana (about 3 small)	3/4 cup	175 mL
Plain (all-purpose) flour	1 1/2 cups	375 mL
Cocoa	1 tbsp	15 mL
Baking powder	1 1/2 tsp	7 mL
Bicarbonate soda (baking soda)	1/4 tsp	1 mL
Salt	1/2 tsp	2 mL
Chopped walnuts (optional)	1/2 cup	125 mL

1. Cream margarine and sugar together in bowl. Beat in eggs. Add banana. Mix.

2. Add remaining 6 ingredients. Stir to moisten. Turn into greased 22 x 12 x 7.5 cm (9 x 5 x 3 inch) loaf pan. Set pan on wire trivet in 5 L (5 quart) oval slow cooker. Place 5 paper towels between top of slow cooker and lid. Put wooden match or an object 3 mm (1/8 inch) thick between paper towels and edge of slow cooker to allow a bit of steam to escape. Do not lift lid for the first 2 hours cooking time. Cook on High for about 2 1/4 hours. A wooden pick inserted in centre should come out clean. Remove pan to wire rack to cool. Let stand for 20 minutes. Loosen sides with knife. Turn out onto rack to cool. Cuts into 18 slices.

1 slice: 494 Kilojoules (118 Calories); 4.2 g Total Fat; 144 mg Sodium; 2 g Protein; 19 g Carbohydrate

Herb Bread

Nicely rounded loaf that's herb coloured and has good flavour.

White (granulated) sugar	1 tsp	5 mL
Warm water	1 1/3 cups	325 mL
Active dry yeast	1 tbsp	15 mL
Plain (all-purpose) flour	2 cups	500 mL
White (granulated) sugar	1 tbsp	15 mL
Cooking oil	2 tbsp	30 mL
Dried oregano	1 tsp	5 mL
Ground sage	1 tsp	5 mL
Garlic powder	1/4 tsp	1 mL
Onion powder	1/4 tsp	1 mL
Salt	1 tsp	5 mL
Plain (all-purpose) flour	1 cup	250 mL

1. Stir first amount of sugar in warm water in large warmed bowl. Sprinkle with yeast. Let stand for 10 minutes. Stir to dissolve yeast.

2. Add next 8 ingredients. Beat on Low to moisten. Beat on Medium for 2 minutes.

3. Work in second amount of flour. Turn into greased 3.5 L (3 1/2 quart) slow cooker. Smooth top with wet spoon or hand. Place 5 paper towels between top of slow cooker and lid. Put wooden match or an object 3 mm (1/8 inch) thick between paper towels and edge of slow cooker to allow a bit of steam to escape. Do not lift lid for the first 2 hours cooking time. Cook on High for about 2 1/2 hours. Loosen sides with knife taking care not to scratch the slow cooker's liner. Turn out onto rack to cool. Cuts into 14 slices.

1 slice: 536 Kilojoules (128 Calories); 2.3 g Total Fat; 195 mg Sodium; 3 g Protein; 23 g Carbohydrate

Sandwich Brisket

Once this fork-tender beef brisket has cooled, slice it up for weekday sandwiches or freeze for later use. Heat the cooking liquid for dipping, or make gravy for hot beef sandwiches. Cooled brisket can also be julienned for stir-fries or salads.

Boneless beef brisket roast	4 lbs	1.8 kg
Chopped onion	1 cup	250 mL
Garlic cloves, minced (or 4 mL, 3/4 tsp, powder)	3	3
Liquid beef stock (prepared beef broth)	1 cup	250 mL
Red wine vinegar	1/4 cup	60 mL

1. Place brisket in 5 to 7 L (5 to 7 quart) slow cooker.

2. Heat medium greased frying pan (skillet) on Medium. Add onion and garlic. Cook, stirring often, for about 10 minutes, until starting to brown. Sprinkle generously with salt and pepper.

3. Add stock (broth) and vinegar to onion mixture. Bring to a boil. Pour over brisket. Cook, covered, on High for 4 1/2 to 5 hours until brisket is very tender. Remove brisket from slow cooker. Cool completely. Wrap in plastic wrap. Let stand in refrigerator for 6 hours or overnight. Chill cooking liquid. Remove and discard fat from brisket and cooking liquid. Makes about 250 mL (1 1/4 cups) cooking liquid. Slice brisket thinly. Serve brisket with cooking liquid. Makes about 1 kg (2.2 lbs) brisket.

85 g (3 oz) portion with 60 mL (1/4 cup) cooking liquid: 850 Kilojoules (203 Calories); 7.0 g Total Fat; 261 mg Sodium; 31 g Protein; 2 g Carbohydrate

Sloppy Joes

An old favourite – quick to put together and easy to serve.

Cooking oil	2 tsp	10 mL
Lean beef mince (ground beef)	2 lbs	900 g
Tomato purée (tomato sauce)	14 oz	398 mL
Chopped onion	1 1/2 cups	375 mL
Thinly sliced celery	1 cup	250 mL
Barbecue sauce	2 tbsp	30 mL
Worcestershire sauce	2 tsp	10 mL
Salt, sprinkle		
Pepper (optional)	1/4 tsp	1 mL
Grated Cheddar cheese	1 1/2 cups	375 mL
Rolls, split (toasted, optional)	8	8

1. Heat cooking oil in large frying pan (skillet) on Medium. Add beef mince (ground beef). Scramble-fry for 5 to 10 minutes until no longer pink. Drain. Transfer to 3.5 to 4 L (3 1/2 to 4 quart) slow cooker.

2. Add next 7 ingredients. Stir well. Cover. Cook on Low for 8 to 9 hours or on High for 4 to 4 1/2 hours.

3. Add cheese. Stir until melted. Makes about 1 L (4 cups) beef mixture. Place 1 bottom half of rolls on each of 8 plates. Divide and spoon beef mixture onto bottom half. Cover with top half of roll on each. Serves 8.

1 serving: 1978 Kilojoules (471 Calories); 20.6 g Total Fat; 886 mg Sodium; 33 g Protein; 38 g Carbohydrate

Basic Spareribs

So easy to do; you end up with nicely browned ribs.

Meaty pork spareribs, cut into 2- or 3- rib sections	3 lbs	1.4 kg
Liquid gravy browner (optional)	2 tsp	10 mL

Brush ribs with gravy browner. Put into 3.5 L (3 1/2 quart) slow cooker. Cover. Cook on Low for 9 to 10 hours or on High for 4 1/2 to 5 hours. Serves 6.

1 serving: 1176 Kilojoules (280 Calories); 20.8 g Total Fat; 133 mg Sodium; 21 g Protein; 1 g Carbohydrate

Sweet-and-Sour Ribs

Superb! Glazed well and delicious.

BROWN SUGAR SAUCE

Brown sugar	2 cups	500 mL
Plain (all-purpose) flour	1/4 cup	60 mL
Water	1/3 cup	75 mL
White vinegar	1/2 cup	125 mL
Soy sauce	2 tbsp	30 mL
Tomato sauce (ketchup)	2 tbsp	30 mL
Ground ginger	1/4 tsp	1 mL
Garlic powder	1/4 tsp	1 mL

Meaty pork spareribs, cut into 2- or 3- rib sections	3 lbs	1.4 kg

1. BROWN SUGAR SAUCE: Mix brown sugar and flour in saucepan. Add water. Stir. Add next 5 ingredients. Heat and stir until boiling and thickened.

2. Layer ribs in a 5 L (5 quart) slow cooker, spooning sauce over each layer. Cover. Cook on Low for 10 to 12 hours or on High for 5 to 6 hours until ribs are very tender. Serves 6.

1 serving: 2511.6 Kilojoules (598 Calories); 20.8 g Total Fat; 516 mg Sodium; 22 g Protein; 82 g Carbohydrate

Red-Peppered Chorizo

This creamy sausage and cheese mixture tastes great on crisp crackers or crostini slices for a hearty snack or appetiser.

Chorizo (or hot Italian) sausage, casing removed	1 1/2 lbs	680 g
Jar of roasted red capsicum (peppers), drained, chopped	12 oz	340 g
Balsamic vinaigrette dressing	2 tbsp	30 mL
Orange cordial (frozen concentrated orange juice, thawed)	2 tbsp	30 mL
Goat (chèvre) cheese	1/3 cup	75 mL

1. Scramble-fry sausage in large frying pan (skillet) on Medium-High for about 12 minutes until no longer pink. Drain. Transfer to 3.5 to 4 L (3 1/2 to 4 quart) slow cooker.

2. Add next 3 ingredients. Stir. Cook, covered, on Low for 3 to 4 hours or on High for 1 1/2 to 2 hours.

3. Add cheese. Stir until melted. Makes about 625 mL (2 1/2 cups).

Pictured between pages 16 & 17 and on front cover.

60 mL (1/4 cup): 1273 Kilojoules (304 Calories); 20.2 g Total Fat; 1191 mg Sodium; 16 g Protein; 11 g Carbohydrate

Garlic Mushrooms

Enjoy these creamy, flavourful mushrooms with crostini or baguette slices – or try serving them alongside a steak dinner!

Fresh small white mushrooms	2 lbs	900 g
Alfredo pasta sauce	1/2 cup	125 mL
Dry (or alcohol-free) white wine	1/4 cup	60 mL
Garlic cloves, minced (or 1 tsp, 5 mL, powder)	4	4
Lemon juice	2 tsp	10 mL

1. Arrange mushrooms on large greased baking tray (sheet) with sides. Grill (broil) on top rack in oven for about 15 minutes, stirring once, until starting to brown. Drain and discard any liquid. Transfer to 3.5 to 4 L (3 1/2 to 4 quart) slow cooker.

2. Add next 3 ingredients and a sprinkle of pepper. Stir. Cook, covered, on Low for 5 to 6 hours or on High for 2 1/2 to 3 hours.

3. Add lemon juice. Stir. Makes about 750 mL (3 cups).

75 mL (1/3 cup): 266 Kilojoules (54 Calories); 2.4 g Total Fat; 83 mg Sodium; 2 g Protein; 5 g Carbohydrate

Lemony Vine Leaves

These Greek-style grape leaves are a great summertime
appetiser to serve with tzatziki dip.

Long-grain white rice	2 cups	500 mL
Finely chopped roasted red capsicum in cream cheese (roasted red pepper cream cheese)	1 cup	250 mL
Greek seasoning	2 tbsp	30 mL
Grape leaves, rinsed and drained, tough stems removed	60	60
Lemon juice	1/3 cup	75 mL

1. Mix first 3 ingredients and a sprinkle of salt and pepper in medium bowl until no dry rice remains.

2. Arrange 38 to 40 grape leaves on work surface, vein-side up, stem end closest to you. Spoon about 15 mL (1 tbsp) rice mixture onto leaf about 12 mm (1/2 inch) from stem end of leaf.

Fold bottom of leaf over rice mixture. Fold in sides. Roll up from bottom to enclose filling (see Note 1). Repeat with remaining leaves and rice mixture. Cover bottom of greased 3.5 to 4 L (3 1/2 to 4 quart) slow cooker with 4 to 5 grape leaves. Arrange rolls, seam-side down, close together in single layer over leaves. Cover with 4 to 5 grape leaves. Repeat with remaining rolls and leaves.

3. Add lemon juice and 1 L (4 cups) water. Do not stir. Place a heatproof plate on top to keep rolls submerged during cooking (see Note 2). Cook, covered, on Low for 7 to 8 hours or on High for 3 1/2 to 4 hours until rice is tender. Let stand, covered, for 20 minutes. Makes 38 to 40 stuffed grape leaves.

NOTE 1: Leaves should be rolled securely, but not too tightly, as the filling will expand during cooking.

NOTE 2: If you have an oval slow cooker that will not fit a round plate, use two smaller, heatproof plates that will fit.

VARIATION: Try them with herb and garlic cream cheese in place of the red capsicum cream cheese.

1 stuffed grape leaf: 239 Kilojoules (57 Calories); 1.6 g Total Fat; 44 mg Sodium; 1 g Protein; 9 g Carbohydrate

Sweet-and-Sour Pork Ribs

The classic flavours of sweet and sour are infused into these delicious pork ribs. Serve with white rice for a crowd-pleasing meal.

Pork side ribs, trimmed of fat and cut into 3-bone portions	3 lbs	1.4 kg
Rice vinegar	2 tbsp	30 mL
Garlic cloves, minced (or 2 mL, 1/2 tsp, powder)	2	2
Grated fresh ginger (or 2 mL, 1/2 tsp, powder)	2 tsp	10 mL
Sweet-and-sour sauce	3 cups	750 mL

1. Heat large greased frying pan (skillet) on Medium-High. Add ribs. Sprinkle with salt and pepper. Cook for about 2 minutes per side until browned. Transfer to 3.5 to 4 L (3 1/2 to 4 quart) slow cooker.

2. Combine next 3 ingredients and 500 mL (2 cups) sweet-and-sour sauce in medium bowl. Pour over ribs. Cook, covered, on Low for 8 to 9 hours or on High for 4 to 4 1/2 hours. Transfer ribs to large shallow bowl. Cover to keep warm. Skim and discard fat from cooking liquid. Add remaining sweet-and-sour sauce. Stir. Pour over ribs. Makes ten 3-bone portions.

1 portion: 2533 Kilojoules (605 Calories); 43.1 g Total Fat; 472 mg Sodium; 33 g Protein; 20 g Carbohydrate

Peachy Ribs

Enjoy the flavours of tender, barbecue-flavoured pork ribs with a touch of summery peach sweetness. Drizzle the smooth, tasty sauce over the ribs for even more flavour.

Pork side ribs, trimmed of fat and cut into 3-bone portions	3 lbs	1.4 kg
Plain (all-purpose) flour	1/4 cup	60 mL
Can of sliced peaches, drained and juice reserved, chopped	14 oz	398 g
Barbecue sauce	1/4 cup	60 mL
Peach jam (jelly)	1/4 cup	60 mL

1. Sprinkle ribs with salt and pepper. Put into large resealable freezer bag. Add flour. Seal bag. Turn until coated. Put ribs into 3.5 to 4 L (3 1/2 to 4 quart) slow cooker.

2. Spoon peaches over top. Combine barbecue sauce, jam (jelly) and reserved peach juice in small bowl. Pour over peaches. Cook, covered, on Low for 8 to 10 hours or on High for 4 to 5 hours. Transfer ribs to large serving platter. Cover to keep warm. Skim and discard fat from cooking liquid. Carefully process in blender until smooth (see Safety Tip). Pour sauce over ribs. Makes ten 3-bone portions.

SAFETY TIP: Follow blender manufacturer's instructions for processing hot liquids.

1 portion: 2336 Kilojoules (558 Calories); 40.4 g Total Fat; 250 mg Sodium; 33 g Protein; 13 g Carbohydrate

Pork and Guacamole Tostadas

Serve this easy, crowd-pleasing appetiser at your next party. About half of the pork mixture will be left over – it can be frozen or made into fajitas for lunch!

Boneless pork shoulder butt roast, trimmed of fat	2 lbs	900 g
Hot salsa	2 cups	500 mL
Corn (nacho) chips	9 oz	250 g
Prepared guacamole	1 1/2 cups	375 mL
Finely chopped jalapeño chillies in grated cheddar cheese (jalapeño Monterey Jack)	1 1/2 cups	375 mL

1. Place roast in 3.5 to 4 L (3 1/2 to 4 quart) slow cooker. Sprinkle with salt and pepper. Pour 375 mL (1 1/2 cups) salsa over top. Cook, covered, on High for 4 1/2 to 5 hours. Transfer roast to large plate. Skim and discard fat from sauce. Shred pork with 2 forks. Return to sauce. Add remaining salsa. Stir.

2. Spoon pork mixture over each chip. Top with guacamole. Sprinkle with cheese. Makes 48 tostadas.

Pictured between pages 16 & 17 and on front cover.

1 tostada: 330 Kilojoules (79 Calories); 4.4 g Total Fat; 155 mg Sodium; 5 g Protein; 5 g Carbohydrate

Porcupine Meatballs

Very colourful starter with rice being the quills.

Lean beef mince (ground beef)	1 1/2 lbs	680 g
Onion flakes (or 60 mL, 1/4 cup, diced onion)	1 1/2 tbsp	25 mL
Salt	1 tsp	5 mL
Pepper	1/4 tsp	1 mL
Large egg, fork-beaten	1	1
Uncooked long-grain (converted) rice	2/3 cup	150 mL
Fine dry breadcrumbs	1/2 cup	125 mL
Milk	2 tbsp	30 mL
Tomato juice	3 cups	750 mL
Water	1 cup	250 mL
White (granulated) sugar	1 tsp	5 mL
Salt	1/2 tsp	2 mL
Liquid gravy browner (optional)	1/2 tsp	2 mL

1. Combine first 8 ingredients in large bowl. Mix well. Shape into 3.8 cm (1 1/2 inch) balls. Place in 3.5 L (3 1/2 quart) slow cooker.

2. Pour tomato juice and water into bowl. Add sugar, second amount of salt and gravy browner. Stir. Pour over meatballs. Cover. Cook on Low for 8 to 10 hours or on High for 4 to 5 hours. Makes 36 meatballs.

3 meatballs (with sauce): 856.8 Kilojoules (204 Calories); 9.3 g Total Fat; 652 mg Sodium; 13 g Protein; 16 g Carbohydrate

Smokin' Smokies

A triple hit of smoky flavour. Serve from the slow cooker on lowest setting with a generous supply of toothpicks.

Smoked sausages (smokies) (cut diagonally into 12 mm, 1/2 inch, slices)	2 lbs	900 g
Chilli sauce	1 3/4 cups	425 mL
Brown sugar, packed	1 tbsp	15 mL
Finely chopped jalapeño chillies and smoky barbecue sauce (chipotle peppers in adobo sauce) (see Tip, page 36)	1 tbsp	15 mL
Smoked sweet paprika	2 tsp	10 mL

Combine all 5 ingredients in 3.5 to 4 L (3 1/2 to 4 quart) slow cooker. Cook, covered, on Low for 6 to 7 hours or on High for 3 to 3 1/2 hours. Makes about 1.25 L (5 cups).

Pictured between pages 16 & 17 and on front cover.

75 mL (1/3 cup): 938 Kilojoules (224 Calories); 16.7 g Total Fat; 1396 mg Sodium; 7 g Protein; 11 g Carbohydrate

Creamy Seafood Filling

Serve this elegant, delicious appetiser over fresh puff pastry cups or points and garnish with sprigs of fresh dill.

Chive and onion cream cheese	2 cups	500 mL
Crayfish meat (can of frozen lobster meat, thawed, drained), larger pieces cut up	11 1/3 oz	320 g
Dry (or alcohol-free) white wine	1/3 cup	75 mL
Prawn (shrimp) and scallop mix, thawed, drained and blotted dry	1 lb	454 g
Chopped fresh dill (dill weed) (or 1/2 tsp, 2 mL, dried)	2 tsp	10 mL

1. Combine first 3 ingredients and a sprinkle of pepper in 3.5 to 4 L (3 1/2 to 4 quart) slow cooker. Cook, covered, on Low for 3 to 4 hours or on High for 1 1/2 to 2 hours. Stir until smooth.

2. Add prawns (shrimp) and scallops. Stir. Cook, covered, on High for about 20 minutes until prawns turn pink.

3. Add dill. Stir. Makes about 1 L (4 cups).

60 mL (1/4 cup): 703 Kilojoules (168 Calories); 10.7 g Total Fat; 220 mg Sodium; 11 g Protein; 3 g Carbohydrate

Hot Wings and Blue Cheese Dip

Dip these nippy little fellows into Blue Cheese Dip for a special treat.

White vinegar	4 tsp	20 mL
White (granulated) sugar	2 tsp	10 mL
Hot chilli (pepper) sauce	1/4 cup	60 mL
Paprika	1 tsp	5 mL
Whole chicken wings (or drumettes)	3 lbs	1.4 kg

BLUE CHEESE DIP

Light salad dressing (or mayonnaise)	1/2 cup	125 mL
Blue cheese, crumbled	1/4 cup	60 mL
Lemon juice	1 tbsp	15 mL
Onion powder	1/4 tsp	1 mL
Garlic powder	1/4 tsp	1 mL
Worcestershire sauce	1/2 tsp	2 mL
Non-fat (or regular) sour cream	1/2 cup	125 mL

1. Combine first 4 ingredients in small cup. Stir. Discard tip and cut wings apart at joint. Brush sauce over both sides of chicken pieces. Place pieces in 3.5 L (3 1/2 quart) slow cooker. Cover. Cook on Low for 7 to 8 hours or on High for 3 1/2 to 4 hours until tender. Serve from slow cooker. Makes about 28 pieces of wing or 18 drumettes.

2. **BLUE CHEESE DIP:** Combine all 7 ingredients in bowl. Beat until smooth. Makes 280 mL (1 1/8 cups). Serve with wings.

1 wing piece (with dip): 339 Kilojoules (81 Calories); 5.8 g Total Fat; 76 mg Sodium; 5 g Protein; 1 g Carbohydrate

Swedish Meatballs

Make a bunch so you can freeze some. Gravy adds the extra touch.

Milk	1 cup	250 mL
Fine dry breadcrumbs	1 1/4 cups	300 mL
Large eggs, fork beaten	2	2
Chopped onion	1 1/4 cups	300 mL
Salt	1 1/2 tsp	7 mL
Pepper	1/4 tsp	1 mL
Ground allspice	1/8 tsp	0.5 mL
Lean beef mince (ground beef)	1 1/2 lbs	680 g

Lean pork mince (ground pork)	1/2 lb	225 g

SAUCE

Plain (all-purpose) flour	1/4 cup	60 mL
Salt	1/2 tsp	2 mL
Condensed beef liquid stock (consommé)	10 oz	284 mL
Water	1 cup	250 mL

1. Mix first 7 ingredients in bowl. Stir well.

2. Add beef and pork mince (ground beef and pork). Shape into 3.8 cm (1 1/2 inch) balls. Arrange on griller (broiler)tray. Brown quickly under griller, turning once. Pile balls into 5 L (5 quart) slow cooker.

3. **SAUCE:** Measure flour and salt in saucepan. Whisk in stock (consommé) and water gradually until no lumps remain. Heat until it boils and thickens slightly. Pour over meatballs. Cover. Cook on Low for 8 to 10 hours or on High for 4 to 5 hours. Makes 57 meatballs.

3 meatballs (with sauce): 634.2 Kilojoules (151 Calories); 7 g Total Fat; 467 mg Sodium; 12 g Protein; 9 g Carbohydrate

Mexi Meatballs

Thaw meatballs overnight in the refrigerator. Adjust heat by using mild, medium or hot salsa. Serve with toothpicks and enjoy!

Cooked meatballs (box of frozen cooked meatballs, thawed)	2 lbs	900 g
Salsa	2 cups	500 mL
Sour cream	1/2 cup	125 mL
Lime juice	2 tbsp	30 mL
Chopped fresh coriander (cilantro) or parsley	1 tbsp	15 mL

1. Combine meatballs and salsa in 3.5 to 4 L (3 1/2 to 4 quart) slow cooker. Cook, covered, on Low for 3 to 4 hours or on High for 1 1/2 to 2 hours.

2. Combine remaining 3 ingredients in small bowl. Add to meatball mixture. Stir. Serves 12.

1 serving: 1147 Kilojoules (274 Calories); 19.4 g Total Fat; 824 mg Sodium; 4 g Protein; 10 g Carbohydrate

Greek Lemon Drumettes

Serve with fresh lemon wedges for an extra squeeze of citrus flavour.

Lemon yoghurt	3/4 cup	175 mL
Chicken drumettes	3 lbs	1.4 kg
Grated Parmesan cheese	1 1/2 cups	375 mL
Fine dry breadcrumbs	1/2 cup	125 mL
Greek seasoning	2 tsp	10 mL

1. Measure yoghurt into large bowl. Add drumettes. Stir until coated.

2. Combine remaining 3 ingredients and a sprinkle of salt and pepper in large resealable freezer bag. Add 1/3 of drumettes. Seal bag. Toss until coated. Repeat with remaining drumettes.

3. Put drumettes into greased 3.5 to 4 L (3 1/2 to 4 quart) slow cooker. Cook, covered, on Low for 8 to 9 hours or High for 4 to 4 1/2 hours. Makes about 24 drumettes.

1 drumette: 724 Kilojoules (173 Calories); 11.5 g Total Fat; 217 mg Sodium; 14 g Protein; 3 g Carbohydrate;

Oriental Chicken Wings

Soy sauce flavour is always a favourite. These marinate as they cook.

Whole chicken wings (or drumettes)	3 lbs	1.4 kg
Soy sauce	1 cup	250 mL
Brown sugar, packed	3/4 cup	175 mL
Water	1/2 cup	125 mL
Lemon juice	1 tsp	5 mL
Mustard powder	1/4 tsp	1 mL
Garlic powder	1/4 tsp	1 mL
Salt	1/2 tsp	2 mL
Ground ginger	1/4 tsp	1 mL

1. Discard tip and cut wings apart at joint. Place pieces in 3 1/2 L (3.5 quart) slow cooker.

2. Measure the remaining 8 ingredients into bowl. Mix well. Pour over chicken pieces. Cover. Cook on Low for 8 to 9 hours or on High for 4 to 4 1/2 hours until tender. Serve from slow cooker or remove to platter. Makes about 28 pieces of wing or about 18 drumettes.

1 wing piece (with sauce): 381 Kilojoules (91 Calories); 4.3 g Total Fat; 692 mg Sodium; 6 g Protein; 7 g Carbohydrate

Mango Ribs

Mango gives these tender, tasty ribs a sweet and fruity flavour twist – perfect for a simple, hands-on appetiser at a casual get-together.

Frozen mango pieces, thawed	1 cup	250 mL
Liquid chicken stock (prepared chicken broth)	1 cup	250 mL
Mango chutney	1/2 cup	125 mL
Brown sugar, packed	1 tbsp	15 mL
Sweet-and-sour-cut pork ribs, trimmed of fat and cut into 1-bone portions	3 1/2 lbs	1.6 kg

1. Combine first 4 ingredients in 4 to 5 L (4 to 5 quart) slow cooker.

2. Arrange ribs on greased baking tray (sheet) with sides. Sprinkle with salt and pepper. Grill (broil) on top rack in oven for about 7 minutes per side until lightly browned. Drain and discard liquid. Add ribs to slow cooker. Stir. Cook, covered, on Low for 6 to 7 hours or on High for 3 to 3 1/2 hours. Transfer ribs with slotted spoon to medium bowl. Cover to keep warm. Skim and discard fat from cooking liquid. Carefully process in blender until smooth (see Safety Tip). Pour over ribs. Makes about 1.5 L (6 cups).

SAFETY TIP: Follow blender manufacturer's instructions for processing hot liquids.

125 mL (1/2 cup): 2374 Kilojoules (567 Calories); 41.3 g Total Fat; 399 mg Sodium; 39 g Protein; 8 g Carbohydrate

Honey Garlic Wings

These tender wings are a real crowd-pleaser with their classic honey garlic flavour. Set them out hot on a platter and watch everyone gather 'round.

Split chicken wings, tips discarded	3 lbs	1.4 kg
Liquid honey	1 cup	250 mL
Soy sauce	1/2 cup	125 mL
Garlic cloves, minced (or 1/2 tsp, 2 mL, powder)	2	2
Ground ginger	1/4 tsp	1 mL

1. Arrange wings on greased baking tray (sheet) with sides. Sprinkle with pepper. Grill (broil) on top rack in oven for about 6 minutes per side until browned. Transfer to 4 to 5 L (4 to 5 quart) slow cooker.

2. Combine remaining 4 ingredients in small bowl. Pour over chicken. Stir until coated. Cook, covered, on Low for 4 to 5 hours or on High for 2 to 2 1/2 hours. Discard liquid from slow cooker. Makes about 32 wings.

1 wing: 477 Kilojoules (114 Calories); 6.7 g Total Fat; 196 mg Sodium; 8 g Protein; 5 g Carbohydrate

Appetiser Ribs

Ribs in golden juice. Deliciously sweet and tangy.

White vinegar	1/2 cup	125 mL
White (granulated) sugar	1 cup	250 mL
Tomato sauce (ketchup)	2/3 cup	150 mL
Onion flakes	1 tbsp	15 mL
Worcestershire sauce	1 tbsp	15 mL
Water	1 cup	250 mL
Pork spareribs, cut into short lengths and into single rib pieces	3 lbs	1.4 kg

1. Place first 6 ingredients in 5 L (5 quart) slow cooker. Stir well.

2. Add ribs. Stir. Cover. Cook on Low for 10 to 12 hours or on High for 5 to 6 hours. Makes about 37 ribs.

1 rib: 306.6 Kilojoules (73 Calories); 3.4 g Total Fat; 79 mg Sodium; 4 g Protein; 7 g Carbohydrate

Sweet-and-Sour Wings

In dark flavourful sauce, these are among the first appetisers to disappear.

Whole chicken wings (or drumettes)	3 lbs	1.4 kg	Garlic powder	1/4 tsp	1 mL
Brown sugar, packed	1 cup	250 mL	Onion flakes	1 tbsp	15 mL
Plain (all-purpose) flour	1/4 cup	60 mL	Salt	1/2 tsp	2 mL
Water	1/2 cup	125 mL	Prepared mustard	1/2 tsp	2 mL
White vinegar	1/4 cup	60 mL			
Tomato sauce (ketchup)	1 1/2 tbsp	25 mL			
Soy sauce	1/4 cup	60 mL			

1. Discard tip and cut wings apart at joint. Place chicken pieces in 5 L (5 quart) slow cooker.

2. Mix brown sugar and flour well in saucepan. Add water, vinegar and tomato sauce (ketchup). Stir. Add remaining 5 ingredients. Heat and stir until boiling and thickened. Pour over wings. Cover. Cook on Low for 8 to 9 hours or on High for 4 to 4 1/2 hours until tender. Serve from slow cooker or remove to platter. Makes about 28 wing pieces or about 18 drumettes.

1 wing piece: 414 Kilojoules (99 Calories); 5 g Total Fat; 4.3 mg Sodium; 241 g Protein; 10 g Carbohydrate

Smoky Meatballs

A hint of smoked flavour makes these irresistible.

Chilli sauce	3/4 cup	175 mL	Smoky barbecue sauce (liquid smoke) (optional)	2 tsp	10 mL
White (granulated) sugar	2/3 cup	150 mL	Garlic powder	1/4 tsp	1 mL
Worcestershire sauce	1 tsp	5 mL	Chilli powder	1 tsp	5 mL
Large egg, fork-beaten	1	1	Salt	1 tsp	5 mL
Water	1/2 cup	125 mL	Pepper	1/4 tsp	1 mL
Fine dry breadcrumbs	2/3 cup	150 mL	Lean beef mince (ground beef)	1 1/2 lbs	680 g
Chopped onion	1/2 cup	125 mL			

1. Measure first 3 ingredients into bowl. Stir well. Set aside.

2. Combine next 9 ingredients in bowl. Stir well.

3. Add beef mince (ground beef). Mix well. Shape into 3.8 cm (1 1/2 inch) balls. Place in 3.5 L (3 1/2 quart) slow cooker. Spoon chilli sauce mixture over top, covering all balls that are visible. Cover. Cook on Low for 8 to 10 hours or on High for 4 to 5 hours. Makes 36 meatballs.

3 meatballs (with sauce): 928.2 Kilojoules (221 Calories); 9.4 g Total Fat; 565 mg Sodium; 13 g Protein; 22 g Carbohydrate

SOUPS

SOUPS

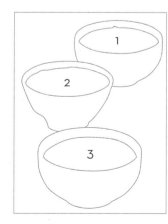

Pictured on reverse:
1. Lamb and Barley Soup, page 37
2. Smoked Pork and Bean Soup, page 55
3. Split Pea Soup, page 44

Butternut Cream Soup

The sweetness and rich texture of pumpkin (squash) and pear blend perfectly with sour cream in this creamy, beautifully golden soup.

Chopped onion	1 1/2 cups	375 mL
Chopped butternut pumpkin (squash)	8 cups	2 L
Can of pear halves in juice (with juice)	28 oz	796 g
Sour cream	1 cup	250 mL
Chopped fresh chives, for garnish		

1. Heat large greased frying pan (skillet) on Medium. Add onion. Cook, stirring often, for about 8 minutes until softened. Transfer to 4 to 5 L (4 to 5 quart) slow cooker.

2. Add pumpkin (squash), pears with juice, a generous sprinkle of salt and 625 mL (2 1/2 cups) water. Cook, covered, on Low for 8 to 10 hours or on High for 4 to 5 hours. Carefully process with hand blender or in blender in batches until smooth (see Safety Tip).

3. Add sour cream. Whisk until smooth. Garnish with chives. Makes about 3 L (12 cups).

Pictured between pages 48 & 49 and on back cover.

SAFETY TIP: Follow blender manufacturer's instructions for processing hot liquids.

250 mL (1 cup): 657 Kilojoules (157 Calories); 3.9 g Total Fat; 113 mg Sodium; 3 g Protein; 30 g Carbohydrate

Borscht

Vegetables, beef and beetroots in an old family favourite. Serve with a swirl of sour cream.

Lean beef mince (ground beef)	1/4 lb	113 g
Shredded green (or red) cabbage, lightly packed	1/3 cup	75 mL
Chopped onion	1/4 cup	60 mL
Grated carrot	2 tbsp	30 mL
Grated swede (yellow turnip)	2 tbsp	30 mL
Fresh large beetroot, peeled, cut julienne	1	1
Water	2 cups	500 mL
Tomato sauce (ketchup)	2 tbsp	30 mL
White vinegar	1 tsp	5 mL
White (granulated) sugar	1/2 tsp	2 mL
Parsley flakes	1/2 tsp	2 mL
Dried dill leaf tips (dill weed)	1/8 tsp	0.5 mL

Bay leaf	1/2	1/2
Salt	1/2 tsp	2 mL
Pepper	1/8 tsp	0.5 mL

1. Scramble-fry beef mince (ground beef) in small frying pan (skillet) on Medium until no longer pink. Drain well.

2. Combine next 4 ingredients in large bowl. Add beef mince. Mix well.

3. Add beetroot. Mix gently. Transfer to 1.5 L (1 1/2 quart) slow cooker.

4. Measure remaining 9 ingredients into small bowl. Stir well. Add to beef mixture. Stir well. Cover. Cook on Low for 8 to 10 hours or on High for 4 to 5 hours. Remove and discard bay leaf half. Makes about 750 mL (3 cups).

250 mL (1 cup): 504 Kilojoules (120 Calories); 5.8 g Total Fat; 574 mg Sodium; 8 g Protein; 9 g Carbohydrate

French Onion Soup

Simple and just like you would have when dining out.

Quartered and thinly sliced white onion	4 1/4 cups	1.1 L
Water	4 cups	1 L
Beef stock (bouillon) powder	4 tsp	20 mL
French bread slices, cut to fit	4	4

Grated mozzarella cheese	1 cup	250 mL
Grated Parmesan cheese, sprinkle		

1. Combine first 3 ingredients in 3.5 L (3 1/2 quart) slow cooker. Cover. Cook on Low for 8 to 10 hours or on High for 4 to 5 hours.

2. Ladle soup into bowls. Place 1 slice of bread in each bowl. Divide mozzarella cheese and sprinkle over each slice. Sprinkle with Parmesan cheese. Grill (broil) until cheese is bubbly and golden brown. If preferred, bread with cheese may be grilled separately, then added to each bowl. Serves 4.

250 mL (1 cup): 883 Kilojoules (211 Calories); 8.3 g Total Fat; 809 mg Sodium; 10 g Protein; 25 g Carbohydrate

Apricot Red Lentil Soup

This simple vegetarian soup, Armenian in origin, is a lovely balance of sweet and peppery flavours. It's low-fat, high-fibre and thick, creamy and satisfying!

Chopped onion	2 cups	500 mL
Liquid vegetable stock (prepared vegetable broth)	4 cups	1 L
Chopped carrot	2 cups	500 mL
Dried red split lentils	2 cups	500 mL
Chopped dried apricot	1 1/2 cups	375 mL

1. Heat large greased frying pan (skillet) on Medium. Add onion and a generous sprinkle of salt. Cook for about 15 minutes, stirring often, until onion is browned. Transfer to 5 to 7 L (5 to 7 quart) slow cooker.

2. Add remaining 4 ingredients and 1.25 L (5 cups) water. Stir. Cook, covered, on Low for 10 to 12 hours or on High for 5 to 6 hours. Carefully process with hand blender or in blender in batches until smooth

(see Safety Tip). Makes about 2.75 L (11 cups).

SAFETY TIP: Follow blender manufacturer's instructions for processing hot liquids.

250 mL (1 cup): 862 Kilojoules (206 Calories); 1.4 g Total Fat; 306 mg Sodium; 11 g Protein; 39 g Carbohydrate

Chilli Corn Chowder

The sweet aroma of this soup will bring a southwestern feel to your kitchen! Enjoy the richness of creamed corn and the flavour of smoky bacon and jalapeño chillies (chipotle peppers).

Chopped onion	1 cup	250 mL
Bacon slices, diced	6	6
Cans of creamed corn (398 g, 14 oz, each)	3	3
Can of red kidney beans, rinsed and drained	14 oz	398 g
Finely chopped jalapeño chillies and smoky barbecue sauce (chipotle peppers in adobo sauce) (see Tip, right)	1 tbsp	15 mL

1. Heat medium frying pan (skillet) on Medium-High. Add onion and bacon. Cook for about 5 minutes, stirring often, until onion is softened. Transfer to 3.5 to 4 L (3 1/2 to 4 quart) slow cooker.

2. Add remaining 3 ingredients and 625 mL (2 1/2 cups) water. Stir. Cook, covered, on Low for 6 to 7 hours or on High for 3 to 3 1/2 hours. Makes about 2.1 L (8 1/2 cups).

TIP: Be sure to wash your hands after handling chillies. To store leftover jalapeño chillies, divide into recipe-friendly portions and freeze, with sauce, in airtight containers for up to one year.

250 mL (1 cup): 829 Kilojoules (198 Calories); 2.7 g Total Fat; 586 mg Sodium; 7 g Protein; 36 g Carbohydrate

Sausage Kale Soup

For added aroma, look for Italian sausage with fennel seeds for a delicious, licorice-like flavour.

Hot (or mild) Italian sausage, casing removed	3/4 lb	340 g
Chopped kale leaves, lightly packed	4 cups	1 L
Can of diced tomatoes (with juice)	28 oz	796 g
Can of black-eyed peas (or cannellini/ navy beans), with liquid	19 oz	540 g
Basil pesto	1/4 cup	60 mL

1. Scramble-fry sausage meat in large frying pan (skillet) on Medium for about 10 minutes until no longer pink. Drain. Transfer to 4 to 5 L (4 to 5 quart) slow cooker.

2. Add next 3 ingredients and 1 L (4 cups) water. Stir. Cook, covered, on Low for 9 to 10 hours or on High for 4 1/2 to 5 hours. Break up mixture with potato masher.

3. Add pesto. Stir. Makes about 2.4 L (9 3/4 cups).

VARIATION: Instead of using sausage with fennel in it, you could add 10 mL (2 tsp) whole fennel seeds to the sausage while it's browning.

37

250 mL (1 cup): 888 Kilojoules (212 Calories); 12.9 g Total Fat; 958 mg Sodium; 12 g Protein; 15 g Carbohydrate

Lamb and Barley Soup

Also known as Scottish broth, this warming soup is a centuries-old favourite.

Lamb shanks, trimmed of fat, cut into 12 mm (1/2 inch) pieces, bones reserved	1 lb	454 g
Diced carrot (6 mm, 1/4 inch, pieces)	1 cup	250 mL
Diced swede (yellow turnip) (rutabaga)	1 cup	250 mL
Pot barley	1/2 cup	125 mL
Packet of onion soup mix	1 1/2 oz	42 g

1. Heat greased large frying pan on Medium-High. Add lamb. Cook for about 8 minutes, stirring occasionally, until browned. Transfer to 4 to 5 L (4 to 5 quart) slow cooker. Add 375 mL (1 1/2 cups) water to same frying pan. Heat and stir, scraping any brown bits from bottom of pan, until boiling. Pour over lamb.

2. Add next 4 ingredients, reserved bones, 1.25 L (5 cups) water and a sprinkle of salt and pepper. Stir. Cook, covered, on Low for 8 to 10 hours or on High for 4 to 5 hours. Remove and discard bones. Makes about 1.9 L (7 1/2 cups).

Pictured between pages 32 & 33.

250 mL (1 cup): 548 Kilojoules (131 Calories); 3.9 g Total Fat; 631 mg Sodium; 8 g Protein; 16 g Carbohydrate

Smoky Salmon Potato Soup

This smooth, smoky-tasting soup is traditionally made with smoked haddock, and has kept generations of people warm on cold, rainy nights. Sprinkle with chopped fresh parsley to serve.

Finely chopped onion	1 1/2 cups	375 mL
Diced, peeled baking potato	4 cups	1 L
Liquid vegetable stock (prepared vegetable broth)	3 cups	750 mL
Milk	2 cups	500 mL
Thinly sliced smoked salmon, chopped	4 oz	113 g

1. Heat large greased frying pan (skillet) on Medium. Add onion. Cook for about 8 minutes, stirring often, until softened. Transfer to 3.5 to 4 L (3 1/2 to 4 quart) slow cooker.

2. Add potato and stock (broth). Cook, covered, on Low for 5 to 6 hours or on High for 2 1/2 to 3 hours until potato is tender.

3. Carefully process with hand blender or in blender in batches until smooth (see Safety Tip). Add milk and smoked salmon. Cook, covered, on High for about 15 minutes until heated through. Sprinkle generously with salt and pepper. Stir. Makes about 2 L (8 cups).

SAFETY TIP: Follow blender manufacturer's instructions for processing hot liquids.

250 mL (1 cup): 716 Kilojoules (171 Calories); 2.2 g Total Fat; 735 mg Sodium; 7 g Protein; 31 g Carbohydrate

Ruby Beetroot Soup

The flavours of pears and beetroots complement each other in this velvety, beautifully coloured soup. Add a sour cream garnish, or try serving it chilled for a refreshing variation.

Chopped onion	3/4 cup	175 mL
Chopped fresh peeled beetroot (see Note)	6 cups	1.5 L
Liquid vegetable stock (prepared vegetable broth)	4 cups	1 L
Can of pear halves, drained and juice reserved	28 oz	796 g
Red wine vinegar	2 tbsp	30 mL

1. Heat medium greased frying pan (skillet) on Medium. Add onion. Cook for about 5 minutes, stirring often, until softened. Transfer to 3.5 to 4 L (3 1/2 to 4 quart) slow cooker.

2. Add next 3 ingredients. Cook, covered, on Low for 8 to 9 hours or High for 4 to 4 1/2 hours until beetroot is tender.

3. Add vinegar and reserved pear juice. Stir. Carefully process with hand blender or in blender in batches until smooth (see Safety Tip). Makes about 2.4 L (9 1/2 cups).

Pictured between pages 48 & 49 and on back cover.

NOTE: Don't get caught red handed! Wear rubber gloves when handling beetroots.

SAFETY TIP: Follow blender manufacturer's instructions for processing hot liquids.

250 mL (1 cup): 389 Kilojoules (93 Calories); 0.9 g Total Fat; 383 mg Sodium; 2 g Protein; 21 g Carbohydrate

Minestrone

A large quantity recipe that will fill your slow cooker with a nourishing tomato and cabbage soup the whole family will enjoy!

Liquid chicken (or vegetable) stock (prepared chicken or vegetable broth)	6 cups	1.5 L
Cans of diced tomatoes (with juice), 398 g (14 oz) each	2	2
Can of cannellini (navy) beans, rinsed and drained	19 oz	540 g
Shredded cabbage, lightly packed	2 cups	500 mL
Sliced celery	1 3/4 cups	425 mL
Diced carrot	1 3/4 cups	425 mL
Medium leeks (white part only), cut in half lengthwise, thinly sliced	3	3
Garlic cloves, minced (or 2 mL, 1/2 tsp, powder)	2	2

White (granulated) sugar	1 tsp	5 mL
Dried basil	1/2 tsp	2 mL
Salt	1/2 tsp	2 mL
Pepper	1/2 tsp	2 mL
Diced zucchini (courgette) (with peel)	1 cup	250 mL
Frozen cut green beans, thawed	1 cup	250 mL
Grated Parmesan cheese, for garnish		

1. Combine first 12 ingredients in 5 to 7 L (5 to 7 quart) slow cooker. Cover. Cook on Low for 9 to 10 hours or on High for 4 1/2 to 5 hours.

2. Add zucchini (courgette) and green beans. Stir well. Cover. Cook on High for about 20 minutes until green beans are tender.

3. Garnish individual servings with Parmesan cheese. Makes about 3.74 L (15 cups).

Pictured between pages 48 & 49.

250 mL (1 cup): 352 Kilojoules (84 Calories); 1 g Total Fat; 568 mg Sodium; 5 g Protein; 15 g Carbohydrate

Pea and Ham Soup

A light, satisfying split pea soup, that's sure to delight! You'll need a 5 to 7 litre (5 to 7 quart) slow cooker for this large-quantity recipe. Freezes well.

Smoked pork hock (or meaty ham bone), about 790 g (1 3/4 lbs)	1	1
Chopped onion	2 cups	500 mL
Chopped carrot	2 cups	500 mL
Chopped celery	1 cup	250 mL
Chopped parsnip	1 cup	250 mL
Yellow split peas, rinsed and drained	2 1/4 cups	550 mL
Bay leaves	2	2
Salt	2 tsp	10 mL
Pepper	1/2 tsp	2 mL
Water	10 cups	2.5 L

1. Put pork hock into 5 to 7 L (5 to 7 quart) slow cooker. Layer next 8 ingredients, in order given, over top.

2. Add water. Do not stir. Cover. Cook on Low for 9 to 10 hours or on High for 4 1/2 to 5 hours. Remove and discard bay leaves. Remove pork hock to cutting board. Let stand until cool enough to handle. Remove meat from bone. Discard bone. Coarsely chop meat. Return meat to vegetable mixture. Stir well. Cover. Cook on High for 10 to 15 minutes until heated through. Makes about 3.74 L (15 cups).

250 mL (1 cup): 781 Kilojoules (186 Calories); 4.1 g Total Fat; 357 mg Sodium; 14 g Protein; 25 g Carbohydrate

Root Soup

A back-to-basics vegetable soup with a sweet, earthy flavour. Delicious with wholegrain bread. Make when celeriac (celery root) is in season.

Liquid vegetable stock (prepared vegetable broth)	8 cups	2 L
Medium potatoes, peeled, chopped	3	3
Chopped onion	3 cups	750 mL
Chopped peeled celeriac (celery root)	2 cups	500 mL
Chopped carrot	2 cups	500 mL
Chopped sweet potato (yam)	2 cups	500 mL

Medium parsnip, chopped	1	1
Salt	1/4 tsp	1 mL
Pepper	1/4 tsp	1 mL

Combine all 9 ingredients in 5 to 7 L (5 to 7 quart) slow cooker. Cover. Cook on Low for 8 to 10 hours or on High for 4 to 5 hours. Carefully process with hand blender or in blender until smooth (see Safety Tip). Makes about 2.75 L (11 cups).

SAFETY TIP: Follow blender manufacturer's instructions for processing hot liquids.

250 mL (1 cup): 504 Kilojoules (120 Calories); 0.7 g Total Fat; 712 mg Sodium; 5 g Protein; 25 g Carbohydrate

Kielbasa Potato Soup

This wholesome soup is thick with cooked-down potato and makes a meal when served with crusty bread. The longer it stands, the more the flavours blend.

Chopped peeled potato	6 cups	1.5 L
Liquid vegetable stock (prepared vegetable broth)	4 cups	1 L
Kielbasa (or other spiced cooked lean sausage), thinly sliced	3/4 lb	340 g
Garlic and herb no-salt seasoning	1/2 tsp	2 mL
Frozen cut green beans, thawed	1 1/2 cups	375 mL

1. Combine first 4 ingredients and 500 mL (2 cups) water in 5 to 7 L (5 to 7 quart) slow cooker. Sprinkle generously with salt and pepper. Cook, covered, on Low for 10 to 11 hours or on High for 5 to 5 1/2 hours.

2. Add green beans. Stir. Cook, covered, on High for about 30 minutes until tender. Break up with potato masher. Makes about 2.75 L (11 cups).

250 mL (1 cup): 674 Kilojoules (161 Calories); 1.1 g Total Fat; 853 mg Sodium; 7 g Protein; 31 g Carbohydrate

Hearty Winter Soup

Warm up with this chunky tomato soup thick with vegetables and bacon.

Bacon rashers, cooked crisp and crumbled	8	8		Sprigs of fresh rosemary (see Note)	2	2
Liquid chicken stock (prepared chicken broth)	6 cups	1.5 L		Chopped fresh parsley (or 7 mL, 1 1/2 tsp, flakes)	2 tbsp	30 mL
Chopped swede (yellow turnip)	3 cups	750 mL		Lemon juice	1 tbsp	15 mL
Can of cannellini (navy) beans, rinsed and drained	19 oz	540 g				
Chopped onion	1 cup	250 mL				
Chopped carrot	1 cup	250 mL				
Chopped celery	1/2 cup	125 mL				
Tomato paste	1/4 cup	60 mL				
Salt	1/4 tsp	1 mL				
Pepper	1/4 tsp	1 mL				
Frozen peas	1 cup	250 mL				

1. Combine first 10 ingredients in 5 to 7 L (5 to 7 quart) slow cooker. Cover. Cook on Low for 9 to 10 hours or on High for 4 1/2 to 5 hours.

2. Add remaining 4 ingredients. Stir well. Cover. Cook on High for about 10 minutes until peas are heated through. Remove and discard rosemary sprigs. Makes about 2.75 L (11 cups).

NOTE: Omit rosemary sprigs. Add 2 mL (1/2 tsp) dried crushed rosemary to first 10 ingredients.

250 mL (1 cup): 500 Kilojoules (119 Calories); 3.4 g Total Fat; 690 mg Sodium; 8 g Protein 15 g Carbohydrate

Split Pea Soup

This simple, classic soup has lots of smoky sausage flavour and a hint of garlic.

Chopped carrots	2 cups	500 mL
Yellow split peas, rinsed and drained	2 cups	500 mL
Diced kielbasa (or other spiced cooked lean sausage)	1 1/2 cups	375 mL
Chopped celery (with leaves)	3/4 cup	175 mL
Chopped onion	3/4 cup	175 mL

1. Combine all 5 ingredients in 3.5 to 4 L (3 1/2 to 4 quart) slow cooker. Add 2 L (8 cups) water. Stir. Cook, covered, on High for 6 to 7 hours until peas are tender. Sprinkle generously with salt and pepper. Stir. Makes about 2.25 L (9 cups).

Pictured between pages 32 & 33.

250 mL (1 cup): 934 Kilojoules (223 Calories); 1.1 g Total Fat; 480 mg Sodium; 17 g Protein; 37 g Carbohydrate

Curried Pumpkin Soup

This thick, creamy soup has apple cider sweetness and a touch of curry heat. With a dollop of sour cream, it's an attractive starter for any meal.

Finely chopped onion	1 1/2 cups	375 mL
Cooked pumpkin	28 oz	796 mL
Liquid chicken stock (prepared chicken broth)	2 cups	500 mL
Sweet apple cider	2 cups	500 mL
Mild curry paste	2 tsp	10 mL

1. Heat large greased frying pan (skillet) on Medium. Add onion. Cook for about 8 minutes, stirring often, until softened. Transfer to 3.5 to 4 L (3 1/2 to 4 quart) slow cooker.

2. Add remaining 4 ingredients. Stir. Cook, covered, on Low for 5 to 6 hours or on High for 2 1/2 to 3 hours. Sprinkle with salt and pepper. Carefully process with hand blender or in blender in batches until smooth (see Safety Tip). Makes about 2 L (8 cups).

SAFETY TIP: Follow manufacturer's instructions for processing liquids.

250 mL (1 cup): 377 Kilojoules (90 Calories); 1.4 g Total Fat; 500 mg Sodium; 2 g Protein; 19 g Carbohydrate

Big Batch Bean Soup

You'll need a 7 litre (7 quart) slow cooker for this soup, or recipe can be divided in half to fit a 3.5 to 4 litre (3 1/2 to 4 quart) slow cooker.
A great soup to freeze in individual containers to take to work or school.

Dried mixed beans (your choice)	2 1/2 cups	625 mL
Boiling water		
Liquid chicken (or vegetable) stock (prepared chicken or vegetable broth)	12 cups	3 L
Bag of dry coleslaw mix	16 oz	500 mL
Finely chopped onion	1 cup	250 mL
Chopped celery	1 cup	250 mL
Diced carrot	1 cup	250 mL
Dried marjoram	1 tsp	5 mL
Dried thyme	1 tsp	5 mL
Bay leaf	1	1
Pepper	1/2 tsp	2 mL
Cans of stewed tomatoes (with juice), 398 g (14 oz) each, chopped	2	2
Chopped smoked ham sausage (or similar deli sausage)	2 cups	500 mL

1. Measure beans into large bowl. Add boiling water until 5 cm (2 inches) above beans. Cover. Let stand for at least 1 hour until cool. Drain. Rinse beans. Drain well. Transfer to 7 L (7 quart) slow cooker.

2. Add next 9 ingredients. Stir well. Cover. Cook on Low for 10 to 12 hours or on High for 5 to 6 hours. Remove and discard bay leaf.

3. Add tomatoes and sausage. Stir well. Cover. Cook on High for about 20 minutes until heated through. Makes about 5.5 L (22 cups).

250 mL (1 cup): 617 Kilojoules (142 Calories); 3 g Total Fat; 697 mg Sodium; 11 g Protein; 19 g Carbohydrate

Autumn Bounty Soup

Vegetables aplenty in this thick, hearty soup topped with French bread and golden cheese. You've just 'gouda' try it!

Liquid vegetable stock (prepared vegetable broth)	4 cups	1 L
Diced sweet potato (or yam)	2 cups	500 mL
Chopped cauliflower	2 cups	500 mL
Diced peeled potato	1 cup	250 mL
Chopped carrot	1 cup	250 mL
Chopped onion	1 cup	250 mL
Bay leaf	1	1
White (granulated) sugar	1 tsp	5 mL
Dried thyme	1/2 tsp	2 mL
Salt	1/2 tsp	2 mL
Pepper	1/2 tsp	2 mL
French bread slices, 12 mm (1/2 inch) thick	6	6
Grated Gouda cheese	1 cup	250 mL

1. Combine first 11 ingredients in 3.5 to 4 L (3 1/2 to 4 quart) slow cooker. Cover. Cook on Low for 8 to 10 hours or on High for 4 to 5 hours. Remove and discard bay leaf. Makes about 1.6 L (6 1/2 cups) soup.

2. Arrange bread slices on ungreased baking tray (sheet). Sprinkle each with 37 mL (2 1/2 tbsp) cheese. Grill (broil) 10 cm (4 inches) from heat in oven for 2 to 3 minutes until cheese is melted and golden. Divide and ladle soup into 6 individual bowls. Top each with 1 bread slice. Serves 6.

1 serving: 1050 Kilojoules (250 Calories); 7.8 g Total Fat; 1087 mg Sodium; 12 g Protein; 34 g Carbohydrate

Hearty Chicken Soup

Chunky vegetables, chicken and chickpeas (garbanzo beans) fill this soup. A tasty combination to serve with rolls or salad.

Liquid chicken stock (prepared chicken broth)	6 cups	1.5 L
Can of chickpeas (garbanzo beans), rinsed and drained	14 oz	398 g
Chopped onion	1 1/2 cups	375 mL
Chopped carrot	1/2 cup	125 mL
Chopped celery	1/2 cup	125 mL
Roma (plum) tomatoes, seeds removed, chopped	3	3
Tomato paste	1/4 cup	60 mL
Bay leaf	1	1
Pepper	1/2 tsp	2 mL
Cooking oil	2 tsp	10 mL
Boneless, skinless chicken thighs, chopped	1 lb	454 g
Chopped fresh parsley (or 7 mL, 1 1/2 tsp, flakes), optional	2 tbsp	30 mL

1. Combine first 9 ingredients in 3.5 to 4 L (3 1/2 to 4 quart) slow cooker.

2. Heat cooking oil in large frying pan (skillet) on Medium. Add chicken. Cook for about 5 minutes, stirring occasionally, until browned. Add to vegetable mixture. Stir. Cover. Cook on Low for 8 to 10 hours or on High for 4 to 5 hours. Remove and discard bay leaf.

3. Add parsley. Stir well. Makes about 2.75 L (11 cups).

Pictured between pages 48 & 49.

250 mL (1 cup): 609 Kilojoules (145 Calories); 4.8 g Total Fat; 511 mg Sodium; 14 g Protein; 12 g Carbohydrate

Orange Sweet Potato Soup

Serve this thick, creamy and vibrant soup either warm or chilled.
Coriander (cilantro) lovers might enjoy a sprinkle of this fresh herb in their bowls.

Fresh peeled orange-fleshed sweet potatoes (yams), chopped	3 lbs	1.4 kg
Liquid vegetable stock (prepared vegetable broth)	4 cups	1 L
Chopped onion	1 cup	250 mL
Large oranges	2	2
Plain yoghurt	1 cup	250 mL

1. Combine sweet potato (yam) and stock (broth) in 3.5 to 4 L (3 1/2 to 4 quart) slow cooker.

2. Heat medium greased frying pan (skillet) on Medium. Add onion. Cook for about 5 minutes, stirring often, until softened. Add to slow cooker. Cook, covered, on Low for 6 to 7 hours or on High for 3 to 3 1/2 hours.

3. Grate 2 mL (1/2 tsp) orange zest into small bowl. Squeeze orange juice into same bowl. Add to slow cooker. Carefully process with hand blender or in blender in batches until almost smooth (see Safety Tip).

4. Add yoghurt. Stir. Makes about 2.5 L (10 cups).

Pictured at right and on back cover.

SAFETY TIP: Follow manufacturer's instructions for processing hot liquids.

1. Ruby Beetroot Soup, page 39
2. Orange Sweet Potato Soup, above
3. Easy Tomato Soup, page 53
4. Butternut Cream Soup, page 33

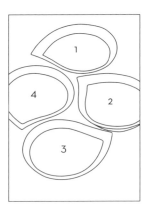

250 mL (1 cup): 662 Kilojoules (158 Calories); 1.1 g Total Fat; 276 mg Sodium; 4 g Protein; 33 g Carbohydrate

Beef Vegetable Soup

Rich colour and a full-meal soup. Serve with garlic bread or crusty rolls.

Lean beef mince (ground beef)	1 lb	454 g
Canned diced tomatoes	14 oz	398 g
Chopped onion	1 cup	250 mL
Frozen mixed vegetables	10 oz	300 g
Thinly sliced or diced carrot	1 cup	250 mL
Diced potato	1 1/2 cups	375 mL
Diced celery	1/2 cup	125 mL
Can of condensed tomato soup	10 oz	284 g
Water	3 cups	750 mL
White (granulated) sugar	1 tsp	5 mL
Salt	1/2 tsp	2 mL
Pepper	1/4 tsp	1 mL
Liquid gravy browner (optional)	1 tsp	5 mL

1. Scramble-fry beef mince (ground beef) in non-stick frying pan (skillet) until no longer pink. Drain well.

2. Combine beef mince and remaining 12 ingredients in 5 L (5 quart) slow cooker. Stir well. Cover. Cook on Low for 9 to 10 hours or on High for 4 1/2 to 5 hours. Makes 2.68 L (10 2/3 cups).

1. Hearty Chicken Soup, page 47
2. Beef Barley Soup, page 59
3. Minestrone, page 40

Props Courtesy Of: Out of the Fire Studio
Scona Clayworks
Treasure Barrel

250 mL (1 cup): 590 Kilojoules (141 Calories); 4.2 g Total Fat; 439 mg Sodium; 10 g Protein; 17 g Carbohydrate

Zesty Southwestern Soup

Turn up the heat with a steaming bowl of this spicy soup.
Serve with corn (nacho) chips instead of crackers.

Liquid vegetable stock (prepared vegetable broth)	5 cups	1.25 L
Diced peeled potato	2 2/3 cups	650 mL
Thinly sliced onion	1 3/4 cups	425 mL
Thinly sliced celery	1 cup	250 mL
Jar of diced green chillies (with juice)	4 oz	113 g
Roma (plum) tomatoes, seeds removed, chopped	2	2
Garlic cloves, minced (or 2 mL, 1/2 tsp, powder)	2	2
Chilli powder	1 tsp	5 mL
Ground cumin	1 tsp	5 mL
Cayenne pepper	1/2 tsp	2 mL
Grated sharp Cheddar cheese	1 cup	250 mL
Medium salsa, for garnish		
Chopped fresh coriander (cilantro) or parsley (or 4 mL, 3/4 tsp, dried), for garnish		

1. Combine first 10 ingredients in 3.5 to 4 L (3 1/2 to 4 quart) slow cooker. Cover. Cook on Low for 8 to 10 hours or on High for 4 to 5 hours. Carefully process with hand blender or in blender until smooth (see Safety Tip).

2. Add cheese. Stir until cheese is melted.

3. Garnish individual servings with salsa and coriander (cilantro). Makes about 1.6 L (6 1/2 cups).

SAFETY TIP: Follow blender manufacturer's instructions for processing hot liquids.

250 mL (1 cup): 739 Kilojoules (176 Calories); 7 g Total Fat; 985 mg Sodium; 10 g Protein; 20 g Carbohydrate

Sausage White Bean Soup

A kaleidoscope of colour and a team of textures produce a wonderful medley of flavour! Make it in the morning, enjoy it for dinner.

Bacon slices, diced	6	6
Chopped onion	1 cup	250 mL
Garlic cloves, minced (or 2 mL, 1/2 tsp, powder)	2	2
Liquid chicken stock (prepared chicken broth)	5 cups	1.25 L
Can of cannellini (navy) beans, rinsed and drained	19 oz	540 g
Chopped sweet potato (yam)	2 cups	500 mL
Sweet (or regular) chilli sauce	2 tbsp	30 mL
Pepper	1/2 tsp	2 mL
Cooking oil	1 tsp	5 mL
Chorizo sausages, casings removed, chopped	2	2
Fresh spinach, stems removed, lightly packed	3 cups	750 mL
Chopped fresh parsley (or 11 mL, 2 1/4 tsp, flakes)	3 tbsp	50 mL
Lemon juice	1 tbsp	15 mL

1. Cook bacon in medium frying pan (skillet) on Medium until crisp. Remove to paper towels to drain. Remove and discard drippings, reserving 15 mL (1 tbsp) in pan.

2. Add onion. Cook for 5 to 10 minutes, stirring often, until softened.

3. Add garlic. Heat and stir for about 1 minute until fragrant. Transfer to 3.5 to 4 L (3 1/2 to 4 quart) slow cooker.

4. Add bacon and next 5 ingredients. Stir well. Cover. Cook on Low for 8 to 10 hours or on High for 4 to 5 hours.

5. Heat cooking oil in same medium frying pan on Medium. Add sausage. Cook for 8 to 10 minutes, stirring occasionally, until no longer pink. Drain. Add to bean mixture. Stir.

6. Add spinach and parsley. Stir well. Cover. Cook on High for about 15 minutes until spinach is wilted.

7. Add lemon juice. Stir well. Makes about 2.25 L (9 cups).

250 mL (1 cup): 1004 Kilojoules (239 Calories); 11.3 g Total Fat; 924 mg Sodium; 13 g Protein; 21 g Carbohydrate

Red Lentil Soup

Smoky sausage adds flavour and substance to this filling soup.
Serve with rolls and salad for a delicious meal.

Water	6 cups	1.5 L
Dried red lentils, rinsed and drained	2 cups	500 mL
Diced garlic ham sausage (or other deli sausage)	1 1/2 cups	375 mL
Chopped onion	1 cup	250 mL
Chopped carrot	1 cup	250 mL

Chopped celery	1/2 cup	125 mL
Basil pesto	1 tbsp	15 mL
Bay leaves	1–2	1–2
Paprika	1/2 tsp	2 mL
Pepper	1/2 tsp	2 mL

Combine all 10 ingredients in 4 to 5 L (4 to 5 quart) slow cooker. Cover. Cook on Low for 8 to 10 hours or on High for 4 to 5 hours. Remove and discard bay leaves. Makes about 2 L (8 cups).

250 mL (1 cup): 1041 Kilojoules (248 Calories); 4.4 g Total Fat; 293 mg Sodium; 19 g Protein; 34 g Carbohydrate

Chicken Vegetable Soup

A colourful soup in a clear broth. Contains lots of chicken.

Boneless, skinless chicken breast halves, diced	3	3
Chopped onion	1 cup	250 mL
Thinly sliced carrot	1 1/3 cups	325 mL
Diced celery	1/2 cup	125 mL
Diced turnip	1/2 cup	125 mL
Diced potato	2 cups	500 mL
Chicken stock (bouillon) powder	1 tbsp	15 mL

Salt	1 tsp	5 mL
Pepper	1/4 tsp	1 mL
Ground thyme	1/4 tsp	1 mL
Water	4 cups	1 L
Liquid gravy browner, to colour slightly (optional)		

1. Place first 11 ingredients in 5 L (5 quart) slow cooker. Stir. Cover. Cook on Low for 8 to 10 hours or on High for 4 to 5 hours. If vegetables are large and not quite tender, turn heat to High for a few minutes.

2. Add gravy browner just before serving. Taste for salt and pepper, adding more if needed. Makes 2 L (8 cups).

250 mL (1 cup): 441 Kilojoules (105 Calories); 0.9 g Total Fat; 635 mg Sodium; 12 g Protein; 12 g Carbohydrate

cooker. Cook, covered, on Low for 5 to 6 hours or on High for 2 1/2 to 3 hours.

2. Add lime juice. Stir. Makes about 3 L (12 cups).

Pictured between pages 48 & 49 and on back cover.

Tomato juice	12 cups	3 L
White (granulated) sugar	2 tbsp	30 mL
Worcestershire sauce	1 tbsp	15 mL
Italian seasoning	2 tsp	10 mL
Lime juice	1 tbsp	15 mL

250 mL (1 cup): 381 Kilojoules (91 Calories); 0.1 g Total Fat; 1329 mg Sodium; 4 g Protein; 23 g Carbohydrate

Coconut Carrot Soup

Try this fragrant, velvety smooth soup with a splash of lime juice – any way you serve it, it's sweet, spicy and absolutely delicious.

Chopped onion	1 1/2 cups	375 mL
Thai red curry paste	2 tsp	10 mL
Sliced carrot	6 cups	1.5 L
Liquid vegetable stock (prepared vegetable broth)	5 cups	1.25 L
Can of coconut milk	14 oz	398 mL

1. Heat large greased frying pan (skillet) on Medium. Add onion. Cook for about 8 minutes, stirring often, until onion is softened.

2. Add curry paste. Heat and stir for 1 minute. Transfer to 3.5 to 4 L (3 1/2 to 4 quart) slow cooker.

3. Add carrot, stock (broth) and a sprinkle of salt. Stir. Cook, covered, on Low for 8 to 10 hours or on High for 4 to 5 hours.

4. Add coconut milk. Stir. Carefully process with hand blender or in blender in batches until smooth (see Safety Tip). Makes about 2.5 L (10 cups).

SAFETY TIP: Follow blender manufacturer's instructions for processing hot liquids.

250 mL (1 cup): 595 Kilojoules (142 Calories); 9.6 g Total Fat; 383 mg Sodium; 2 g Protein; 14 g Carbohydrate

SOUPS

53

Chinese Mushroom Soup

A mingling of light ingredients, reminiscent of hot and sour soup.

Chinese dried mushrooms, stems removed	15	15
Boiling water		
Liquid chicken stock (prepared chicken broth)	6 cups	1.5 L
Can of sliced water chestnuts, drained	8 oz	227 g
Can of bamboo shoots, drained	8 oz	227 g
Rice vinegar	1/3 cup	75 mL
Soy sauce	1/4 cup	60 mL
Dried crushed chillies	1 tsp	5 mL
Diced cooked pork	1 cup	250 mL
Sliced spring (green) onion	2 tbsp	30 mL

1. Place mushrooms in small bowl. Add boiling water until 5 cm (2 inches) above mushrooms. Let stand for about 20 minutes until softened. Drain. Thinly slice mushrooms. Transfer to 3.5 to 4 L (3 1/2 to 4 quart) slow cooker.

2. Add next 6 ingredients. Stir well. Cover. Cook on Low for 8 to 10 hours or on High for 4 to 5 hours.

3. Add pork and onion. Stir well. Cover. Cook on High for 10 to 15 minutes until pork is heated through. Makes about 2.1 L (8 1/2 cups).

VARIATION: Omit pork. Use same amount of diced cooked beef, chicken or prawns. For meatless soup, use same amount of diced tofu.

250 mL (1 cup): 491 Kilojoules (117 Calories); 3.9 g Total Fat; 1110 mg Sodium; 10 g Protein; 11 g Carbohydrate

Smoked Pork and Bean Soup

Make sure about a third of the legumes are split peas and/or red lentils because they break up during cooking, giving the soup a great texture.

Dried mixed beans and lentils	1 1/2 cups	375 mL
Smoked pork hock (or meaty ham bone)	1 1/2 lbs	680 g
Chopped onion	1 cup	250 mL
Can of diced tomatoes (with juice)	14 oz	398 g
Packet of vegetable soup mix	1 1/4 oz	40 g

1. Measure beans and lentils into medium bowl. Add water until 5 cm (2 inches) above beans. Let stand overnight (see Tip). Drain. Rinse beans. Drain. Transfer to 5 to 7 L (5 to 7 quart) slow cooker.

2. Add pork hock, onion and 2.25 L (9 cups) water. Cook, covered, on High for 4 to 5 hours until beans are tender. Remove pork hock. Let stand until cool enough to handle. Remove and discard skin, bones and fat. Chop meat. Return to slow cooker.

3. Add tomatoes, soup mix and a sprinkle of salt and pepper. Stir. Cook, covered, on High for about 45 minutes until vegetables are tender. Makes about 3.4 L (13 1/2 cups).

Pictured between pages 32 & 33.

TIP: If you would like a quicker method for soaking the beans, place beans in a heatproof dish, cover with boiling water and let stand for at least one hour until cool.

250 mL (1 cup): 917 Kilojoules (219 Calories); 12.1 g Total Fat; 304 mg Sodium; 17 g Protein; 10 g Carbohydrate

Simple Bean Soup

A good soup born of convenience food that you can have ready in record time.

Canned cannellini (navy) beans (398 g, 14 oz, each)	2	2
Canned flakes of ham, with liquid, broken up (or 1 cup, 250 mL, diced ham)	6.5 oz	184 g
Chopped onion	1 1/2 cups	375 mL
Beef stock (bouillon) powder	1 tbsp	15 mL
Warm water	2 1/2 cups	625 mL
Tomato sauce (ketchup)	1 tbsp	15 mL

Combine all 6 ingredients in 3.5 L (3 1/2 quart) slow cooker. Stir. Cover. Cook on Low for 8 to 10 hours or on High for 4 to 5 hours. Makes 1.75 L (7 cups).

250 mL (1 cup): 942 Kilojoules (225 Calories); 5.7 g Total Fat; 1208 mg Sodium; 14 g Protein; 30 g Carbohydrate

Meaty Chicken Soup

The broth is tasty and can be used in other dishes – it also freezes well.
Egg noodles or cooked rice may be added for an even heartier soup.

Chicken legs, back attached (310–340 g, 11–12 oz, each), skin removed	4	4
Chopped onions	2 1/2 cups	625 mL
Chopped celery (with leaves)	1 cup	250 mL
Sprig of fresh rosemary	1	1
Chopped carrot	1 1/2 cups	375 mL

1. Put chicken into 5 to 7 L (5 to 7 quart) slow cooker. Add next 3 ingredients, 2 L (8 cups) water and a generous sprinkle of salt and pepper. Cook, covered, on Low for 6 hours or on High for 3 hours.

2. Add carrot. Cook, covered, on High for about 2 hours until chicken and carrot are tender. Remove and discard rosemary. Transfer chicken and bones with slotted spoon to cutting board.

Let stand until cool enough to handle. Remove chicken from bones. Discard bones. Coarsely chop chicken. Skim and discard fat from broth. Return chicken to broth. Sprinkle generously with salt and pepper. Stir. Makes about 3.25 L (13 cups).

250 mL (1 cup): 519 Kilojoules (124 Calories); 4.7 g Total Fat; 245 mg Sodium; 15 g Protein; 5 g Carbohydrate

Bean Soup

A brownish soup with tomato adding some colour.
Thick and simple soup with a good flavour.

Dried cannellini (navy) beans (454 g, 1 lb)	2 1/3 cups	575 mL
Chopped onion	1 1/4 cups	300 mL
Garlic clove, minced (or 1 mL, 1/4 tsp, powder)	1	1
Canned flakes of ham, with liquid, broken up (or 250 mL, 1 cup, diced ham)	6.5 oz	184 g
Canned tomatoes, with juice, broken up	14 oz	398 g
Water	6 cups	1.5 L
Salt	1 tsp	5 mL
Pepper	1/4 tsp	1 mL

Measure all 8 ingredients into 5 L (5 quart) slow cooker. Stir well. Cover. Cook on Low for 8 to 10 hours or on High for 4 to 5 hours. Taste for salt and pepper, adding more if needed. Makes 2.4 L (9 2/3 cups).

250 mL (1 cup): 974.4 Kilojoules (232 Calories); 4.4 g Total Fat; 616 mg Sodium; 15 g Protein; 35 g Carbohydrate

Sweet Onion Soup

An easy take on onion soup – and no need to caramelise the onions on the stove! For a real treat, serve this delicious soup with slices of toast topped with melted smoked cheddar or havarti.

Thinly sliced sweet onion (see Note 1)	6 cups	1.5 L
Olive (or cooking) oil	3 tbsp	50 mL
Liquid beef stock (prepared beef broth) (see Note 2)	6 cups	1.5 L
Dark beer	1 1/2 cups	375 mL
Sprig of fresh thyme (or 2 mL, 1/2 tsp, dried)	1	1

1. Combine onion and olive oil in 3.5 to 4 L (3 1/2 to 4 quart) slow cooker. Cook, covered, on High for about 6 hours, stirring once at halftime, until onion is caramelised.

2. Add next 3 ingredients and a sprinkle of salt and pepper. Cook, covered, on High for about 45 minutes until heated through. Remove and discard thyme sprig. Makes about 2.2 L (8 3/4 cups).

NOTE 1: If you prefer not to have long strands of onion, cut onions in half before slicing for shorter strands.

NOTE 2: When adding liquid to a hot slow cooker, make sure the liquid is at least at room temperature, as cold liquids could cause the liner to crack

250 mL (1 cup): 511 Kilojoules (122 Calories); 5.4 g Total Fat; 1017 mg Sodium; 2 g Protein; 15 g Carbohydrate

Mushroom Dill Soup

A light and refreshing combination. Earthy mushrooms blend
with the tanginess of dill in a wine-accented broth.

Chopped assorted fresh mushrooms (see Note)	6 cups	1.5 L
Dry (or alcohol-free) white wine	1 cup	250 mL
Liquid vegetable stock (prepared vegetable broth)	4 cups	1 L
Grated peeled potato	1 1/2 cups	375 mL
Dried dill (dillweed)	2 tsp	10 mL

1. Heat large greased frying pan (skillet) or pot on Medium-High. Add mushrooms. Cook for about 10 minutes, stirring occasionally, until mushrooms start to brown.

2. Add wine and a generous sprinkle of salt and pepper. Heat and stir for 2 minutes. Transfer to 3.5 to 4 L (3 1/2 to 4 quart) slow cooker.

3. Add remaining 3 ingredients. Stir. Cook, covered, on Low for 4 to 5 hours or on High for 2 to 2 1/2 hours. Makes about 1.75 L (7 cups).

NOTE: If using portobello mushrooms, remove gills before chopping.

250 mL (1 cup): 458 Kilojoules (109 Calories); 1.2 g Total Fat; 553 mg Sodium; 3 g Protein; 16 g Carbohydrate

Curry Corn Soup

This rich, smooth soup blends the lovely flavours of mild
curry, sweet coconut and creamed corn.

Chopped onion	1 1/2 cups	375 mL
Hot curry paste	1 tbsp	15 mL
White (granulated) sugar	1 tsp	5 mL
Can of coconut milk	14 oz	398 mL
Frozen corn kernels, thawed	4 cups	1 L

1. Heat large greased frying pan (skillet) on Medium. Add onion. Cook for about 8 minutes, stirring often, until softened.

2. Add curry paste and sugar. Heat and stir for 1 minute. Add coconut milk. Stir. Transfer to 4 to 5 L (4 to 5 quart) slow cooker.

3. Add corn, 500 mL (2 cups) water and a generous sprinkle of salt. Stir. Cook, covered, on Low for 5 to 6 hours or on High for 2 1/2 to 3 hours. Carefully process with hand blender or in blender in batches until smooth (see Safety Tip). Makes about 1.5 L (6 cups).

SAFETY TIP: Follow blender manufacturer's instructions for processing hot liquids.

250 mL (1 cup): 1022 Kilojoules (244 Calories); 15.9 g Total Fat; 352 mg Sodium; 5 g Protein; 24 g Carbohydrate

Beef Barley Soup

Quick to assemble in the morning – ready when the family arrives in the evening.

Water	5 cups	1.25 L
Cans of condensed beef stock (broth) (284 mL, 10 oz, each)	2	2
Can of sliced mushrooms, drained	10 oz	284 g
Chopped onion	1 cup	250 mL
Chopped carrot	1 cup	250 mL
Tomato purée (tomato sauce)	7 1/2 oz	213 mL
Pearl barley	1/2 cup	125 mL
Bay leaves	2	2
Dried thyme	1 tsp	5 mL
Salt	1/4 tsp	1 mL
Pepper	1/8 tsp	0.5 mL
Beef stewing meat, cut into 12 mm (1/2 inch) pieces	1 lb	454 g
Frozen peas	1 cup	250 mL
Chopped fresh parsley (or 4 mL, 3/4 tsp, flakes)	1 tbsp	15 mL

1. Combine first 12 ingredients in 4 to 5 L (4 to 5 quart) slow cooker. Cover. Cook on Low for 8 to 10 hours or on High for 4 to 5 hours. Remove and discard bay leaves.

2. Add peas and parsley. Stir well. Cover. Cook on High for 3 to 5 minutes until peas are heated through. Makes about 3 L (12 cups).

Pictured between pages 48 & 49.

250 mL (1 cup): 554 Kilojoules (132 Calories); 3.7 g Total Fat; 571 mg Sodium; 12 g Protein; 13 g Carbohydrate

Pizza Topping Soup

Pizza you can eat with a spoon! Enjoy all the pizza toppings you love in a hearty soup. Serve with focaccia or crusty bread.

Cooking oil	1 tsp	5 mL
Hot Italian sausages, casings removed, chopped	1 lb	454 g
Cans of diced tomatoes (with juice), 398 g (14 oz) each	2	2
Sliced fresh white mushrooms	2 cups	500 mL
Sliced green capsicum	1 3/4 cups	425 mL
Can of condensed beef stock (broth)	10 oz	284 mL
Chopped onion	1 cup	250 mL
Water	1 cup	250 mL
Tomato purée (tomato sauce)	7 1/2 oz	213 mL
Dried oregano	1/2 tsp	2 mL
Dried basil	1/2 tsp	2 mL
Cayenne pepper	1/8 tsp	0.5 mL
Grated reduced fat (part-skim) mozzarella cheese (or normal mozzarella)	1 cup	250 mL

1. Heat cooking oil in medium frying pan (skillet) on Medium. Add sausage. Scramble-fry for 8 to 10 minutes until no longer pink. Drain. Transfer to 4 to 5 L (4 to 5 quart) slow cooker.

2. Add next 10 ingredients. Stir well. Cover. Cook on Low for 8 to 9 hours or on High for 4 to 4 1/2 hours. Makes about 2.3 L (9 1/3 cups) soup.

3. Divide and ladle soup into 6 individual bowls. Sprinkle each with cheese. Serves 6.

1 serving: 1016 Kilojoules (242 Calories); 13.3 g Total Fat; 1182 mg Sodium; 16 g Protein; 16 g Carbohydrate

Tortilla Soup

A perfect starter for a casual or Mexican-themed party. Adjust the heat by choosing mild, medium or hot salsa.

Liquid chicken stock (prepared chicken broth)	4 cups	1 L
Chunky salsa	1 1/2 cups	375 mL
Processed cheese spread (can of condensed Cheddar cheese soup)	10 oz	284 g
Sour cream	2/3 cup	150 mL
Corn (tortilla) chips, broken up	1 cup	250 mL

1. Combine first 3 ingredients in 3.5 to 4 L (3 1/2 to 4 quart) slow cooker. Cook, covered, on Low for 4 to 6 hours or on High for 2 to 3 hours.

2. Add sour cream. Stir until smooth.

3. Put corn (tortilla) chips into 4 soup bowls. Ladle soup over chips. Serves 4.

1 serving: 1089 Kilojoules (260 Calories); 13.9 g Total Fat; 2834 mg Sodium; 5 g Protein; 27 g Carbohydrate

Creamy Clam Chowder

Everyone's favourite seafood soup with five ingredients! This version is rich and creamy with the delicious flavours of potatoes, clams and dill.

Cans of minced clams (85 g, 3 oz, each), drained and liquid reserved	3	3
Can of condensed cream of mushroom and onion soup	10 oz	284 g
Diced peeled potato	3 cups	750 mL
Dried dill (dillweed)	1/2 tsp	2 mL
Homogenised milk	1 1/2 cups	375 mL

1. Combine clam liquid, soup and 250 mL (1 cup) water in 3.5 to 4 L (3 1/2 to 4 quart) slow cooker. Stir until smooth. Chill clams.

2. Add potato and dill (dillweed) to slow cooker. Stir. Cook, covered, on Low for 6 to 8 hours or on High for 3 to 4 hours.

3. Add milk and reserved clams. Cook, covered, on High for about 15 minutes until heated through. Makes about 1.75 L (7 cups).

250 mL (1 cup): 774 Kilojoules (185 Calories); 5.2 g Total Fat; 739 mg Sodium; 10 g Protein; 26 g Carbohydrate

Curried Split Pea Soup

This curried soup topped with croutons is sure to satisfy a dinnertime crowd.

Smoked pork hock (or meaty ham bone), about 790 g (1 3/4 lbs)	1	1
Green split peas, rinsed and drained	2 cups	500 mL
Chopped onion	1 cup	250 mL
Chopped carrot	1 cup	250 mL
Chopped celery	1 cup	250 mL
Curry powder	1 tbsp	15 mL
Dried thyme	1 tsp	5 mL
Bay leaf	1	1
Pepper	1/2 tsp	2 mL
Cans of condensed chicken stock (broth) (284 mL, 10 oz, each)	2	2
Water	5 cups	1.25 L

CURRIED CROUTONS

White bread slices (with crusts), cubed	6	6
Grated Parmesan cheese	2 tsp	10 mL
Curry powder	1/2 tsp	2 mL
Hard margarine (or butter)	1/4 cup	60 mL

1. Put pork hock into 5 to 7 L (5 to 7 quart) slow cooker. Layer next 8 ingredients, in order given, over top.

2. Pour stock (broth) and water over top. Do not stir. Cover. Cook on Low for 8 to 10 hours or on High for 4 to 5 hours. Remove and discard bay leaf. Remove pork hock to cutting board. Let stand until cool enough to handle. Remove meat from bone. Discard bone. Cut meat into 12 mm (1/2 inch) pieces. Carefully process vegetable mixture with hand blender or in blender until smooth (see Safety Tip). Return meat to vegetable mixture. Stir well. Makes about 2.5 L (10 cups) soup.

3. CURRIED CROUTONS: Put bread cubes into large bowl. Add Parmesan cheese and curry powder. Toss well.

4. Melt margarine in large frying pan (skillet) on Medium. Add coated bread cubes. Heat and stir for about 10 minutes until bread cubes are toasted. Makes about 500 mL (2 cups) croutons. Divide and ladle soup into 8 individual bowls. Top each serving with 60 mL (1/4 cup) croutons. Serves 8.

SAFETY TIP: Follow blender manufacturer's instructions for processing hot liquids.

1 serving: 1852 Kilojoules (441 Calories); 15.6 g Total Fat; 714 mg Sodium; 29 g Protein; 47 g Carbohydrate

Tomato Bean Soup

A hearty, deep red tomato soup full of tender beans and vegetables. Top individual servings with a dollop of sour cream and serve with slices of crusty wholemeal bread.

Dried chickpeas, (garbanzo beans) rinsed and drained	1 cup	250 mL
Dried red kidney beans, rinsed and drained	1 cup	250 mL
Boiling water		
Chopped onion	1 cup	250 mL
Chopped celery	1 cup	250 mL
Chopped carrot	1 cup	250 mL
Ground cumin	1 tbsp	15 mL
Paprika	1 tbsp	15 mL
Ground coriander	1 tbsp	15 mL
Garlic cloves, minced (or 2 mL, 1/2 tsp, powder)	2	2
Liquid chicken (or vegetable) stock (prepared chicken or vegetable broth)	6 cups	1.5 L
Can of diced tomatoes (with juice)	28 oz	796 g

Tomato paste	2 tbsp	30 mL
White (granulated) sugar	1 tsp	5 mL
Salt, sprinkle		
Box of frozen chopped spinach, thawed and squeezed dry	10 oz	284 g

1. Measure chickpeas (garbanzo beans) and kidney beans into large bowl. Add boiling water until 5 cm (2 inches) above beans. Cover. Let stand for at least 1 hour until cool. Drain. Rinse beans. Drain well. Transfer to 5 to 7 L (5 to 7 quart) slow cooker.

2. Layer next 3 ingredients, in order given, on top of beans.

3. Sprinkle next 4 ingredients over carrot. Add stock (broth). Do not stir. Cover. Cook on Low for 8 to 10 hours or on High for 4 to 5 hours.

4. Add next 4 ingredients. Stir well. Cover. Cook on High for about 30 minutes until heated through.

5. Add spinach. Stir well. Cover. Cook for 1 to 2 minutes until spinach is wilted. Makes about 3.1 L (12 1/2 cups).

250 mL (1 cup): 718 Kilojoules (171 Calories); 2.4 g Total Fat; 535 mg Sodium; 11 g Protein; 28 g Carbohydrate

White Bean Borscht

Creamy beetroot and bean soup with a dash of dill.
Sour cream and fresh parsley garnishes are a nice touch.

Dried cannellini (navy) beans, rinsed and drained	1 cup	250 mL
Boiling water		
Liquid chicken (or vegetable) stock (prepared chicken or vegetable broth)	8 cups	2 L
Fresh medium beetroots, peeled, cut into 12 mm (1/2 inch) pieces	3	3
Finely chopped onion	1 cup	250 mL
Diced carrot	2/3 cup	150 mL
Finely chopped brown (or white) mushrooms	1/2 cup	125 mL
Garlic clove, minced (or 1 mL, 1/4 tsp, powder), optional	1	1
Bay leaf	1	1
Unthickened (half-and-half) cream	1/2 cup	125 mL
Plain (all-purpose) flour	2 tbsp	30 mL

Lemon juice	1 tbsp	15 mL
Dried dill leaf tips (dillweed)	1 tsp	5 mL
Salt	1 tsp	5 mL
Pepper	1/2 tsp	2 mL
Sour cream (or unthickened/half-and-half-cream, for garnish)		
Chopped fresh parsley, for garnish		

1. Measure beans into medium bowl. Add boiling water until 5 cm (2 inches) above beans. Cover. Let stand for at least 1 hour until cool. Drain. Rinse beans. Drain well. Transfer to 4 to 5 L (4 to 5 quart) slow cooker.

2. Add next 7 ingredients. Stir well. Cover. Cook on Low for 9 to 12 hours or on High for 4 1/2 to 6 hours. Remove and discard bay leaf.

3. Stir cream into flour in small bowl until smooth. Add to bean mixture. Stir well. Cover. Cook on High for about 15 minutes until boiling and slightly thickened.

4. Add next 4 ingredients. Stir well.

5. Garnish individual servings with sour cream and parsley. Makes about 2.4 L (9 3/4 cups).

250 mL (1 cup): 651 Kilojoules (155 Calories); 2.9 g Total Fat; 964 mg Sodium; 10 g Protein; 22 g Carbohydrate

RICE & PASTA

RICE & PASTA

Pictured on reverse:

1. Italiano Pasta Sauce, page 76
2. Veggie Pasta Sauce, page 82
3. Chicken Sausage Pasta Sauce, page 83

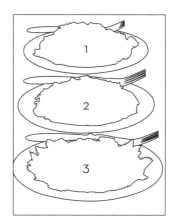

Lasagne

Tastes just like lasagne but doesn't have layers.

Lasagne noodles, broken into bite-size pieces	8	8
Boiling water	3 qts	3 L
Cooking oil (optional)	2 tsp	10 mL
Salt	2 tsp	10 mL
Lean beef mince (ground beef)	1 1/2 lbs	680 g
Finely chopped onion	3/4 cup	175 mL
Canned tomatoes, 398 g (14 oz) each with juice, broken up	2	2
Tomato paste	5 1/2 oz	156 mL
Creamed cottage cheese	1 cup	250 mL
Grated mozzarella cheese	2 cups	500 mL
White (granulated) sugar	2 tsp	10 mL

Parsley flakes	1 tsp	5 mL
Dried oregano	1/2 tsp	2 mL
Garlic powder	1/4 tsp	1 mL
Dried basil	1/4 tsp	1 mL
Salt	1 1/4 tsp	6 mL
Pepper	1/2 tsp	2 mL

1. Cook lasagne noodle pieces in boiling water, cooking oil and salt in large uncovered pot for 14 to 16 minutes until tender but firm. Drain.

2. Scramble-fry beef mince (ground beef) in non-stick frying pan (skillet) until browned. Drain well. Turn into 3.5 L (3 1/2 quart) slow cooker.

3. Add remaining 12 ingredients. Stir well. Add lasagne noodle pieces. Stir. Cover. Cook on Low for 7 to 9 hours or on High for 3 1/2 to 4 1/2 hours. Makes (2.5 L) 10 cups.

250 mL (1 cup): 1235 Kilojoules (295 Calories); 12.4 g Total Fat; 708 mg Sodium; 24 g Protein; 22 g Carbohydrate

Chicken Tetrazzini

A complete meal.

Chopped onion	1 cup	250 mL
Sliced fresh mushrooms	3 cups	750 mL
Chopped, boneless, skinless chicken (white or dark meat)	3 cups	750 mL
Plain (all-purpose) flour	3 tbsp	50 mL
Salt	1 tsp	5 mL
Pepper	1/4 tsp	1 mL
Chicken stock (bouillon) powder	1 tbsp	15 mL
Water	1 1/2 cups	375 mL
Skim evaporated milk	1 cup	250 mL
Sherry (or alcohol-free sherry)	3 tbsp	50 mL
Spaghetti noodles, broken into short pieces	8 oz	250 g
Grated Parmesan cheese, sprinkle		

1. Combine first 7 ingredients in 5 L (5 quart) slow cooker. Stir well to coat chicken with flour.

2. Pour water, evaporated milk and sherry into bowl. Stir. Pour over top. Cover. Cook on Low for 6 to 8 hours or on High for 3 to 4 hours.

3. Add noodles. Stir well to avoid sticking together. Push under liquid. Sprinkle with cheese. Cook on High for 15 to 20 minutes until tender. Makes 1.75 L (7 cups).

250 mL (1 cup): 1239 Kilojoules (296 Calories); 3.4 g Total Fat; 780 mg Sodium; 26 g Protein; 38 g Carbohydrate

Spicy Spaghetti Sauce

Serve this chunky sauce over spaghetti, noodles or other pasta.

Canned diced tomatoes	19 oz	540 g
Tomato sauce (ketchup)	1/4 cup	60 mL
Canned sliced mushrooms, drained	10 oz	284 g
Chopped green capsicum (pepper)	1/3 cup	75 mL
Lemon juice	1 1/2 tbsp	25 mL
Dried oregano	3/4 tsp	4 mL
Dried basil	1/2 tsp	2 mL
Bay leaf	1	1
Chilli powder	2 tsp	10 mL
Garlic powder	1/4 tsp	1 mL
White (granulated) sugar (optional)	1 tsp	5 mL
Salt	1 1/2 tsp	7 mL

Pepper	1/4 tsp	1 mL
Lean beef mince (ground beef)	1 lb	454 g
Chopped onion	1 cup	250 mL

1. Combine first 13 ingredients in 3.5 L (3 1/2 quart) slow cooker.

2. Scramble-fry beef mince (ground beef) and onion in non-stick frying pan (skillet) until beef is no longer pink. Drain well. Add to slow cooker. Stir. Cover. Cook on Low for 6 to 7 hours or on High for 3 to 3 1/2 hours. Discard bay leaf. Makes 1.3 L (5 1/4 cups).

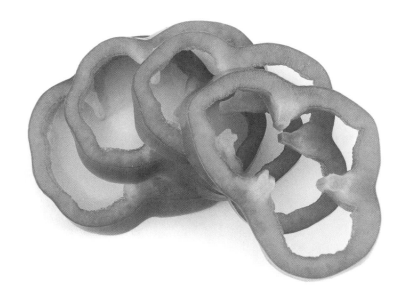

250 mL (1 cup): 808 Kilojoules (193 Calories); 7.8 g Total Fat; 1267 mg Sodium; 18 g Protein; 14 g Carbohydrate

Greek Pasta Bake

This filling dish features tomato-saucy pasta with lots of lemony lamb for Greek flair. Round it out with a Greek salad and garlic toast.

Lean lamb mince (ground lamb)	1 1/2 lbs	680 g
Greek seasoning	1 tbsp	15 mL
Grated lemon zest	1 tsp	5 mL
Four-cheese tomato pasta sauce	4 cups	1 L
Cooked rigatoni pasta (about 750 mL, 3 cups, uncooked)	5 cups	1.25 L

1. Scramble-fry lamb in large greased frying pan (skillet) on Medium-High for about 10 minutes until no longer pink.

2. Add Greek seasoning, lemon zest and a sprinkle of salt and pepper. Stir.

3. To assemble, layer ingredients in greased 5 to 7 L (5 to 7 quart) slow cooker as follows:
   a) 175 mL (3/4 cup) pasta sauce
   b) 1/3 of pasta
   c) 250 mL (1 cup) lamb mixture

4. Repeat steps a to c to make 2 more layers. Top with remaining pasta sauce.

5. Cook, covered, on Low for 3 to 4 hours or on High for 1 1/2 to 2 hours until heated through. Serves 8.

1 serving: 1884 Kilojoules (450 Calories); 20.7 g Total Fat; 792 mg Sodium; 27 g Protein; 37 g Carbohydrate

Pesto Chicken Pasta

Light, mildly spiced sauce coats pasta, red capsicum (peppers) and chicken.

Chopped red onion	1 cup	250 mL
Dry white (or alcohol-free) wine	1 cup	250 mL
Red capsicums (peppers), seeds and ribs removed, cut into strips	2	2
Garlic cloves, minced (or 2 mL, 1/2 tsp, powder)	2	2
Chilli powder	1 tsp	5 mL
Salt	1/2 tsp	2 mL
Pepper	1/2 tsp	2 mL
Boneless, skinless chicken thighs (57–85 g, 2–3 oz, each), halved	12	12
Lemon juice	1 tbsp	15 mL
Cornflour (cornstarch)	1 tbsp	15 mL
Sun-dried tomato pesto	3 tbsp	50 mL
Penne pasta (about 285 g, 10 oz)	3 cups	750 mL

Boiling water	12 cups	3 L
Salt	1 1/2 tsp	7 mL
Grated Parmesan cheese	1/3 cup	75 mL

1. Combine first 7 ingredients in 3.5 to 4 L (3 1/2 to 4 quart) slow cooker. Add chicken. Stir well. Cover. Cook on Low for 7 to 8 hours or on High for 3 1/2 to 4 hours.

2. Stir lemon juice into cornflour (cornstarch) in small cup until smooth. Add pesto. Stir well. Add to chicken mixture. Stir. Cover. Cook on High for about 15 minutes until sauce is thickened.

3. Cook pasta in boiling water and second amount of salt in large uncovered pot for about 15 minutes, stirring occasionally, until tender but firm. Drain. Return pasta to pot. Add chicken mixture. Toss gently until coated. Remove to large serving bowl.

4. Sprinkle with Parmesan cheese. Serves 6.

1 serving: 1768 Kilojoules (421 Calories); 9.4 g Total Fat; 328 mg Sodium; 31 g Protein; 45 g Carbohydrate

Creamy Cauliflower Rotini

A little spice is always nice! Use less jalapeño chilli, if desired, to cut the heat of this creamy, cheesy dish. Sauce freezes well to reheat and add to pasta another day.

Cauliflower florets	3 cups	750 mL
Liquid vegetable stock (prepared vegetable broth)	3 cups	750 mL
Can of cannellini (navy) beans, rinsed and drained	19 oz	540 g
Chopped red capsicum (pepper)	1 cup	250 mL
Chopped carrot	1 cup	250 mL
Finely chopped onion	1 cup	250 mL
Ground cumin	1 tsp	5 mL
Chilli powder	1 tsp	5 mL
Salt	1/4 tsp	1 mL
Pepper	1/4 tsp	1 mL
Plain (all purpose) flour	2 tbsp	30 mL
Grated white Cheddar cheese	1 cup	250 mL
Frozen peas	1 cup	250 mL
Block of cream cheese, cut up, softened	4 oz	125 g

Finely chopped canned jalapeño chilli	2 tbsp	30 mL
Rotini pasta (about 681 g, 24 oz), or other spiral pasta	9 cups	2.25 L
Boiling water	24 cups	6 L

1. Combine first 10 ingredients in 4 to 5 L (4 to 5 quart) slow cooker. Cover. Cook on Low for 8 to 9 hours or on High for 4 to 4 1/2 hours.

2. Measure flour into small bowl. Add Cheddar cheese. Toss until coated. Add to cauliflower mixture. Stir.

3. Add next 3 ingredients. Stir well. Cover. Cook on High for about 30 minutes until sauce is slightly thickened.

4. Cook pasta in boiling water and second amount of salt in large uncovered pot for 10 to 12 minutes, stirring occasionally, until tender but firm. Drain. Return pasta to pot. Add cauliflower mixture. Toss until coated. Serves 8.

1 serving: 2247 Kilojoules (535 Calories); 12.5 g Total Fat; 682 mg Sodium; 22 g Protein; 83 g Carbohydrate

Bacon Chicken Pasta

Tender chicken and spiral pasta coated with a light, creamy sauce and a pungent pairing of feta cheese and smoky bacon. Serve with a crisp salad.

Bacon rashers, diced	6	6
Chopped onion	1 cup	250 mL
Boneless, skinless chicken thighs, quartered	1 lb	454 g
Liquid chicken stock (prepared chicked broth)	1 cup	250 mL
Salt	1/4 tsp	1 mL
Pepper	1/2 tsp	2 mL
Milk	1/2 cup	125 mL
Cornflour (cornstarch)	1 tbsp	15 mL
Frozen peas	2/3 cup	150 mL
Chopped fresh parsley (or 7 mL, 1 1/2 tsp, flakes)	2 tbsp	30 mL
Rotini (or other spiral) pasta (about 225 g, 8 oz)	3 cups	750 mL
Boiling water	8 cups	2 L
Salt	1 tsp	5 mL
Crumbled feta cheese	1 cup	250 mL

1. Cook bacon in large frying pan (skillet) on Medium until almost crisp. Drain, reserving bacon and about 5 mL (1 tsp) drippings in pan.

2. Add onion. Cook for 5 to 10 minutes, stirring often, until onion is softened. Transfer to 1.5 L (1 1/2 quart) slow cooker.

3. Add next 4 ingredients. Stir well. Cover. Cook on Low for 8 to 10 hours or on High for 4 to 5 hours.

4. Stir milk into cornflour (cornstarch) in small bowl until smooth. Add to chicken mixture. Stir.

5. Add peas and parsley. Stir well. Cover. Cook on High for 15 to 20 minutes until sauce is thickened.

6. Cook pasta in boiling water and second amount of salt in large uncovered pot for 10 to 15 minutes, stirring occasionally, until tender but firm. Drain. Return pasta to pot.

7. Add chicken mixture and feta cheese. Toss gently until coated. Serves 4.

Pictured between pages 80 & 81 and on front cover.

1 serving: 2339 Kilojoules (557 Calories); 18.8 g Total Fat; 882 mg Sodium; 40 g Protein; 54 g Carbohydrate

Tomato Chickpea Pasta

Spicy chickpea and tomato sauce tossed with penne pasta.
A great way to introduce legumes!

Can of diced tomatoes (with juice)	28 oz	796 g
Can of chickpeas (garbanzo beans), rinsed and drained	19 oz	540 g
Dry white (or alcohol-free) wine	1/2 cup	125 mL
Olive (or cooking) oil	2 tbsp	30 mL
Balsamic vinegar	1 tbsp	15 mL
Garlic cloves, minced (or 2 mL, 1/2 tsp, powder)	2	2
Dried crushed chillies	1/2–1 tsp	2–5 mL
White (granulated) sugar	1/2 tsp	2 mL
Salt	1/4 tsp	1 mL
Pepper	1/4 tsp	1 mL
Chopped fresh parsley (or 11 mL, 2 1/4 tsp, flakes)	3 tbsp	50 mL

Penne pasta (about 285 g, 10 oz)	3 cups	750 mL
Boiling water	12 cups	3 L
Salt	1 1/2 tsp	7 mL
Grated Parmesan cheese	1/3 cup	75 mL

1. Combine first 10 ingredients in 3.5 to 4 L (3 1/2 to 4 quart) slow cooker. Cover. Cook on Low for 8 to 9 hours or on High for 4 to 4 1/2 hours.

2. Add parsley. Stir well.

3. Cook pasta in boiling water and second amount of salt in large uncovered pot for 8 to 10 minutes, stirring occasionally, until tender but firm. Drain. Return pasta to pot. Add tomato mixture. Toss until coated. Remove to large serving bowl.

4. Sprinkle with Parmesan cheese. Serves 6.

Pictured between pages 80 & 81 and on front cover.

1 serving: 1487 Kilojoules (354 Calories); 8.5 g Total Fat; 531 mg Sodium; 13 g Protein; 54 g Carbohydrate

Sweet Potato and Spinach Pasta

'Pasta sweet potato and spinach, please!' will be music to your ears
when you serve this savoury dish the whole family will love.
Add a little milk or cream if you like a thinner sauce.

Hard margarine (or butter)	1 tbsp	15 mL
Chopped onion	1 cup	250 mL
Sliced fresh white mushrooms	1 1/2 cups	375 mL
Garlic cloves, minced (or 2 mL, 1/2 tsp, powder)	2	2
Hard margarine (or butter)	1 tbsp	15 mL
Plain (all-purpose) flour	2 tbsp	30 mL
Liquid vegetable stock (prepared vegetable broth)	1 cup	250 mL
Dry white (or alcohol-free) wine	1/2 cup	125 mL
Chopped sweet potato (yam)	3 cups	750 mL
Chopped fresh rosemary leaves (or 1 mL, 1/4 tsp, dried, crushed)	1 tsp	5 mL
Salt	1/4 tsp	1 mL
Pepper	1/4 tsp	1 mL
Fresh spinach, stems removed, lightly packed	2 cups	500 mL
Liquid vegetable stock (prepared vegetable broth)	1/2 cup	125 mL
Chopped spring (green) onion	1/3 cup	75 mL
Sour cream	1/4 cup	60 mL

Dijon mustard (with whole seeds)	1 tbsp	15 mL
Penne pasta (about 170 g, 6 oz)	2 cups	500 mL
Boiling water	10 cups	2.5 L
Salt	1 1/4 tsp	6 mL
Grated Parmesan cheese	1/3 cup	75 mL

1. Melt first amount of margarine in medium frying pan (skillet) on Medium. Add onion. Cook for 5 to 10 minutes, stirring often, until softened.

2. Add mushrooms and garlic. Cook for 3 to 5 minutes, stirring occasionally, until mushrooms are softened. Transfer to 3.5 to 4 L (3 1/2 to 4 quart) slow cooker.

3. Melt second amount of margarine in same medium frying pan on Medium. Add flour. Heat and stir for 1 minute. Slowly add first amount of stock (broth), stirring constantly until smooth. Add wine. Heat and stir for about 3 minutes until boiling and thickened. Add to mushroom mixture. Stir.

4. Add next 4 ingredients. Stir well. Cover. Cook on Low for 6 to 7 hours or on High for 3 to 3 1/2 hours. Mash sweet potato slightly.

5. Add next 5 ingredients. Stir well. Cover. Cook on High for about 10 minutes until spinach is wilted.

6. Cook pasta in boiling water and second amount of salt in large uncovered pot for 8 to 10 minutes, stirring occasionally, until tender but firm. Drain. Return pasta to pot. Add sweet potato mixture. Toss until coated.

7. Add Parmesan cheese. Stir gently. Serves 6.

1 serving: 1516 Kilojoules (361 Calories); 8.3 g Total Fat; 528 mg Sodium; 11 g Protein; 58 g Carbohydrate

Hamburger Stroganoff

Stroganoff over noodles makes a favourite dish.

Lean beef mince (ground beef)	1 1/2 lbs	680 g
Plain (all-purpose) flour	2 tbsp	30 mL
Salt	1 tsp	5 mL
Pepper	1/4 tsp	1 mL
Chopped onion	1 cup	250 mL
Condensed cream of chicken soup	10 oz	284 g
Red wine vinegar	1 tsp	5 mL
Orange juice	2 tbsp	30 mL
Light sour cream	1 cup	250 mL
Fettuccine noodles	1 lb	454 g
Boiling water	4 qts	4 L
Cooking oil (optional)	1 tbsp	15 mL
Salt	1 tbsp	15 mL

1. Scramble-fry beef mince (ground beef) in non-stick frying pan (skillet) until browned. Do not drain.

2. Mix in flour, first amount of salt, pepper and onion. Stir in soup, vinegar and orange juice. Turn into 3.5 L (3 1/2 quart) slow cooker. Cover. Cook on Low for 5 to 6 hours or on High for 2 1/2 to 3 hours.

3. Stir in sour cream. Heat through. Makes 1.25 L (5 cups).

4. Cook noodles in boiling water, cooking oil and second amount of salt in large uncovered pot for 5 to 7 minutes until tender. Drain. Serve stroganoff over noodles. Serves 6.

1 serving: 2642 Kilojoules (631 Calories); 24.1 g Total Fat; 946 mg Sodium; 34 g Protein; 67 g Carbohydrate

Chicken Pesto Lasagne

Make this rich, cheesy lasagne for Italian night and serve with a green salad and toasty garlic bread. Customise the flavour by using your favourite pasta sauce!

Chopped cooked chicken	3 cups	750 mL
Basil pesto	1/4 cup	60 mL
Tomato pasta sauce	4 cups	1 L
Cooked lasagne sheets (noodles)	9	9
Grated Parmesan, Mozzarella and Romano cheese (Italian cheese blend)	4 cups	1 L

1. Combine chicken and pesto in medium bowl.

2. To assemble, layer ingredients in greased 5 to 7 L (5 to 7 quart) slow cooker as follows:

   a) 250 mL (1 cup) pasta sauce

   b) 3 lasagne sheets (noodles)

   c) 250 mL (1 cup) chicken mixture

   d) 250 mL (1 cup) cheese

   e) 250 mL (1 cup) pasta sauce

   f) 3 lasagne sheets

   g) 250 mL (1 cup) chicken mixture

   h) 250 mL (1 cup) cheese

   i) 250 mL (1 cup) pasta sauce

   j) Remaining lasagne sheets

   k) Remaining chicken mixture

   l) Remaining pasta sauce

   m) Remaining cheese

3. Cook, covered, on Low for 4 to 5 hours or on High for 2 to 2 1/2 hours until heated through. Let stand, uncovered, for 10 minutes. Serves 6.

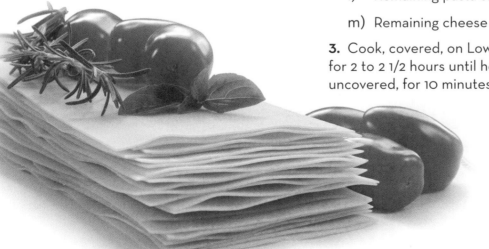

1 serving: 2713 Kilojoules (648 Calories); 34.0 g Total Fat; 1312 mg Sodium; 48 g Protein; 36 g Carbohydrate

Macaroni and Cheese

A simple one-pot meal everyone will enjoy.

Plain (all-purpose) flour	1/4 cup	60 mL	Grated medium or sharp Cheddar cheese	1 cup	250 mL	
Salt	1 tsp	5 mL	Uncooked elbow macaroni	2 cups	500 mL	
Pepper	1/4 tsp	1 mL				
Minced onion flakes	2 tbsp	30 mL				
Paprika	1/2 tsp	2 mL				
Milk	3 cups	750 mL				

1. Stir first 5 ingredients in saucepan.

2. Whisk in milk gradually until no lumps remain. Heat and stir until boiling and thickened.

3. Add cheese and macaroni. Stir. Turn into 3.5 L (3 1/2 quart) slow cooker. Cover. Cook on Low for 2 to 2 1/2 hours or on High for about 1 hour. Makes 1 L (4 cups).

250 mL (1 cup): 1880 Kilojoules (449 Calories); 13 g Total Fat; 965 mg Sodium; 22 g Protein; 60 g Carbohydrate

Italiano Pasta Sauce

Serve this sweet tomato sauce over your favourite pasta for a delicious meal anytime! Sausage, onion and artichoke add richness and hearty textures.

Cans of Italian-style stewed tomatoes (540 g, 19 oz, each), cut up	2	2
Hot Italian sausage, casing removed	1 lb	454 g
Chopped onion	1 cup	250 mL
Cans of artichoke hearts (398 g, 14 oz, each), drained, quartered	2	2
Tomato basil pasta sauce	4 cups	1 L

1. Put tomatoes into 4 to 5 L (4 to 5 quart) slow cooker.

2. Scramble-fry sausage and onion in large greased frying pan (skillet) on Medium-High for about 8 minutes until sausage is no longer pink. Drain. Add to slow cooker.

3. Add artichoke and pasta sauce. Stir. Cook, covered, on Low for 6 to 8 hours or on High for 3 to 4 hours. Makes about 3 L (12 cups).

Pictured between pages 64 & 65.

175 mL (3/4 cup): 762 Kilojoules (182 Calories); 9.3 g Total Fat; 849 mg Sodium; 9 g Protein; 14 g Carbohydrate

Meatballs in Sauce

Serve over your favourite pasta with garlic toast on the side.

Cans of diced tomatoes (with juice), 540 mL (19 oz) each	2	2
Jalapeño chilli (chipotle pepper), finely chopped	1	1
White (granulated) sugar	1 tsp	5 mL
Bacon slices, cooked almost crisp and chopped	4	4
Fresh breadcrumbs	1 cup	250 mL
Finely chopped onion	2/3 cup	150 mL
Chopped fresh parsley (or 15 mL, 1 tbsp, flakes)	1/4 cup	60 mL
Large egg, fork-beaten	1	1
Garlic cloves, minced (or 2 mL, 1/2 tsp, powder)	2	2
Dry mustard	1 tsp	5 mL
Salt	1/4 tsp	1 mL
Lean beef mince (ground beef)	1 1/2 lbs	680 g
Cooking oil	1 tbsp	15 mL
Sour cream	2 tbsp	30 mL
Finely chopped fresh parsley, for garnish	1 tbsp	15 mL

1. Put tomatoes, jalapeño chilli (chipotle pepper) and sugar into 3.5 to 4 L (3 1/2 to 4 quart) slow cooker. Stir well.

2. Combine next 8 ingredients in large bowl. Add beef mince (ground beef). Mix well. Roll mixture into 5 cm (2 inch) balls, using 60 mL (1/4 cup) for each. Makes about 18 meatballs.

3. Heat cooking oil in large frying pan (skillet) on Medium. Add meatballs in 2 batches. Cook for 8 to 10 minutes per batch, turning occasionally, until browned. Add to tomato mixture. Stir gently. Cover. Cook on Low for 8 to 10 hours or on High for 4 to 5 hours. Remove meatballs with slotted spoon to large serving bowl. Skim and discard any fat from surface of tomato mixture.

4. Add sour cream to tomato mixture. Stir well. Pour over meatballs. Toss gently. Garnish with second amount of parsley. Serves 6.

Pictured between pages 80 & 81 and on front cover.

1 serving: 1839 Kilojoules (438 Calories); 24.7 g Total Fat; 718 mg Sodium; 28 g Protein; 26 g Carbohydrate

Stuffed Cabbage Wraps

An easy version of traditional cabbage rolls, these rice and bean wraps have great tomato taste. Try serving them as a side.

Large head of green cabbage	1	1
Chopped onion	3/4 cup	175 mL
Cooked long-grain brown rice (about 125 mL, 1/2 cup, uncooked)	1 1/2 cups	375 mL
Can of black beans, rinsed and drained	19 oz	540 g
Tomato pasta sauce	3 cups	750 mL

1. Remove core from cabbage. Trim about 12 mm (1/2 inch) slice from bottom. Place, cut-side down, in 4 to 5 L (4 to 5 quart) slow cooker. Cover with boiling water. Let stand, covered, for 5 minutes. Drain. Let stand until cool enough to handle. Carefully remove 8 large outer leaves from cabbage (see Note). Cut 'V' shape along tough ribs of leaves to remove. Discard ribs. Set leaves aside.

2. Heat medium greased frying pan (skillet) on Medium. Add onion. Cook for about 5 minutes, stirring often, until starting to soften. Transfer to medium bowl.

3. Add rice, beans, 125 mL (1/2 cup) pasta sauce and a sprinkle of salt and pepper. Stir. Place about 75 mL (1/3 cup) rice mixture on 1 cabbage leaf. Fold in sides. Roll up tightly from bottom to enclose filling. Repeat with remaining rice mixture and cabbage leaves. Pour remaining pasta sauce into slow cooker. Arrange cabbage rolls in 2 layers, seam-side down, over sauce. Cook, covered, on Low for 7 to 8 hours or on High for 3 1/2 to 4 hours. Transfer rolls with slotted spoon to serving plate. Serve with sauce. Makes 375 mL (1 1/2 cups) sauce and 8 rolls.

NOTE: Discard any other outer leaves that are partially steamed. Save the remaining cabbage in the refrigerator for another use.

1 cabbage roll with 50 mL (3 tbsp) sauce: 1101 Kilojoules (263 Calories); 4.1 g Total Fat; 643 mg Sodium; 9 g Protein; 46 g Carbohydrate

Seafood Marinara

Delicious prawns (shrimp) in an Italian-spiced sauce. Serve over rice or pasta.

Canned tomatoes, with juice, broken up	14 oz	398 g
Finely chopped onion	1 cup	250 mL
Garlic cloves, minced (or 2 mL, 1/2 tsp, garlic powder)	2	2
Dried oregano	3/4 tsp	4 mL
Salt	1 tsp	5 mL
Pepper	1/4 tsp	1 mL
Parsley flakes	1/2 tsp	2 mL
White (granulated) sugar	1/2 tsp	2 mL
Cooked fresh (or cooked frozen, thawed) shelled prawns (shrimp)	1 lb	454 g
Grated Parmesan cheese, sprinkle		

1. Combine first 8 ingredients in 3.5 L (3 1/2 quart) slow cooker. Cover. Cook on Low for 6 to 7 hours or on High for 3 to 3 1/2 hours until onion is cooked.

2. Add prawns (shrimp). Stir. Cook on High for about 15 minutes until heated through.

3. Serve over rice or pasta. Sprinkle with cheese. Makes 825 mL (3 1/3 cups).

175 mL (3/4 cup): 586 Kilojoules (140 Calories); 1.4 g Total Fat; 992 mg Sodium; 23 g Protein; 8 g Carbohydrate

Beefy Macaroni

This has to be one of the best-looking casseroles to come from a slow cooker. Tastes great too!

Finely chopped onion	1 cup	250 mL
Uncooked elbow macaroni	2 cups	500 mL
Lean beef mince (ground beef)	1 1/2 lbs	680 g
Plain (all-purpose) flour	1/4 cup	60 mL
Salt	1 tsp	5 mL
Pepper	1/4 tsp	1 mL
Milk	3 cups	750 mL
Canned sliced mushrooms, drained	10 oz	284 g
Frozen peas, thawed	10 oz	300 g

1. Place onion and macaroni in 3.5 L (3 1/2 quart) slow cooker.

2. Scramble-fry beef mince (ground beef) in non-stick frying pan (skillet) until no longer pink. Drain. Add to slow cooker.

3. Stir flour, salt and pepper together in small saucepan. Whisk in milk gradually until no lumps remain. Heat, stirring constantly, until boiling and thickened. Pour over beef mince in slow cooker. Stir.

4. Sprinkle mushrooms and peas over top. Cover. Cook on Low for 3 to 4 hours or on High for 1 1/2 to 2 hours. Makes 2.1 L (8 1/2 cups).

1. Tomato Chickpea Pasta, page 72
2. Bacon Chicken Pasta, page 71
3. Meatballs In Sauce, page 77

Props Courtesy Of: Cherison Enterprises Inc
Danesco Inc
Out of the Fire Studio

250 mL (1 cup): 1294 Kilojoules (309 Calories); 8.3 g Total Fat; 507 mg Sodium; 23 g Protein; 34 g Carbohydrate

Tasty Mex Casserole

Green chillies add spice to this colourful casserole.

Lean beef mince (ground beef)	1 1/2 lbs	680 g
White vinegar	3 tbsp	50 mL
Chilli powder	1 tbsp	15 mL
Dried oregano	1 tsp	5 mL
Garlic powder	1/4 tsp	1 mL
Salt	1 1/2 tsp	7 mL
Pepper	1/4 tsp	1 mL
Chopped onion	1 1/2 cups	375 mL
Medium green capsicum (pepper), chopped	1	1
Canned chopped green chillies, drained (optional)	4 oz	114 g
Canned corn kernels, drained	12 oz	341 g
Elbow macaroni, partially cooked, drained and rinsed	1 cup	250 mL

Canned tomatoes, 398 g (14 oz) each, with juice, broken up	2	2
Chilli powder	2 tsp	10 mL
Parsley flakes	1 tsp	5 mL
Dried oregano	1/2 tsp	2 mL
White (granulated) sugar	2 tsp	10 mL
Salt	1/2 tsp	2 mL
Pepper	1/4 tsp	1 mL

1. Mix first 7 ingredients in bowl. Scramble-fry in non-stick frying pan (skillet) until browned. Drain.

2. Put onion into 3.5 L (3 1/2 quart) or 5 L (5 quart) slow cooker. Add green capsicum (pepper), green chillies, corn and partially cooked macaroni. Add beef mixture. Stir.

3. Combine remaining 7 ingredients in bowl. Stir well. Pour over top. Stir. Cover. Cook on Low for 8 hours or on High for 4 hours. Makes 2.5 L (10 cups).

1. Easy Burritos, page 100
2. Spicy Beans And Rice, page 100

Props Courtesy Of: Hamilton Beach®
Canada Pier 1 Imports

250 mL (1 cup): 862 Kilojoules (206 Calories); 6.5 g Total Fat; 874 mg Sodium; 16 g Protein; 23 g Carbohydrate

Lentil Pasta Sauce

A pasta sauce that will satisfy the family and add a vegetarian meal option to your weekly menu. Complete the meal with a salad and garlic bread.

Diced zucchini (courgette) (with peel)	2 cups	500 mL
Chopped onion	1 cup	250 mL
Grated carrot	1 cup	250 mL
Roasted garlic tomato pasta sauce	6 cups	1.5 L
Can of lentils, rinsed and drained	19 oz	540 g

1. Heat large greased frying pan (skillet) on Medium. Add first 3 ingredients. Cook for about 10 minutes, stirring often, until onion is softened and starts to brown. Transfer to 3.5 to 4 L (3 1/2 to 4 quart) slow cooker.

2. Add pasta sauce and lentils. Stir. Cook, covered, on Low for 6 to 8 hours or on High for 3 to 4 hours. Makes about 2.25 L (9 cups).

175 mL (3/4 cup): 477 Kilojoules (114 Calories); 1.2 g Total Fat; 334 mg Sodium; 6 g Protein; 23 g Carbohydrate

Veggie Pasta Sauce

This easy-to-prepare pasta sauce has a hearty, meaty texture, but without the meat. It's perfect on pasta and can be used to make lasagna.

Tomato basil pasta sauce	4 cups	1 L
Soy-based meat substitute (veggie ground round)	12 oz	340 g
Chopped carrot	1 cup	250 mL
Chopped onion	1 cup	250 mL
Chopped zucchini (courgette) (with peel)	1 cup	250 mL

Combine all 5 ingredients in 3.5 to 4 L (3 1/2 to 4 quart) slow cooker. Cook, covered, on Low for 7 to 8 hours or on High for 3 1/2 to 4 hours. Makes about 1.5 L (6 cups).

Pictured between pages 64 & 65.

175 mL (3/4 cup): 602 Kilojoules (144 Calories); 2.6 g Total Fat; 692 mg Sodium; 11 g Protein; 17 g Carbohydrate

Chicken Sausage Pasta Sauce

A thick and chunky pasta sauce that's best served with bite-sized pasta. This can also be used in your favourite lasagne recipe.

Chicken (or turkey) sausage, casing removed	1 1/2 lbs	680 g
Finely chopped onion	1/2 cup	125 mL
Tomato basil pasta sauce	3 cups	750 mL
Chopped fresh white mushrooms	1 cup	250 mL
Chopped zucchini (courgette) (with peel)	1 cup	250 mL

1. Scramble-fry sausage and onion in large greased frying pan (skillet) on Medium-High for about 10 minutes, until sausage is no longer pink. Drain. Transfer to 4 to 5 L (4 to 5 quart) slow cooker.

2. Add remaining 3 ingredients. Stir. Cook, covered, on Low for 4 to 5 hours or on High for 2 to 2 1/2 hours. Makes about 1.5 L (6 cups).

Pictured between pages 64 & 65.

125 mL (1/2 cup): 624 Kilojoules (149 Calories); 7.5 g Total Fat; 277 mg Sodium; 13 g Protein; 6 g Carbohydrate

Meat Sauce for Many

When you make a meat sauce in the slow cooker, all that's left to do is cook up some noodles and toss a salad. Freeze in portions to save for pasta nights!

Lean beef mince (ground beef)	2 lbs	900 g
Hot Italian sausage, casing removed	1 lb	454 g
Sliced fresh white mushrooms	4 cups	1 L
Tomato pasta sauce	10 cups	2.5 L
Italian seasoning	2 tbsp	30 mL

1. Scramble-fry beef and sausage in large greased frying pan (skillet) on Medium-High for about 10 minutes until no longer pink. Drain. Transfer to 4 to 5 L (4 to 5 quart) slow cooker.

2. Add mushrooms to same greased frying pan. Cook on Medium-High for about 5 minutes until softened. Add to slow cooker.

3. Add pasta sauce and Italian seasoning. Stir well. Cook, covered, on Low for 6 to 8 hours or on High for 3 to 4 hours. Makes about 3.25 L (13 cups).

125 mL (1/2 cup): 569 Kilojoules (136 Calories); 6.7 g Total Fat; 377 mg Sodium; 10 g Protein; 10 g Carbohydrate

Ham and Noodles

This tasty dish has a delicious Parmesan cheese sauce with mushrooms.

Cubed cooked ham	1 1/2 cups	375 mL
Canned whole or sliced mushrooms, drained	10 oz	284 g
Condensed cream of mushroom soup	10 oz	284 g
Water	1/2 cup	125 mL
Horseradish	1 1/2 tsp	7 mL

Grated Parmesan cheese	1/4 cup	60 mL
Sherry (or alcohol-free sherry)	2 tbsp	30 mL
Uncooked broad egg noodles	2 cups	500 mL
Water	1 cup	250 mL

1. Place ham cubes and mushrooms in 3.5 L (3 1/2 quart) slow cooker.

2. Combine soup and first amount of water in bowl. Add horseradish, cheese and sherry. Stir. Add to slow cooker. Cover. Cook on Low for 6 to 8 hours or on High for 3 to 4 hours.

3. Add noodles and second amount of water. Stir. Cover. Cook on High for 15 to 20 minutes until noodles are tender. Makes scant 1 L (4 cups).

250 mL (1 cup): 1143 Kilojoules (273 Calories); 11.5 g Total Fat; 1701 mg Sodium; 18 g Protein; 23 g Carbohydrate

Tuna Casserole

Good combo of ingredients, and a good-looking dish.

Chopped onion	1/2 cup	125 mL
Condensed cream of chicken soup 284 g (10 oz) each	2	2
Milk	1 cup	250 mL
Frozen peas	10 oz	300 g
Uncooked medium egg noodles	8 oz	225 g
Canned flaked tuna 184 g (6 1/2 oz) each, drained	2	2

1. Sprinkle onion in 3.5 L (3 1/2 quart) slow cooker.

2. Mix soup and milk in large bowl. Add peas, egg noodles and tuna. Stir well. Turn into slow cooker. Smooth top with spoon. Cover. Cook on Low for 5 to 6 hours or on High for 2 1/2 to 3 hours. Stir before serving. Makes 1.65 L (6 2/3 cups).

250 mL (1 cup): 1377 Kilojoules (329 Calories); 7.5 g Total Fat; 952 mg Sodium; 25 g Protein; 40 g Carbohydrate

Mushroom Beef Sauce

Serve over potatoes, rice or pasta for a complete meal,
and garnish with chopped fresh parsley.

Stewing beef, trimmed of fat, cut into 2.5 cm (1 inch) cubes	2 lbs	900 g
Packet of mushroom pasta sauce mix	1 1/4 oz	38 g
Butter (or hard margarine)	1 tbsp	15 mL
Sliced fresh mixed mushrooms	4 cups	1 L
Dry (or alcohol-free) red wine	3/4 cup	175 mL

1. Combine beef and sauce mix in 4 to 5 L (4 to 5 quart) slow cooker.

2. Melt butter in large frying pan (skillet) on Medium. Add mushrooms. Cook for about 8 minutes, stirring often, until browned. Transfer to slow cooker.

3. Add wine and 175 mL (3/4 cup) water. Cook, covered, on Low for 8 to 9 hours or on High for 4 to 4 1/2 hours. Skim and discard fat. Makes about 1.4 L (5 1/2 cups).

85

125 mL (1/2 cup): 812 Kilojoules (194 Calories); 11.8 g Total Fat; 203 mg Sodium; 15 g Protein; 3 g Carbohydrate

Chilli Pasta Bake

This home-style bake is reddish in colour and has a great taste.

Lean beef mince (ground beef)	1 1/2 lbs	680 g
Chopped onion	1 cup	250 mL
Canned tomatoes, 398 g (14 oz), each with juice, mashed	2	2
Chilli powder	2 tsp	10 mL
Dried oregano	1/2 tsp	2 mL
Tomato purée (tomato sauce)	7.5 oz	213 mL
Salt	1 tsp	5 mL
Pepper	1/4 tsp	1 mL
Uncooked elbow macaroni	1 1/4 cups	300 mL
Grated medium Cheddar (Monterey Jack) cheese	1 cup	250 mL

1. Scramble-fry beef mince (ground beef) in non-stick frying pan (skillet) until browned. Drain well. Transfer to 3.5 L (3 1/2 quart) slow cooker.

2. Add next 8 ingredients. Stir. Cover. Cook on Low for 5 to 7 hours or on High for 2 1/2 to 3 1/2 hours.

3. Sprinkle cheese over top. Cook on High for 10 to 15 minutes until cheese is melted. Makes 1.75 L (7 cups).

250 mL (1 cup): 1377 Kilojoules (329 Calories); 14 g Total Fat; 904 mg Sodium; 26 g Protein; 25 g Carbohydrate

Hearty Creole

Lots of healthy ingredients for colour such as green capsicum (pepper), tomato, mushrooms and prawns (shrimp) make an eye-catching meal. Serve over rice.

Finely chopped onion	1 cup	250 mL
Chopped celery	1/2 cup	125 mL
Medium green capsicum (pepper), chopped	1	1
Canned tomatoes, with juice, broken up	14 oz	398 g
Tomato sauce (ketchup)	2 tbsp	30 mL
Canned sliced mushrooms, drained	10 oz	284 g
Salt	1 tsp	5 mL
Pepper	1/4 tsp	1 mL
Garlic powder	1/4 tsp	1 mL
Cayenne pepper	1/4 tsp	1 mL
Lemon juice	1 tsp	5 mL
Parsley flakes	1 tsp	5 mL
Cooked fresh (or cooked frozen, thawed) shelled prawns (shrimp) (or 2 cans, 114 g, 4 oz, each, drained)	1 lb	454 g

1. Put onion, celery and green capsicum (pepper) into 3.5 L (3 1/2 quart) slow cooker.

2. Combine next 9 ingredients in bowl. Stir. Pour over top. Cover. Cook on Low for 6 to 8 hours or on High for 3 to 4 hours.

3. Add prawns (shrimp). Stir. Cook on High for 20 to 30 minutes until prawns are heated through. Stir before serving over cooked rice. Makes 1 L (4 1/4 cups).

250 mL (1 cup): 691 Kilojoules (165 Calories); 1.7 g Total Fat; 1285 mg Sodium; 25 g Protein; 13 g Carbohydrate

Cajun Chicken and Rice

A colourful concoction with a cheeky Cajun kick!

Can of red kidney beans, rinsed and drained	19 oz	540 g
Sliced red capsicum (pepper)	1 1/2 cups	375 mL
Frozen corn kernels	1 cup	250 mL
Liquid chicken stock (prepared chicken broth)	1 cup	250 mL
Cajun seasoning	1 tbsp	15 mL
Ground cumin	1 tsp	5 mL
Boneless, skinless chicken thighs, chopped	1 lb	454 g
Can of diced tomatoes (with juice)	14 oz	398 g
Long-grain white rice	1/2 cup	125 mL
Sliced zucchini (courgette) (with peel)	1 cup	250 mL
Chopped fresh coriander (cilantro) or parsley (or 7 mL, 1 1/2 tsp, dried)	2 tbsp	30 mL

1. Combine first 7 ingredients in 3.5 to 4 L (3 1/2 to 4 quart) slow cooker. Cover. Cook on Low for 8 to 10 hours or on High for 4 to 5 hours.

2. Add tomatoes and rice. Stir gently. Cover. Cook on High for 30 to 40 minutes until rice is almost tender.

3. Add zucchini (courgette) and coriander (cilantro). Stir gently. Cover. Cook on High for 10 to 15 minutes until rice and zucchini are tender. Serves 4.

1 serving: 1747 Kilojoules (416 Calories); 8.2 g Total Fat; 547 mg Sodium; 34 g Protein; 54 g Carbohydrate

Chicken Jambalaya

Chicken, sausage, prawns (shrimp) and juicy vegetables – there's something for everyone in this spicy rice dish!

Boneless, skinless chicken thighs (57–85 g, 2–3 oz, each), halved	8	8
Cooking oil	1 tsp	5 mL
Chorizo sausage, cut into 12 mm (1/2 inch) slices	1 lb	454 g
Can of diced tomatoes (with juice)	14 oz	398 g
Chopped green capsicum (pepper)	1 1/2 cups	375 mL
Chopped onion	1 cup	250 mL
Chopped celery	1 cup	250 mL
Tomato purée (tomato sauce)	7 1/2 oz	213 mL
Garlic cloves, minced (or 2 mL, 1/2 tsp, powder)	2	2
Dried basil	1/2 tsp	2 mL
Paprika	1/2 tsp	2 mL

Dried crushed chillies	1/4–1/2 tsp	1–2 mL
Dried thyme	1/4 tsp	1 mL
Cooked long-grain white rice (about 175 mL, 3/4 cup, uncooked)	2 cups	500 mL
Fresh uncooked medium prawns (shrimp), peeled and deveined	1 lb	454 g

1. Put chicken into 3.5 to 4 L (3 1/2 to 4 quart) slow cooker.

2. Heat cooking oil in large frying pan (skillet) on Medium. Add sausage. Cook for about 5 minutes, stirring occasionally, until starting to brown. Remove to paper towels to drain.

3. Combine next 10 ingredients in large bowl. Pour over chicken. Add sausage. Stir well. Cover. Cook on Low for 8 to 9 hours or on High for 4 to 4 1/2 hours.

4. Add rice and prawns (shrimp). Stir gently. Cover. Cook on High for 15 to 20 minutes until prawns are pink and curled. Serves 8.

1 serving: 2129 Kilojoules (507 Calories); 26.8 g Total Fat; 1051 mg Sodium; 39 g Protein; 26 g Carbohydrate

West Indies Rice Casserole

Salty ham bites are nicely balanced with sweet potato
and curry seasoning in this fluffy rice dish.

Liquid chicken stock (prepared chicken broth)	2 cups	500 mL
Curry (jerk seasoning) paste	1 tbsp	15 mL
Cubed fresh peeled orange-fleshed sweet potato (yam)	2 cups	500 mL
Long-grain white rice	2 cups	500 mL
Ham steak (about 454 g, 1 lb), cut into quarters	1	1

1. Whisk stock (broth) and curry (jerk seasoning) paste in 4 to 5 L (4 to 5 quart) slow cooker until smooth. Add sweet potato (yam), rice, 250 mL (1 cup) water and a sprinkle of salt and pepper. Stir.

2. Heat large greased frying pan (skillet) on Medium-High. Add ham. Cook for about 1 minute per side until starting to brown. Place over rice mixture. Cook, covered, on Low for 5 to 6 hours or on High for 2 1/2 to 3 hours. Transfer ham to work surface. Dice. Return to slow cooker. Stir gently to distribute the ham and sweet potato evenly. Makes about 1.75 L (7 cups).

250 mL (1 cup): 1407 Kilojoules (336 Calories); 4.2 g Total Fat; 1472 mg Sodium; 18 g Protein; 54 g Carbohydrate

Stuffed Peppers

Green capsicums (peppers) with a deliciously mild filling and red soup topping.

Boiling water	1/4 cup	60 mL
Instant white rice	1/4 cup	60 mL
Finely chopped onion	1/4 cup	60 mL
Grated carrot	1/4 cup	60 mL
Corn kernels, frozen or canned	1/4 cup	60 mL
Worcestershire sauce	1/2 tsp	2 mL
Horseradish	1/2 tsp	2 mL
Salt	1/2 tsp	2 mL
Pepper	1/8 tsp	0.5 mL
Lean beef mince (ground beef)	1/2 lb	225 g
Medium green capsicums (peppers), tops cut off, ribs and seeds removed	4	4
Can of condensed tomato soup	10 oz	284 mL

1. Pour boiling water over rice in bowl. Cover. Let stand for 5 minutes.

2. Add next 8 ingredients. Mix well.

3. Stuff capsicums (peppers) with rice mixture. Place in 5 L (5 quart) slow cooker.

4. Spoon soup over top and around capsicums. Cover. Cook on Low for 7 to 9 hours or on High for 3 1/2 to 4 1/2 hours. Serves 4.

1 serving: 980 Kilojoules (234 Calories); 9.9 g Total Fat; 915 mg Sodium; 14 g Protein; 24 g Carbohydrate

Orange Chicken and Rice

Vibrant citrus flavour infuses light and fluffy rice, served alongside tender, seasoned chicken.

Medium oranges	2	2
Long-grain white rice	2 cups	500 mL
Liquid chicken stock (prepared chicken broth)	2 cups	500 mL
Italian dressing, divided	1/3 cup	75 mL
Boneless, skinless chicken thighs	1 1/2 lbs	680 g

1. Grate 5 mL (1 tsp) orange zest into 3.5 to 4 L (3 1/2 to 4 quart) slow cooker. Squeeze 125 mL (1/2 cup) orange juice and pour into slow cooker.

2. Add rice, stock (broth), 30 mL (2 tbsp) dressing, 250 mL (1 cup) water and a generous sprinkle of salt and pepper. Stir.

3. Put chicken into medium bowl. Sprinkle with salt. Pour remaining dressing over top. Stir until coated. Heat large greased frying pan (skillet) on Medium-High. Add chicken. Discard any remaining dressing. Cook for about 3 minutes per side until browned. Arrange over rice mixture. Cook, covered, on Low for 4 to 5 hours or High for 2 to 2 1/2 hours. Serves 6.

1 serving: 1951 Kilojoules (466 Calories); 13.8 g Total Fat; 1012 mg Sodium; 26 g Protein; 56 g Carbohydrate

Beef 'n' Beans

Lots of beef, beans and rice. A meal in one.

Lean beef mince (ground beef)	1 lb	454 g
Canned mixed beans, with liquid	19 oz	540 g
Canned kidney beans (black-eyed peas), with liquid	14 oz	398 g
Canned tomatoes, with juice, broken up	14 oz	398 g
Finely chopped onion	1/2 cup	125 mL

Mild or medium salsa	1 cup	250 mL
Uncooked long-grain rice	2/3 cup	150 mL
Salt	1 tsp	5 mL
Pepper	1/4 tsp	1 mL
Garlic powder	1/4 tsp	1 mL
Water	1 cup	250 mL

1. Scramble-fry beef mince (ground beef) in non-stick frying pan (skillet). Drain well. Turn into 3.5 L (3 1/2 quart) slow cooker.

2. Add remaining 10 ingredients. Stir. Cover. Cook on Low for 8 to 9 hours or on High for 4 to 4 1/2 hours. Makes a generous 2 L (8 cups).

250 mL (1 cup): 1176 Kilojoules (281 Calories); 5.7 g Total Fat; 1303 mg Sodium; 19 g Protein; 39 g Carbohydrate

Seafood Casserole

Mild seafood flavour with a golden cheese topping.

Can of condensed cream of mushroom soup	10 oz	284 g
Water	1 cup	250 mL
Sherry (or alcohol-free sherry)	2 tbsp	30 mL
Jars of chopped roasted red capsicum (pimento), 57 g (2 oz) each, drained	2	2

Onion flakes	1 tbsp	15 mL
Dill (dill weed)	1/2 tsp	2 mL
Paprika	1/2 tsp	2 mL
Parsley flakes	1 tsp	5 mL
Cayenne pepper	1/8 tsp	0.5 mL
Canned prawns (shrimp), drained	4 oz	113 g
Canned crabmeat, drained, cartilage removed	4.2 oz	120 g

Uncooked instant white rice	1 1/2 cups	375 mL
Grated medium Cheddar cheese	1 cup	250 mL

1. Mix first 9 ingredients in bowl.

2. Place prawns (shrimp), crabmeat and rice in 3.5 L (3 1/2 quart) slow cooker. Pour soup mixture over top. Stir lightly.

3. Sprinkle with cheese. Cover. Cook on Low for 3 to 4 hours or on High for 1 1/2 to 2 hours. Makes 1.25 L (5 cups).

250 mL (1 cup): 1369 Kilojoules (327 Calories); 13.3 g Total Fat; 832 mg Sodium; 18 g Protein; 33 g Carbohydrate

Chicken Siciliana

Sicily traditionally specialises in tube-shaped pasta, so serve with tubetti, macaroni or penne for an authentic touch.

Boneless, skinless chicken thighs, quartered	1 1/2 lbs	680 g
Balsamic vinegar	2 tbsp	30 mL
Chopped peeled eggplant (aubergine) (12 mm, 1/2 inch, pieces)	4 cups	1 L
Spicy tomato pasta sauce	3 cups	750 mL
Black olive tapenade	1/4 cup	60 mL

1. Heat large greased frying pan (skillet) on Medium-High. Add chicken. Cook for 3 minutes per side until browned. Add balsamic vinegar. Stir. Transfer to 3.5 to 4 L (3 1/2 to 4 quart) slow cooker.

2. Add eggplant (aubergine) and tomato sauce. Stir. Cook, covered, on Low for 8 to 10 hours or on High for 4 to 5 hours.

3. Add tapenade. Stir. Makes about 1.75 L (7 cups).

250 mL (1 cup): 888 Kilojoules (212 Calories); 9.6 g Total Fat; 748 mg Sodium; 20 g Protein; 11 g Carbohydrate

Beefy Rice Casserole

A good mixture, with a mild chilli flavour addition.

Cooking oil	1 tbsp	15 mL
Lean beef mince (ground beef)	1 1/2 lbs	680 g
Canned tomatoes, with juice	28 oz	796 g
Chopped onion	1 1/2 cups	375 mL
Chopped green capsicum (pepper)	1/4 cup	60 mL
Uncooked long-grain rice	1 cup	250 mL

Salt	1 1/2 tsp	7 mL
Chilli powder	1 tsp	5 mL
Water	1 cup	250 mL

1. Heat cooking oil in frying pan (skillet). Add beef mince (ground beef). Scramble-fry until browned. Drain well. Turn into 3.5 L (3 1/2 quart) slow cooker.

2. Add remaining 7 ingredients. Stir. Cover. Cook on Low for 6 to 8 hours or on High for 3 to 4 hours. Makes 1.8 L (7 1/2 cups).

250 mL (1 cup): 1193 Kilojoules (285 Calories); 7.4 g Total Fat; 766 mg Sodium; 14 g Protein; 29 g Carbohydrate

Jamaican Rice and Beans

This creamy, mildly seasoned dish can be served as a vegetarian main course or as a side.

Chopped onion	1 cup	250 mL
Cans of red kidney beans (398 g, 14 oz each), rinsed and drained	2	2
Long-grain brown rice	2 cups	500 mL
Ground allspice	1 tsp	5 mL
Can of coconut milk	14 oz	398 mL

1. Heat medium greased frying pan (skillet) on Medium. Add onion and a generous sprinkle of salt and pepper. Cook for about 5 minutes, stirring often, until softened. Transfer to 4 to 5 L (4 to 5 quart) slow cooker.

2. Add next 4 ingredients, 550 mL (2 1/4 cups) water and a generous sprinkle of salt and pepper. Stir. Cook, covered, on Low for 6 to 7 hours or on High for 3 to 3 1/2 hours. Makes about 2 L (8 cups).

250 mL (1 cup): 1520 Kilojoules (363 Calories); 12.6 g Total Fat; 413 mg Sodium; 11 g Protein; 54 g Carbohydrate

Herbed Barley Risotto

A flavourful risotto made with barley instead of rice. Try replacing the barley with short-grain rice for a more traditional dish.

Cooking oil	1 tbsp	15 mL
Finely chopped onion	1 cup	250 mL
Sliced fresh white mushrooms	2 cups	500 mL
Garlic cloves, minced (or 5 mL, 1 tsp, powder)	4	4
Liquid vegetable stock (prepared vegetable broth)	2 2/3 cups	650 mL
Medium tomatoes, peeled, quartered, seeds removed	3	3
Pearl barley, rinsed and drained	1 cup	250 mL
Dry white (or alcohol-free) wine	1/2 cup	125 mL
Dried oregano	1/2 tsp	2 mL
Dried rosemary, crushed	1/2 tsp	2 mL
Salt	1/4 tsp	1 mL
Pepper	1/4 tsp	1 mL
Grated Parmesan cheese	1/3 cup	75 mL
Chopped fresh parsley (or 7 mL, 1 1/2 tsp, flakes)	2 tbsp	30 mL

1. Heat cooking oil in medium frying pan (skillet) on Medium. Add onion. Cook for 5 to 10 minutes, stirring often, until softened.

2. Add mushrooms and garlic. Cook for 3 to 5 minutes, stirring occasionally, until mushrooms are softened. Transfer to 3.5 to 4 L (3 1/2 to 4 quart) slow cooker.

3. Add next 8 ingredients. Stir well. Cover. Cook on Low for 8 to 9 hours or on High for 4 to 4 1/2 hours.

4. Add Parmesan cheese and parsley. Stir well. Serves 4.

1 serving: 1432 Kilojoules (341 Calories); 7.7 g Total Fat; 882 mg Sodium; 13 g Protein; 53 g Carbohydrate

Spicy Beans and Rice

Serve with corn (nacho) chips and crisp vegetables.
Great topped with a dollop of sour cream and a spoonful of salsa.

Can of red kidney beans, 19 oz, rinsed and drained		540 g
Liquid vegetable stock (prepared vegetable broth)	1 1/4 cups	300 mL
Chopped red capsicum (pepper)	1 cup	250 mL
Chopped tomato	1 cup	250 mL
Chopped onion	1 cup	250 mL
Chopped celery	1/2 cup	125 mL
Smoked jalapeño chilli (chipotle pepper), chopped	1/2	1/2
Chilli powder	1 tsp	5 mL
Dried oregano	1 tsp	5 mL
Salt	1/2 tsp	2 mL
Pepper	1/4 tsp	1 mL
Parboiled (converted) white (or brown) rice	1/2 cup	125 mL

Chopped spring (green) onion	1/3 cup	75 mL
Chopped fresh parsley (or 7 mL, 1 1/2 tsp, flakes)	2 tbsp	30 mL
Lime juice	1 tbsp	15 mL

1. Combine first 11 ingredients in 3.5 to 4 L (3 1/2 to 4 quart) slow cooker. Cover. Cook on Low for 7 to 8 hours or on High for 3 1/2 to 4 hours.

2. Add rice. Stir well. Cover. Cook on High for 30 to 45 minutes until rice is tender.

3. Add remaining 3 ingredients. Stir gently. Serves 4.

EASY BURRITOS: Spoon about 125 mL (1/2 cup) Spicy Beans and Rice down centre of each of eight 22 cm (9 inch) flour tortillas. Layer chopped or torn lettuce, sour cream, salsa, grated Cheddar cheese and chopped tomato on top of each. Fold sides of tortillas over filling. Roll up each from bottom to enclose filling.

Pictured between pages 80 & 81.

1 serving: 957 Kilojoules (228 Calories); 1.2 g Total Fat; 731 mg Sodium; 10 g Protein; 46 g Carbohydrate

Chicken Seafood Paella

Mildly spiced with smoked paprika, this paella's (pie-AY-yuh) combination of rice, chicken and seafood is a great introduction to the wonderful world of Spanish cuisine.

Boneless, skinless chicken thighs, halved	1 lb	454 g
Smoked sweet paprika	3/4 tsp	4 mL
Package of Spanish-style rice mix	14 oz	397 g
Marinara mix (frozen seafood medley, thawed)	1/2 lb	340 g
Frozen peas, thawed	1 cup	250 mL

1. Heat large greased frying pan (skillet) on Medium-High. Add chicken. Sprinkle with paprika, salt and pepper. Cook for about 3 minutes per side until browned. Transfer to 3.5 to 4 L (3 1/2 to 4 quart) slow cooker.

2. Add rice mix and 875 mL (3 1/2 cups) water to slow cooker. Stir. Cook, covered, on Low for 6 to 7 hours or on High for 3 to 3 1/2 hours.

3. Add seafood and peas. Stir gently. Cook, covered, on High for about 20 minutes until seafood is cooked. Makes about 2.1 L (8 1/2 cups).

250 mL (1 cup): 678 Kilojoules (162 Calories); 5.6 g Total Fat; 274 mg Sodium; 17 g Protein; 11 g Carbohydrate

Chicken and Rice Casserole

When you're in need of comfort food, settle in with a bowl of this creamy rice casserole full of broccoli and tender chicken pieces.

Long-grain brown rice	1 1/2 cups	375 mL
Can of condensed cream of broccoli soup	10 oz	284 g
Can of condensed cream of chicken soup	10 oz	284 g
Boneless, skinless chicken thighs	1 1/2 lbs	680 g
Frozen chopped broccoli, thawed	3 cups	750 mL

1. Combine first 3 ingredients and 375 mL (1 1/2 cups) water in greased 3.5 to 4 L (3 1/2 to 4 quart) slow cooker.

2. Heat large greased frying pan (skillet) on Medium-High. Add chicken. Sprinkle with salt and pepper. Cook for about 3 minutes per side until browned. Arrange chicken over rice mixture in slow cooker. Cook, covered, on Low for 6 to 7 hours or on High for 3 to 3 1/2 hours.

3. Add broccoli. Stir. Cook, covered, on High for about 15 minutes until broccoli is tender. Makes about 1.9 L (7 1/2 cups).

250 mL (1 cup): 1541 Kilojoules (368 Calories); 12.3 g Total Fat; 687 mg Sodium; 24 g Protein; 41 g Carbohydrate

Chicken and Rice

Pre-cooked chicken makes this an easy dish to prepare.

Chopped onion	1 cup	250 mL
Chopped fresh mushrooms	1 cup	250 mL
Medium green capsicum (pepper), chopped	1	1
Uncooked rice	3/4 cup	175 mL
Chopped cooked chicken	2 cups	500 mL
Chicken stock (bouillon) powder	2 tsp	10 mL

Warm water	1 cup	250 mL
Canned tomatoes, with juice, broken up	14 oz	398 g

1. Layer onion, mushrooms, green capsicum (pepper), rice and chicken in 3.5 L (3 1/2 quart) slow cooker.

2. Stir stock (bouillon) powder and warm water together in bowl. Add tomato. Stir. Pour over chicken. Cover. Cook on Low for 6 to 7 hours or on High for 3 to 3 1/2 hours. Stir before serving. Makes 1.75 L (7 cups).

250 mL (1 cup): 775 Kilojoules (185 Calories); 4.7 g Total Fat; 546 mg Sodium; 14 g Protein; 21 g Carbohydrate

Turkey and Wild Rice

This filling dish combines earthy wild rice and tender turkey pieces in a creamy sauce. Serve with a fresh veggie side like steamed asparagus.

Bacon slices, diced	3	3
Boneless, skinless turkey thighs, cut into 2.5 cm (1 inch) pieces	1 lb	454 g
Can of condensed cream of wild mushroom soup	10 oz	284 g
Liquid chicken stock (prepared chicken broth)	1 cup	250 mL
Wild rice	1 cup	250 mL

1. Cook bacon in large frying pan (skillet) on Medium until crisp. Transfer with slotted spoon to paper towel-lined plate to drain. Drain and discard all but 15 mL (1 tbsp) drippings.

2. Add turkey to same frying pan. Cook for about 10 minutes, stirring occasionally, until browned. Transfer to 3.5 to 4 L (3 1/2 to 4 quart) slow cooker. Scatter bacon over turkey.

3. Add remaining 3 ingredients, 500 mL (2 cups) water and a sprinkle of pepper to same frying pan. Heat and stir, scraping any brown bits from bottom of pan, until boiling. Add to slow cooker. Stir. Cook, covered, on Low for 6 to 7 hours or on High for 3 to 3 1/2 hours until rice is tender. Makes about 1.5 L (6 cups).

250 mL (1 cup): 779 Kilojoules (186 Calories); 6.7 g Total Fat; 664 mg Sodium; 6 g Protein; 26 g Carbohydrate

VEGETABLES & LEGUMES

VEGETABLES & LEGUMES

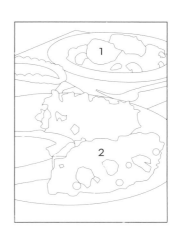

Pictured on reverse:

1. Pumpkin And Dumplings, page 104
2. Pumpkin And Lentil Curry, page 126

Props Courtesy Of: Emile Henry
Pfaltzgraff Canada

Lentil Rice Rolls

Flavours of the world unite in these interesting cabbage rolls.
Definitely worth a try when you're looking for something different.

Medium head of green cabbage (about 1.4 kg, 3 lbs)	1	1
Boiling water		
Can of lentils, rinsed and drained	19 oz	540 g
Tomato purée (tomato sauce)	7 1/2 oz	213 mL
Long-grain brown (or white) rice	1/2 cup	125 mL
Finely chopped carrot	1/2 cup	125 mL
Finely chopped celery	1/2 cup	125 mL
Finely chopped onion	1/2 cup	125 mL
Garlic clove, minced (or 1 mL, 1/4 tsp, powder)	1	1
Dried oregano	1/2 tsp	2 mL
Tomato pasta sauce	25 oz	680 mL
Raisins	1/4 cup	60 mL
Lemon juice	3 tbsp	50 mL
Brown sugar, packed	2 tbsp	30 mL
Grated lemon zest	2 tsp	10 mL
Ground cinnamon	1/2 tsp	2 mL

1. Remove 10 larger outer leaves from cabbage head. Place leaves in large bowl. Add boiling water until 5 cm (2 inches) above leaves. Let stand for about 5 minutes until softened. Cut 'V' shape with knife along tough ribs of cabbage leaves to remove. Discard ribs. Set leaves aside. Shred remaining cabbage. Put into 5 to 7 L (5 to 7 quart) slow cooker.

2. Combine next 8 ingredients in large bowl. Spoon about 75 mL (1/3 cup) lentil mixture onto centre of each cabbage leaf. Fold sides of leaves over filling. Roll up each tightly from bottom to enclose filling. Makes 10 cabbage rolls.

3. Measure remaining 6 ingredients into medium bowl. Stir. Add 375 mL (1 1/2 cups) tomato sauce mixture to shredded cabbage in slow cooker. Stir well. Spread evenly in slow cooker. Arrange rolls, seam-side down, on top of cabbage mixture. Pour remaining tomato sauce mixture on top of rolls. Cover. Cook on Low for 8 to 10 hours or on High for 4 to 5 hours. Carefully transfer rolls to large plate. Remove cabbage mixture to large serving platter. Arrange rolls on top. Serves 10.

1 serving: 634 Kilojoules (151 Calories); 0.9 g Total Fat; 654 mg Sodium; 6 g Protein; 33 g Carbohydrate

Cauliflower Potato Scallop

This rich and creamy scallop is a decadent way to eat your vegetables. It's full of creamy Alfredo sauce and tender kale, potato and cauliflower.

Alfredo pasta sauce	2 cups	500 mL
Thinly sliced peeled potato	5 cups	1.25 L
Chopped kale leaves, lightly packed (see Tip, below)	3 cups	750 mL
Cauliflower florets	3 cups	750 mL
Grated Parmesan cheese	1 cup	250 mL

1. Combine pasta sauce and 250 mL (1 cup) water in small bowl.

2. To assemble, layer ingredients in well-greased 4 to 5 L (4 to 5 quart) slow cooker as follows:
   a) Half of potato
   b) Half of kale
   c) Half of cauliflower
   d) Half of sauce mixture
   e) Half of cheese
   f) Remaining potato
   g) Remaining kale
   h) Remaining cauliflower
   i) Remaining sauce mixture
   j) Remaining cheese

3. Cook, covered, on Low for 8 to 9 hours or on High for 4 to 4 1/2 hours. Makes about 2.5 L (10 cups).

TIP: To remove the centre rib from lettuce or kale, fold the leaf in half along the rib and then cut along the length of the rib. To store, place leaves in large freezer bag. Once frozen, crumble in bag.

250 mL (1 cup): 1093 Kilojoules (261 Calories); 11.9 g Total Fat; 778 mg Sodium; 10 g Protein; 31 g Carbohydrate

Ratatouille

This ra-tuh-TOO-ee is made up of six different vegetables.

Canned tomatoes, with juice, broken up (or 4 fresh medium tomatoes, diced)	19 oz	540 g
Small eggplant, (aubergine) with peel, cut into 12 mm (1/2 inch) cubes	1	1
Finely chopped onion	1 cup	250 mL
Chopped celery	1 cup	250 mL

Medium green or red capsicum (pepper), chopped	1	1
Tomato sauce (ketchup) (or chilli sauce)	1/4 cup	60 mL
White (granulated) sugar	2 tsp	10 mL
Sliced zucchini, (courgettes) with peel (6 mm, 1/4 inch, thick)	3 cups	750 mL
Parsley flakes	1 tsp	5 mL

Salt	1/2 tsp	2 mL
Pepper	1/8 tsp	0.5 mL
Garlic powder	1/4 tsp	1 mL
Dried oregano	1/2 tsp	2 mL
Dried basil	1/2 tsp	2 mL

Measure all 14 ingredients into a 5 L (5 quart) slow cooker. Stir. Cover. Cook on Low for 8 to 9 hours or on High for 4 to 4 1/2 hours. Makes 1.6 L (6 1/2 cups).

Pictured between pages 112 & 113.

250 mL (1 cup): 268 Kilojoules (64 Calories); 0.5 g Total Fat; 500 mg Sodium; 2 g Protein; 15 g Carbohydrate

Stuffed Sweet Potatoes

The delicious pineapple flavour comes through with pecans giving a nice crunch.

Medium sweet potatoes (yams)	6	6
Canned crushed pineapple, with juice	1 cup	250 mL
Grated medium Cheddar cheese	1/4 cup	60 mL
Hard margarine (or butter), melted	1 tbsp	15 mL
Salt	3/4 tsp	4 mL
Pepper	1/8 tsp	0.5 mL

Finely chopped pecans	2 tbsp	30 mL
Paprika, sprinkle		

1. Place sweet potato (yams), pointed ends up, in a 5 L (5 quart) slow cooker. Cover. Cook on Low for 7 to 8 hours. Cut thick slice from top lengthwise. Scoop out pulp into bowl, leaving shell 6 mm (1/4 inch) thick.

2. Add next 5 ingredients to potato pulp. Mash well. Spoon back into shells.

3. Sprinkle with pecans and paprika. Arrange on baking pan. Bake in 20°C (425°F) oven for 15 to 20 minutes until hot. Serves 6.

1 stuffed potato: 907.2 Kilojoules (216 Calories); 5.6 Total Fat; 409 mg Sodium; 4 g Protein; 39 g Carbohydrate; good source of Dietary Fibre

Asparagus Bake

The asparagus retains its shape and rich colour.

Fresh asparagus	1 lb	454 g
Plain (all-purpose) flour	1 1/2 tbsp	25 mL
Salt	1/4 tsp	1 mL
Pepper	1/8 tsp	0.5 mL
Skim evaporated milk	3/4 cup	175 mL
Grated sharp Cheddar cheese	1/4 cup	60 mL

1. Cut off any tough ends of asparagus. Lay spears in 5 L (5 quart) slow cooker.

2. Stir flour, salt and pepper together in saucepan. Whisk in evaporated milk gradually until no lumps remain. Heat and stir until boiling and thickened.

3. Stir in cheese to melt. Pour over asparagus. Cover. Cook on Low for 3 to 4 hours. If you like your asparagus crunchy, check if cooked after 2 to 2 1/2 hours. Remove asparagus with slotted spoon. Serves 6.

1 serving: 297 Kilojoules (71 Calories); 1.9 g Total Fat; 185 mg Sodium; 6 g Protein; 8 g Carbohydrate

Glazed Carrots

These are best cooked on High to keep the great carrot taste. Nicely glazed.

Peeled baby carrots	2 lbs	900 g
Water	1/4 cup	60 mL
Cornflour (cornstarch)	1 tbsp	15 mL
Brown sugar, packed	1/2 cup	125 mL
Hard margarine (or butter), melted	1 tbsp	15 mL

1. Place carrots in 3.5 L (3 1/2 quart) slow cooker.

2. Stir water, cornflour (cornstarch), brown sugar and margarine together in small bowl. Pour over carrots. Cover. Cook on High for 3 to 4 hours. Stir before serving. Makes 1.25 L (5 cups).

125 mL (1/2 cup): 398 Kilojoules (95 Calories); 1.2 g Total Fat; 48 mg Sodium; 1 g Protein; 21 g Carbohydrate

Creamed Cabbage

In a delicious cream sauce.

Medium cabbage, finely chopped	1	1
Finely chopped onion	1/2 cup	125 mL
Water	1/4 cup	60 mL
Plain (all-purpose) flour	3 tbsp	50 mL
Chicken stock (bouillon) powder	1/2 tsp	2 mL
Salt	1/2 tsp	2 mL
Pepper	1/8 tsp	0.5 mL
Milk	2 cups	500 mL

TOPPING

Hard margarine (or butter)	1 tbsp	15 mL
Fine dry breadcrumbs	1/4 cup	60 mL

1. Place cabbage, onion and water in 5 L (5 quart) slow cooker. Cover. Cook on Low for 4 to 6 hours or on High for 2 to 3 hours. Drain.

2. Stir next 4 ingredients in saucepan. Whisk in milk gradually until no lumps remain. Heat and stir until boiling and thickened. Pour over cabbage. Stir.

3. **TOPPING**: Melt margarine in saucepan. Stir in breadcrumbs. Heat and stir until browned. Sprinkle over cabbage mixture before serving. Makes 1 L (4 cups).

125 mL (1/2 cup): 435 Kilojoules (104 Calories); 2.8 g Total Fat; 317 mg Sodium; 5 g Protein; 17 g Carbohydrate

Chilli Black Beans

A colourful, spicy blend of veggies and beans. Add a dollop of sour cream or salsa and sprinkle with spring (green) onion or coriander (cilantro), if desired.

Cans of black beans (540 g, 19 oz, each), rinsed and drained (or kidney or other canned beans)	2	2
Chopped butternut pumpkin (squash)	2 cups	500 mL
Can of diced tomatoes (with juice)	14 oz	398 g
Chopped onion	1 1/2 cups	375 mL
Liquid vegetable stock (broth)	1/2 cup	125 mL
Jalapeño chilli (pepper) (with seeds), finely diced (see Tip, page 36)	1	1
Chilli powder	1 tbsp	15 mL
Bay leaves	2	2
Garlic cloves, minced (or 2 mL, 1/2 tsp, powder)	2	2
Salt	1/4 tsp	1 mL
Chopped green capsicum (pepper)	1 cup	250 mL

1. Combine first 10 ingredients in 3.5 to 4 L (3 1/2 to 4 quart) slow cooker. Cover. Cook on Low for 8 to 10 hours or on High for 4 to 5 hours.

2. Add green capsicum (pepper). Stir gently. Cover. Cook on High for about 20 minutes until capsicum is tender but crisp. Remove and discard bay leaves. Serves 6.

MAKE AHEAD: The night before, combine first 10 ingredients in slow cooker liner. Cover. Chill overnight. Cook as directed.

Pictured on back cover.

1 serving: 768 Kilojoules (183 Calories); 1.1 g Total Fat; 504 mg Sodium; 10 g Protein; 36 g Carbohydrate

Chunky Vegetable Chilli

Colourful, chunky chilli loaded with a variety of tender veggies. Cheddar cheese garnish adds just the right touch. Serve with rolls or salad.

Medium carrots, cut into 2.5 cm (1 inch) pieces	4	4
Celery sticks, cut into 2.5 cm (1 inch) pieces	4	4
Medium onions, cut into 2.5 cm (1 inch) pieces	2	2
Large green capsicum (pepper), seeds and ribs removed, cut into 2.5 cm (1 inch) pieces	1	1
Can of chickpeas, (garbanzo beans) rinsed and drained	19 oz	540 g
Can of baby corn, drained	14 oz	398 g
Can of diced tomatoes, drained and juice reserved	14 oz	398 g
Tomato paste	1/3 cup	75 mL
Reserved juice from tomatoes	1/3 cup	75 mL
Medium salsa	1/3 cup	75 mL
Chilli powder	1 1/2–2 tsp	7–10 mL
Ground cumin	1–1 1/2 tsp	5–7 mL

Dried oregano	1/2–1 tsp	2–5 mL
Salt	1/2 tsp	2 mL
Pepper	1/2 tsp	2 mL
Small zucchini (courgette) (with peel), halved lengthwise, cut into 2.5 cm (1 inch) pieces	2	2
Medium red capsicum (pepper), seeds and ribs removed, cut into 2.5 cm (1 inch) pieces	1	1
Grated Cheddar cheese, for garnish		

1. Layer first 7 ingredients, in order given, in 5 to 7 L (5 to 7 quart) slow cooker.

2. Combine next 8 ingredients in medium bowl. Pour over tomatoes. Do not stir. Cover. Cook on Low for 8 to 10 hours or on High for 4 to 5 hours.

3. Add zucchini (courgette) and capsicum (pepper). Stir well. Cover. Cook on High for 20 to 25 minutes until capsicum is tender but crisp. Makes about 2.75 L (11 cups) chilli.

4. Garnish individual servings with cheese. Serves 8.

1 serving: 626 Kilojoules (149 Calories); 1.6 g Total Fat; 470 mg Sodium; 6 g Protein; 31 g Carbohydrate

Pumpkin and Dumplings

A subtly spiced, meatless stew topped with cheesy polenta dumplings. Enticing Italian flavours and a variety of textures make this dish particularly pleasing!

Butternut pumpkin (squash), cut into 12 mm (1/2 inch) pieces (about 750 mL, 3 cups)	3/4 lb	340 g
Cans of Italian-style stewed tomatoes (398 g, 14 oz, each)	2	2
Can of mixed beans, rinsed and drained	19 oz	540 g
Small fresh white mushrooms, halved	2 cups	500 mL
Water	1 cup	250 mL
Garlic cloves, minced (or 2 mL, 1/2 tsp, powder)	2	2
Italian seasoning	2 tsp	10 mL
Pepper	1/4 tsp	1 mL

POLENTA DUMPLINGS

Plain (all-purpose) flour	1/2 cup	125 mL
Polenta (yellow cornmeal)	1/3 cup	75 mL
Grated Parmesan cheese	2 tbsp	30 mL
Baking powder	1 tsp	5 mL
Paprika	1/8 tsp	0.5 mL
Large egg	1	1
Milk	2 tbsp	30 mL
Cooking oil	2 tbsp	30 mL
Basil pesto	1 tsp	5 mL

1. Combine first 8 ingredients in 4 to 5 L (4 to 5 quart) slow cooker. Cover. Cook on Low for 8 to 9 hours or on High for 4 to 4 1/2 hours.

2. POLENTA DUMPLINGS: Measure first 5 ingredients into medium bowl. Stir. Make a well in centre.

3. Beat remaining 4 ingredients with fork in small cup. Add to well. Stir until just moistened. Spoon mounds of batter, using 30 mL (2 tbsp) for each, in single layer on top of pumpkin mixture. Cover. Cook on High for 40 to 50 minutes until wooden pick inserted in centre of dumpling comes out clean. Serves 6.

Pictured between pages 96 & 97.

1 serving: 1146 Kilojoules (273 Calories); 7.5 g Total Fat; 742 mg Sodium; 10 g Protein; 45 g Carbohydrate

Barley Primavera

Creamy and appealing, this comfort food has a risotto-like texture and lots of colourful, tender but crisp vegetables, with the added nutritional value of barley.

Liquid vegetable stock (prepared vegetable broth)	4 cups	1 L
Pot barley	2 cups	500 mL
Frozen Italian mixed vegetables, thawed	4 cups	1 L
Alfredo pasta sauce	1 2/3 cups	400 mL
Chunky tomato and basil pasta sauce (prepared bruschetta topping)	1 1/2 cups	375 mL

1. Combine stock (broth), barley and 500 mL (2 cups) water in 4 to 5 L (4 to 5 quart) slow cooker. Cook, covered, on Low for 5 to 6 hours or on High for 2 1/2 to 3 hours until barley is tender and liquid is absorbed.

2. Add vegetables and pasta sauces. Stir. Cook, covered, on High for about 30 minutes until vegetables are tender. Makes about 3 L (12 cups).

Pictured between pages 112 & 113.

250 mL (1 cup): 1130 Kilojoules (270 Calories); 12.7 g Total Fat; 577 mg Sodium 6 g Protein; 34 g Carbohydrate

Curried Cauliflower Paneer

This mild vegetarian dish is best served over basmati rice. Garnish with a dollop of plain thick yoghurt and coriander (cilantro) sprigs.

Can of tikka masala curry sauce (see Note)	10 oz	284 g
Cauliflower florets	4 cups	1 L
Cubed paneer cheese	3 cups	750 mL
Fresh spinach leaves, lightly packed	4 cups	1 L
Chopped fresh coriander (cilantro) (or parsley)	1 tbsp	15 mL

1. Combine curry sauce and 250 mL (1 cup) water in 3.5 to 4 L (3 1/2 to 4 quart) slow cooker. Add cauliflower, paneer and a generous sprinkle of salt. Stir. Cook, covered, on Low for 5 to 6 hours or on High for 2 1/2 to 3 hours.

2. Add spinach, coriander (cilantro) and a sprinkle of salt and pepper. Stir. Makes about 1.5 L (6 cups).

NOTE: Jarred cooking sauce, which does not require the addition of water, may be used. Omit water and use 550 mL (2 1/4 cups) cooking sauce.

250 mL (1 cup): 2600 Kilojoules (621 Calories); 50.5 g Total Fat; 2126 mg Sodium; 29 g Protein; 12 g Carbohydrate

Vegetarian Winter Stew

Tender vegetables, fragrant with dill, patiently wait beneath a buttermilk scone (biscuit) topping for a hungry family. Just add a side salad, and dinner is served!

Cooking oil	2 tsp	10 mL
Thinly sliced onion	2 1/2 cups	625 mL
Thinly sliced celery	1 1/2 cups	375 mL
Garlic cloves, minced (or 2 mL, 1/2 tsp, powder)	2	2
Dried thyme	1 tsp	5 mL
Pepper	1 tsp	5 mL
Plain (all-purpose) flour	2 tbsp	30 mL
Can of sliced mushrooms (with liquid)	10 oz	284 g
Can of condensed cream of mushroom soup	10 oz	284 g
Thinly sliced peeled potato	3 cups	750 mL
Thinly sliced carrot	2 cups	500 mL
Thinly sliced parsnip	2 cups	500 mL
Frozen peas	1 cup	250 mL
Tomato juice	1/4 cup	60 mL
Chopped fresh dill (or 15 mL, 1 tbsp, dill leaf tips/dillweed)	1/4 cup	60 mL

SCONE (BISCUIT) TOPPING

Plain (all-purpose) flour	1 1/2 cups	375 mL
Baking powder	1 tbsp	15 mL
Parsley flakes	2 tsp	10 mL
Salt	1/2 tsp	2 mL
Large egg, fork-beaten	1	1
Buttermilk (or reconstituted from powder)	1 cup	250 mL

1. Heat cooking oil in large frying pan (skillet) on Medium. Add onion and celery. Cook for 5 to 10 minutes, stirring often, until onion is softened.

2. Add garlic, thyme and pepper. Heat and stir for about 1 minute until fragrant.

3. Add flour. Heat and stir for 1 minute. Add mushrooms and soup. Heat and stir for about 1 minute until boiling and thickened. Transfer to 4 to 5 L (4 to 5 quart) slow cooker.

4. Add potato, carrot and parsnip. Stir well. Cover. Cook on Low for 8 to 9 hours or on High for 4 to 4 1/2 hours.

5. Add peas, tomato juice and dill. Stir well. Cover.

6. SCONE TOPPING: Combine first 4 ingredients in medium bowl. Make a well in centre. Add egg and buttermilk to well. Stir until just moistened. Spoon batter evenly on top of vegetable mixture. Cover. Cook on High for 30 to 40 minutes until wooden pick inserted in centre of topping comes out clean. Serves 6.

1 serving: 1726 Kilojoules (411 Calories); 7.6 g Total Fat; 1090 mg Sodium; 13 g Protein; 75 g Carbohydrate

Carrot Onion Casserole

The slow cooking really brings out the carrot and onion flavours.

Diagonally sliced carrot	6 cups	1.5 L
Sliced onion	1 1/2 cups	375 mL
Salt	1/2 tsp	2 mL
Water	1/2 cup	125 mL

SAUCE

Plain (all-purpose) flour	1 tbsp	15 mL
Salt, sprinkle		
Pepper, sprinkle		
Milk	1/2 cup	125 mL
Grated medium or sharp Cheddar cheese	1/2 cup	125 mL

TOPPING

Hard margarine (or butter)	1 tbsp	15 mL
Fine dry breadcrumbs	1/4 cup	60 mL

1. Place carrot, onion, salt and water in 3.5 L (3 1/2 quart) slow cooker. Stir. Cover. Cook on High for 4 to 5 hours. Drain. Place in serving bowl.

2. SAUCE: Stir flour, salt and pepper together in small saucepan. Whisk in milk gradually until no lumps remain. Heat and stir until boiling and thickened.

3. Add cheese. Stir to melt. Pour over vegetables. Stir.

4. TOPPING: Melt margarine in saucepan. Stir in breadcrumbs. Heat and stir until browned. Sprinkle over vegetables before serving. Makes 1.5 L (6 cups).

125 mL (1/2 cup): 385 Kilojoules (92 Calories); 3.1 g Total Fat; 177 mg Sodium; 3 g Protein; 14 g Carbohydrate

Red Cabbage

It does lose its brightness but keeps the good taste.

Small red cabbage, quartered, cored and thinly sliced (about 900 g, 2 lbs)	1	1
Chopped onion	1 1/2 cups	375 mL
Medium cooking apples, peeled, cored and chopped	3	3

Brown sugar, packed	1/4 cup	60 mL
Water		1/2 cup 125 mL
White vinegar	1/4 cup	60 mL
Hard margarine (or butter), melted	1 tbsp	15 mL
Salt	1 tsp	5 mL
Pepper	1/4 tsp	1 mL

Place all 9 ingredients in 5 L (5 quart) slow cooker. Stir to coat all with liquid. Cover. Cook on Low for 5 to 6 hours or on High for 2 1/2 to 3 hours. Makes 1.75 L (7 cups).

125 mL (1/2 cup): 268 Kilojoules (64 Calories); 1.1 g Total Fat; 213 mg Sodium; 1 g Protein; 14 g Carbohydrate

Pumpkin and Couscous

This comforting dish has the earthiness of pumpkin (squash) and the sweetness of apricots, all with an eastern Mediterranean flair.

Chopped dried apricots	2/3 cup	150 mL
Cubed butternut pumpkin (squash) (2.5 cm, 1 inch, pieces)	6 cups	1.5 L
Butter (or hard margarine), melted	2 tbsp	30 mL
Box of couscous	7 oz	198 g
Pine nuts, toasted	2 tbsp	30 mL

1. Combine apricots and 375 mL (1 1/2 cups) boiling water in small bowl. Let stand for 10 minutes. Drain, reserving 250 mL (1 cup) water. Transfer apricots to greased 4 to 5 L (4 to 5 quart) slow cooker.

2. Add pumpkin (squash). Drizzle with melted butter. Sprinkle with salt and pepper. Stir well. Cook, covered, on Low for 6 to 7 hours or on High for 3 to 3 1/2 hours until tender.

3. Combine couscous and reserved water. Add to pumpkin mixture. Stir gently. Cook, covered, on High for about 10 minutes until couscous is tender and liquid is absorbed.

4. Sprinkle with pine nuts. Makes about 1.75 L (7 cups).

250 mL (1 cup): 1130 Kilojoules (270 Calories); 5.7 g Total Fat; 375 mg Sodium; 7 g Protein; 54 g Carbohydrate

Vegetable Curry

A colourful combination of chickpeas (garbanzo beans) and vegetables, seasoned with a mellow blend of ginger, curry and coconut milk.

Can of coconut milk	14 oz	398 mL
Curry powder	2 tsp	10 mL
Plain (all-purpose) flour	1 1/2 tbsp	25 mL
Cauliflower florets	3 cups	750 mL
Chopped peeled fresh potato	3 cups	750 mL
Can of chickpeas (garbanzo beans), rinsed and drained	19 oz	540 g
Chopped carrot	2 cups	500 mL
Chopped onion	1 2/3 cups	400 mL
Finely grated, peeled fresh ginger (gingeroot)	1 tbsp	15 mL
Garlic cloves, minced (or 2 mL, 1/2 tsp, powder)	2	2
Salt	1 tsp	5 mL
Frozen peas	1/2 cup	125 mL

1. Beat first 3 ingredients with whisk in small bowl until smooth.

2. Put next 8 ingredients into 5 to 7 L (5 to 7 quart) slow cooker. Add coconut milk mixture. Stir well. Cover. Cook on Low for 7 to 8 hours or on High for 3 1/2 to 4 hours.

3. Add peas. Stir gently. Cover. Cook on High for 5 to 10 minutes until peas are heated through. Serves 8.

1 serving: 1096 Kilojoules (261 Calories); 12.7 g Total Fat; 133 mg Sodium; 7 g Protein; 33 g Carbohydrate

Stuffed Baked Potatoes

Arrive home to hot baked potatoes. Prepare stuffing while oven heats.

Medium baking potatoes	6	6
Water	2 tbsp	30 mL
STUFFING		
Light cream, cheese softened	4 oz	125 g
Non-fat sour cream	2/3 cup	150 mL
Onion salt	1 1/2 tsp	7 mL
Chopped chives	1 tbsp	15 mL
Salt	1/2 tsp	2 mL
Pepper	1/8 tsp	0.5 mL
Grated medium Cheddar cheese	1/3 cup	75 mL
Paprika, sprinkle		

1. Arrange potatoes in 3.5 L (3 1/2 quart) slow cooker, stacking if necessary. Add water. Cover. Cook on Low for 8 to 10 hours.

2. **STUFFING:** Mash first 6 ingredients together in bowl. Cut lengthwise slice from top of each potato. Scoop hot potato into same bowl leaving shells intact. Mash well. Spoon back into shells.

3. Sprinkle with cheese and paprika. Arrange in single layer in 22 x 33 cm (9 x 13 inch) baking pan. Bake in 220°C (425°F) oven for about 15 minutes until hot. Makes 6 stuffed potatoes.

1 stuffed potato: 787 Kilojoules (188 Calories); 5.8 g Total Fat; 827 mg Sodium; 8 g Protein; 27 g Carbohydrate

Veggie Shepherd's Pie

A hearty vegetarian dish with the comforting flavours of home, this slow cooker casserole has a nice blend of seasonings and a hint of spicy heat.

Soy-based meat substitute (veggie ground round)	24 oz	680 g
Chunky tomato and basil pasta sauce (prepared bruschetta topping)	1 1/2 cups	375 mL
Frozen peas, thawed	1 cup	250 mL
Can of corn kernels, drained	7 oz	199 g
Mashed potatoes (about 900 g, 2 lbs, uncooked)	4 1/2 cups	1.1 L

1. Combine first 3 ingredients in 3.5 to 4 L (3 1/2 to 4 quart) slow cooker.

2. Scatter corn over soy product. Do not stir. Sprinkle mashed potatoes with salt and pepper. Stir. Spread mashed potatoes over corn. Do not stir. Lay double layer of tea towel over slow cooker liner. Cover with lid. Cook on Low for 6 to 7 hours or on High for 3 to 3 1/2 hours. Makes about 2.5 L (10 cups).

250 mL (1 cup): 909 Kilojoules (217 Calories); 2.9 g Total Fat; 902 mg Sodium; 15 g Protein; 32 g Carbohydrate

Classic 'Baked' Beans

Cooking dry beans in a slow cooker is not only easy, but healthy and inexpensive, too!

Dried cannellini (navy) beans	5 cups	1.25 L
Chopped onion	1 cup	250 mL
Tomato sauce (ketchup)	1 1/2 cups	375 mL
Treacle (molasses)	1/3 cup	75 mL
Prepared mustard	2 tbsp	30 mL

1. Measure beans into large bowl or pot. Add water until 5 cm (2 inches) above beans. Soak overnight (See Tip, page 55). Drain. Rinse beans. Drain. Transfer to 5 to 7 L (5 to 7 quart) slow cooker.

2. Add onion and 1.25 L (5 cups) water. Cook, covered, on High for 4 to 4 1/2 hours until beans are tender (see Note).

3. Add remaining 3 ingredients and a generous sprinkle of salt and pepper. Stir. Cook, covered, on High for 30 minutes. Sprinkle generously with salt and pepper. Stir. Makes about 3 L (12 cups).

NOTE: Cooking beans on Low setting is not recommended as they may not cook fully.

Pictured between pages 112 & 113.

250 mL (1 cup): 862 Kilojoules (206 Calories); 0.5 g Total Fat; 939 mg Sodium; 8 g Protein; 45 g Carbohydrate

Pineapple Bean Bake

These smoky, sweet and tangy beans would make a great side at your next barbecue – spoon some up with a steak hot from the grill (broiler).

Cans of red kidney beans (540 g, 19 oz, each), rinsed and drained	2	2
Cans of baked beans in tomato sauce (398 g, 14 oz, each)	2	2
Can of crushed pineapple (with juice)	19 oz	540 g
Finely chopped onion	1 cup	250 mL
Smoky (hickory) barbecue sauce	1/2 cup	125 mL

Combine all 5 ingredients in 3.5 to 4 L (3 1/2 to 4 quart) slow cooker. Cook, covered, on Low for 8 to 9 hours or on High for 4 to 4 1/2 hours. Makes about 2.1 L (8 1/2 cups).

250 mL (1 cup): 1231 Kilojoules (294 Calories); 1.2 g Total Fat; 471 mg Sodium; 14 g Protein; 58 g Carbohydrate

Chickpea Stew

Saucy, beany and meaty. Serve with crusty rolls.

Dried chickpeas, (garbanzo beans) 625 mL (2 1/2 cups)	1 lb	454 g
Chopped onion	1 1/2 cups	375 mL
Medium carrots, cut julienne	2	2
Dried sweet basil	1/2 tsp	2 mL
Pepper	1/4 tsp	1 mL
Water	5 1/2 cups	1.4 L
Beef (or pork) stew meat, cut into 12 mm (1/2 inch) cubes	1 lb	454 g
Cooking oil	1 1/2 tsp	7 mL
Canned tomatoes, drained, juice reserved	14 oz	398 g

Beef stock (bouillon) powder	1 tbsp	15 mL
Salt	1 tsp	5 mL
Reserved tomato juice		
Plain (all-purpose) flour	3 tbsp	50 mL

1. Combine first 6 ingredients in 3.5 L (3 1/2 quart) slow cooker.

2. Brown beef quickly in hot cooking oil in frying pan (skillet). Add to slow cooker. Cover. Cook on Low for 8 to 10 hours or on High for 4 to 5 hours.

3. Add tomato, stock (bouillon) powder and salt.

4. Slowly whisk tomato juice into flour in small bowl. Stir into slow cooker. Cover. Cook on Low for 2 hours or on High for 1 hour. Stir before serving. Makes 2.3 L (9 1/2 cups).

1. Classic 'Baked' Beans, page 111
2. Ratatouille, page 99
3. Barley Primavera, page 105

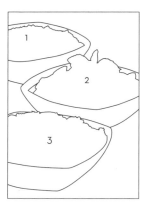

Cauliflower Dhal

Dinner's ready, DHAL-ings! Treat the ones you love to this spicy, traditional East Indian dish. Perfect with pappadum, a crispy Indian flatbread.

Cauliflower florets	4 cups	1 L
Chopped peeled potato	2 cups	500 mL
Yellow split peas, rinsed and drained	1 cup	250 mL
Chopped onion	1 cup	250 mL
Garlic clove, minced (or 1 mL, 1/4 tsp, powder)	1	1
Liquid vegetable stock (prepared vegetable broth)	3 cups	750 mL
Balsamic vinegar	2 tbsp	30 mL
Red curry paste	1 tsp	5 mL
Turmeric	1/4 tsp	1 mL
Ground ginger	1/4 tsp	1 mL
Ground nutmeg	1/4 tsp	1 mL
Salt	1/2 tsp	2 mL
Pepper	1/2 tsp	2 mL

1. Combine first 5 ingredients in 4 to 5 L (4 to 5 quart) slow cooker.

2. Measure remaining 8 ingredients into medium bowl. Stir well. Pour over cauliflower mixture. Stir well. Cover. Cook on Low for 8 to 9 hours or on High for 4 to 4 1/2 hours. Makes about 1.9 L (7 1/2 cups).

1. Full-of-Beans Turkey Pot, p 115
2. Chicken and Beans, page 116
3. Beef and Lentils, page 120

Props Courtesy Of: Casa Bugatti
Island Pottery Inc.
Out of the Fire Studio
Totally Bamboo
Treasure Barrel

250 mL (1 cup): 424 Kilojoules (101 Calories); 0.8 g Total Fat; 575 mg Sodium; 6 g Protein; 19 g Carbohydrate

Beans and Fennel

A wholesome, hearty mix of beans, fennel and spicy sausage deliciously dotted with dill. Serve with a crisp salad.

Fennel bulb (white part only), thinly sliced	1	1
Finely chopped carrot	1 cup	250 mL
Thinly sliced red onion	1 cup	250 mL
Cooking oil	1 tsp	5 mL
Chorizo sausages, casings removed, cut into 12 mm (1/2 inch) slices	3	3
Can of diced tomatoes (with juice)	28 oz	796 g
Can of chickpeas (garbanzo beans), rinsed and drained	19 oz	540 g
Can of cannellini (navy) beans, rinsed and drained	19 oz	540 g
Can of borlotti (pinto) beans, rinsed and drained	19 oz	540 g
Balsamic vinegar	1 tbsp	15 mL
White (granulated) sugar	1 tsp	5 mL
Salt	1/4 tsp	1 mL
Pepper	1/2 tsp	2 mL
Chopped fresh dill (or 7 mL, 1 1/2 tsp, dried dill leaf tips/ dill weed)	2 tbsp	30 mL

1. Layer fennel, carrot and onion in 4 to 5 L (4 to 5 quart) slow cooker.

2. Heat cooking oil in large frying pan (skillet) on Medium. Add sausage. Cook for 8 to 10 minutes, stirring occasionally, until browned. Drain. Set aside.

3. Combine next 8 ingredients in large bowl. Pour over vegetables. Do not stir. Scatter sausage over top. Cover. Cook on Low for 8 to 10 hours or on High for 4 to 5 hours.

4. Add dill. Stir well. Serves 8.

1 serving: 1323 Kilojoules (315 Calories); 13.6 g Total Fat; 874 mg Sodium; 17 g Protein; 33 g Carbohydrate

Full-of-Beans Turkey Pot

A mild curry-flavoured dish that's definitely full of beans!

Cans of sliced peaches in light syrup (with juice), 398 g (14 oz) each	2	2
Can of red kidney beans, rinsed and drained	19 oz	540 g
Can of cannellini (navy) beans, rinsed and drained	19 oz	540 g
Can of black beans, rinsed and drained (or other canned beans)	19 oz	540 g
Can of baked beans in tomato sauce	14 oz	398 g
Chopped green capsicum (pepper)	1 cup	250 mL
Chopped onion	1 cup	250 mL
Sweet (or regular) chilli sauce	1/2 cup	125 mL
Curry powder	1 tsp	5 mL
Boneless, skinless turkey thighs, cut into 2.5 cm (1 inch) pieces	1 1/2 lbs	680 g

1. Combine first 9 ingredients in 5 to 7 L (5 to 7 quart) slow cooker.

2. Add turkey. Stir well. Cover. Cook on Low for 8 to 10 hours or on High for 4 to 5 hours. Serves 8.

Pictured between pages 112 & 113.

1 serving: 1432 Kilojoules (341 Calories); 3.8 g Total Fat; 690 mg Sodium; 27 g Protein; 54 g Carbohydrate

Chicken and Beans

Bacon adds a satisfying smoky flavour to this filling dish.

Bacon slices, diced	8	8
Plain (all-purpose) flour	2 tbsp	30 mL
Boneless, skinless chicken thighs, halved	1 lb	454 g
Can of diced tomatoes (with juice)	28 oz	796 g
Can of cannellini (navy) beans, rinsed and drained	19 oz	540 g
Chopped red capsicum (pepper)	1 1/2 cups	375 mL
Chopped onion	1 cup	250 mL
Salt	1/4 tsp	1 mL
Pepper	1/4 tsp	1 mL

1. Cook bacon in large frying pan (skillet) on Medium until almost crisp. Remove to paper towels to drain. Remove and discard drippings, reserving 15 mL (1 tbsp) in pan.

2. Measure flour into large resealable freezer bag. Add 1/2 of chicken. Seal bag. Toss until coated. Repeat with remaining chicken. Heat reserved drippings in same large frying pan on Medium. Add chicken in 2 batches. Cook for 8 to 10 minutes per batch, stirring occasionally, until browned. Transfer to 3.5 to 4 L (3 1/2 to 4 quart) slow cooker.

3. Combine bacon and remaining 6 ingredients in large bowl. Pour over chicken. Do not stir. Cover. Cook on Low for 8 to 10 hours or on High for 4 to 5 hours. Serves 4.

Pictured between pages 112 & 113.

1 serving: 1634 Kilojoules (389 Calories); 13.4 g Total Fat; 834 mg Sodium; 34 g Protein; 34 g Carbohydrate

Ranch-Style Beans

Containing both beef and ham, this thick and meaty dish is a touch on the sweet side.

Extra lean beef mince (ground beef)	1 lb	454 g
Diced smoked ham (or 1 can, 184 g, 6.5 oz, with liquid)	1 cup	250 mL
Chopped onion	1 cup	250 mL
Canned beans in tomato sauce, 398 g (14 oz) each	2	2
Canned kidney beans, drained	19 oz	540 g

Tomato sauce (ketchup)	1/2 cup	125 mL
Treacle (molasses)	1/4 cup	60 mL
Brown sugar, packed	1/4 cup	60 mL
Salt	3/4 tsp	4 mL
Pepper	1/8 tsp	0.5 mL
Liquid gravy browner (optional)	1/4 tsp	1 mL

Measure all 11 ingredients into 3.5 L (3 1/2 quart) slow cooker. Mix well to break up and distribute beef and ham. Cover. Cook on Low for 8 to 9 hours or on High for 4 to 4 1/2 hours. Stir before serving. Makes 2 L (8 cups).

250 mL (1 cup): 1612 Kilojoules (385 Calories); 9.7 g Total Fat; 1273 mg Sodium; 27 g Protein; 51 g Carbohydrate

Overnight Baked Beans

When you start the beans cooking, have the rest of the ingredients measured and ready to add when needed.

Dried cannellini (navy) beans	2 cups	500 mL
Water	4 cups	1 L
Diced bacon, cooked crisp (about 5 slices)	3/4 cup	175 mL
Tomato sauce (ketchup)	1/4 cup	60 mL
Brown sugar, packed	1/3 cup	75 mL
Treacle (molasses)	2 tbsp	30 mL

1. Combine beans and water in 3.5 L (3 1/2 quart) slow cooker. Stir well. Cover. Cook on Low for 8 to 10 hours or overnight until beans are soft.

2. Add remaining 4 ingredients. Stir well. Cover. Cook on High for about 30 minutes to blend flavours. Makes 1 L (4 cups).

125 mL (1/2 cup): 1072 Kilojoules (256 Calories); 2.7 g Total Fat; 183 mg Sodium; 13 g Protein; 47 g Carbohydrate

Saucy Beans and Chicken

A can of beans, a few slices of bacon and some chicken thighs
are all you need for this delicious, all-in-one meal – perfect
for when you're hosting a crowd for the finals!

Chopped onion	1 cup	250 mL
Bacon slices, diced	3	3
Bone-in chicken thighs, skin removed	3 lbs	1.4 kg
Can of baked beans in tomato sauce	14 oz	398 g
Grated Cheddar cheese	1/2 cup	125 mL

1. Heat large frying pan (skillet) on Medium-High. Add onion and bacon. Cook for about 5 minutes, stirring often, until onion is softened. Transfer with slotted spoon to 4 to 5 L (4 to 5 quart) slow cooker.

2. Add chicken to same frying pan. Sprinkle with salt and pepper. Cook on Medium-High for about 3 minutes per side until browned. Transfer to slow cooker. Cook, covered, on Low for 6 to 7 hours or on High for 3 to 3 1/2 hours. Transfer chicken with slotted spoon to medium bowl. Skim and discard fat from cooking liquid.

3. Add beans and cheese. Stir. Return chicken to slow cooker. Cook, covered, on High for about 15 minutes until heated through. Serves 4.

1 serving: 2424 Kilojoules (579 Calories); 27.9 g Total Fat; 869 mg Sodium; 56 g Protein; 23 g Carbohydrate

Lamb and Bean Hot Pot

Rosemary adds just the right touch to this well-seasoned dish. The answer to dinner when there's company scheduled to arrive just after you do!

Plain (all-purpose) flour	3 tbsp	50 mL
Lamb loin chops (about 1.1 kg, 2 1/2 lbs)	12	12
Cooking oil	1 tbsp	15 mL
Medium potatoes, peeled, cut into 6 mm (1/4 inch) slices	2	2
Sliced carrot	1 1/3 cups	325 mL
Thinly sliced onion	1 cup	250 mL
Salt	1/2 tsp	2 mL
Pepper	1/2 tsp	2 mL
Can of cannellini (navy) beans, rinsed and drained	19 oz	540 g
Liquid chicken stock (prepared chicken broth)	1 cup	250 mL
Dry sherry	1/2 cup	125 mL
Chopped fresh rosemary leaves (or 4 mL, 3/4 tsp, dried, crushed)	1 tbsp	15 mL
Grated lemon zest	1 tsp	5 mL
White (granulated) sugar	1 tsp	5 mL
Worcestershire sauce	1 tsp	5 mL
Chopped fresh mint leaves (or 4 mL, 3/4 tsp, dried), for garnish	1 tbsp	15 mL

1. Measure flour into large resealable freezer bag. Add 1/2 of lamb chops. Seal bag. Toss until coated. Repeat with remaining lamb chops. Heat cooking oil in large frying pan (skillet) on Medium-High. Add lamb chops in 2 batches. Cook for about 3 minutes per batch, turning occasionally, until browned.

2. Layer potato, carrot and onion, in order given, in 4 to 5 L (4 to 5 quart) slow cooker. Sprinkle with salt and pepper. Arrange lamb chops, slightly overlapping, on top of onion.

3. Combine next 7 ingredients in medium bowl. Pour over lamb chops. Do not stir. Cover. Cook on Low for 8 to 10 hours or on High for 4 to 5 hours. Transfer lamb chops to large plate. Remove vegetable mixture with slotted spoon to large serving platter. Arrange lamb chops on top of vegetables. Sprinkle with mint. Serves 6.

1 serving: 2058 Kilojoules (490 Calories); 26.3 g Total Fat; 552 mg Sodium; 32 g Protein; 27 g Carbohydrate

Beef and Lentils

Tangy tomato and barbecue flavours add zip to beef mince (ground beef) and lentils. Simple to prepare. Serve on its own or over rice.

Can of diced tomatoes (with juice)	28 oz	796 g
Can of lentils, rinsed and drained	19 oz	540 g
Finely chopped onion	1 1/2 cups	375 mL
Finely chopped celery	1/2 cup	125 mL
Barbecue sauce	3 tbsp	50 mL
Sweet (or regular) chilli sauce	2 1/2 tbsp	37 mL
Balsamic vinegar	1 tbsp	15 mL
Bay leaf	1	1
Salt	1/4 tsp	1 mL
Pepper	1/8 tsp	0.5 mL
Cooking oil	2 tsp	10 mL
Lean beef mince (ground beef)	1 lb	454 g
Plain (all-purpose) flour	1 1/2 tbsp	25 mL

Liquid beef stock (prepared beef broth)	1/4 cup	60 mL
Finely chopped fresh parsley (or 11 mL, 2 1/4 tsp, flakes), optional	3 tbsp	50 mL

1. Combine first 10 ingredients in 3.5 to 4 L (3 1/2 to 4 quart) slow cooker.

2. Heat cooking oil in large frying pan (skillet) on Medium. Add beef mince (ground beef). Scramble-fry for 5 to 10 minutes until no longer pink. Drain.

3. Sprinkle flour over beef. Heat and stir on Medium for 1 minute. Slowly add stock (broth), stirring constantly and scraping any brown bits from bottom of pan. Add to tomato mixture. Stir well. Cover. Cook on Low for 8 to 10 hours or on High for 4 to 5 hours. Remove and discard bay leaf.

4. Add parsley. Stir well. Serves 6.

Pictured between pages 112 & 113.

1 serving: 1251 Kilojoules (298 Calories); 13.7 g Total Fat; 688 mg Sodium; 21 g Protein; 24 g Carbohydrate

Rice and Bean Tacos

Hearty, meatless taco filling with a slight nuttiness from the wild rice. Topped with sour cream, lettuce and cheese, these look great on a finger food buffet.

RICE AND BEAN FILLING

Cans of mixed beans (540 g, 19 oz, each), rinsed and drained	2	2
Can of diced tomatoes (with juice)	28 oz	796 g
Liquid vegetable stock (prepared vegetable broth)	1 cup	250 mL
Wild rice	1/2 cup	125 mL
Can of diced green chillies	4 oz	113 g
Chilli powder	2 tsp	10 mL
White (granulated) sugar	1 tsp	5 mL
Ground cumin	1 tsp	5 mL
Dried oregano	1 tsp	5 mL
Pepper	1/2 tsp	2 mL

Taco shells	24	24
Sour cream (optional)	1 cup	250 mL
Chopped or torn lettuce	1 1/2 cups	375 mL
Grated Cheddar cheese	1 1/2 cups	375 mL

1. RICE AND BEAN FILLING: Combine first 10 ingredients in 3.5 to 4 L (3 1/2 to 4 quart) slow cooker. Cover. Cook on Low for 8 to 10 hours or on High for 4 to 5 hours. Makes about 1.5 L (6 cups) filling.

2. Heat taco shells according to package directions. Spoon 60 mL (1/4 cup) filling into each shell.

3. Spoon 10 mL (2 tsp) sour cream over filling in each shell. Divide and sprinkle lettuce and cheese over sour cream. Makes 24 tacos.

1 taco: 592 Kilojoules (141 Calories); 5.8 g Total Fat; 291 mg Sodium; 6 g Protein; 18 g Carbohydrate

African Quinoa Stew

Quinoa (KEEN-wah), beans and peanut butter are a delicious, creative combination that packs a protein punch in this rich and colourful African-inspired stew.

Chopped onion	1 1/2 cups	375 mL
Cans of red kidney beans (540 g, 19 oz, each), rinsed and drained	2	2
Tomato purée (tomato sauce)	2 cups	500 mL
Quinoa, rinsed and drained	1 cup	250 mL
Peanut butter	6 tbsp	100 mL

1. Heat large greased frying pan (skillet) on Medium. Add onion. Cook for about 8 minutes, stirring often, until softened. Transfer to 3.5 to 4 L (3 1/2 to 4 quart) slow cooker.

2. Add remaining 4 ingredients, 250 mL (1 cup) water and a generous sprinkle of salt and pepper. Stir. Cook, covered, on Low for 5 to 6 hours or on High for 2 1/2 to 3 hours. Makes about 2 L (8 cups).

250 mL (1 cup): 1457 Kilojoules (348 Calories); 8.9 g Total Fat; 547 mg Sodium; 17 g Protein; 53 g Carbohydrate

Black Beans and Barley

Flavourful onion and a mild malt taste make this combination of black beans and tender barley a treat – tastes great with a crisp side salad.

Liquid vegetable stock (prepared vegetable broth)	3 cups	750 mL
Pot barley	2 cups	500 mL
Can of beer	12 1/2 oz	355 mL
Packet of onion soup mix	1 1/4 oz	38 g
Cans of black beans (540 g, 19 oz, each), rinsed and drained	2	2

1. Combine first 4 ingredients and 375 mL (1 1/2 cups) water in 4 to 5 L (4 to 5 quart) slow cooker. Cook, covered, on Low for 5 to 6 hours or on High for 2 1/2 to 3 hours until barley is tender and liquid is absorbed.

2. Add beans. Stir. Cook, covered, on High for 10 minutes until heated through. Makes about 2.75 L (11 cups).

250 mL (1 cup): 1030 Kilojoules (246 Calories); 1.8 g Total Fat; 723 mg Sodium; 10 g Protein; 45 g Carbohydrate

Meatless Moussaka

Lentils replace the meat in this comforting Greek dish with simple and distinct tastes. For less fuss and more flavour, the traditional béchamel topping was traded up for a quick and easy sprinkle of creamy goat (chèvre) cheese.

Cans of lentils (540 g, 19 oz, each), rinsed and drained	2	2
Tomato pasta sauce	3 cups	750 mL
Ground cinnamon	1/4 tsp	1 mL
Medium eggplants (aubergines) (with peel), cut into 6 mm (1/4 inch) slices	2	2
Goat (chèvre) cheese, crumbled	8 oz	225 g

1. Combine first 3 ingredients and a sprinkle of salt and pepper in large bowl.

2. To assemble, layer ingredients in greased 5 to 7 L (5 to 7 quart) slow cooker as follows:

   a) 500 mL (2 cups) lentil mixture
   b) Half of eggplant (aubergine)
   c) 500 mL (2 cups) lentil mixture
   d) Remaining eggplant
   e) Remaining lentil mixture

3. Cook, covered, on Low for 8 to 9 hours or on High for 4 to 4 1/2 hours.

4. Sprinkle with cheese. Cook, covered, on High for about 10 minutes until cheese is softened. Makes about 2.25 L (9 cups).

250 mL (1 cup): 1076 Kilojoules (257 Calories); 6.5 g Total Fat; 386 mg Sodium; 18 g Protein; 42 g Carbohydrate

Veggie Lentil Stew

A rich, tomato-based stew packed with earthy lentils and vegetables. Perfect with wholemeal bread.

Dried green lentils, rinsed and drained	2 1/4 cups	550 mL
Medium carrots, quartered lengthwise, cut into 5 cm (2 inch) pieces	4	4
Medium leeks (white part only), halved lengthwise, cut into 12 mm (1/2 inch) slices	3	3
Chopped celery	1 cup	250 mL
Cubed red potato (with skin)	2 cups	500 mL
Garlic cloves, minced (or 2 mL, 1/2 tsp, powder), optional	2	2
Can of diced tomatoes (with juice)	28 oz	796 g
Liquid vegetable stock (prepared vegetable broth)	3 cups	750 mL
Can of condensed cream of mushroom soup (or your favourite)	10 oz	284 g
Tomato juice	3/4 cup	175 mL
Dried basil	3/4 tsp	4 mL
Dried thyme	1/2 tsp	2 mL
Pepper	1/2 tsp	2 mL

1. Measure lentils into 5 to 7 L (5 to 7 quart) slow cooker.

2. Layer next 5 ingredients, in order given, on top of lentils.

3. Combine remaining 7 ingredients in large bowl. Pour over vegetables. Do not stir. Cover. Cook on Low for 9 to 10 hours or on High for 4 1/2 to 5 hours. Serves 8.

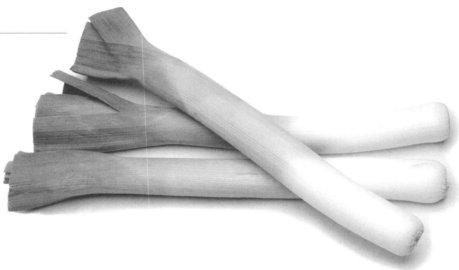

1 serving: 1482 Kilojoules (353 Calories); 4.2 g Total Fat; 914 mg Sodium; 21 g Protein; 61 g Carbohydrate

Simple Dhal

Delicious served over rice or with flatbread. For more heat, add another tablespoon of curry paste or use hot paste instead of mild.

Chopped onion	1 cup	250 mL
Dried red split lentils	2 1/2 cups	625 mL
Mild curry paste	3 tbsp	50 mL
Can of diced tomatoes, drained	14 oz	398 g
Chopped fresh coriander (cilantro)	1/2 cup	125 mL

1. Heat medium greased frying pan (skillet) on Medium. Add onion. Cook for about 5 minutes, stirring often, until softened. Transfer to 3.5 to 4 L (3 1/2 to 4 quart) slow cooker.

2. Add lentils, curry paste and 1.4 L (5 1/2 cups) water. Stir. Cook, covered, on Low for 6 to 7 hours or on High for 3 to 3 1/2 hours.

3. Add tomatoes and a generous sprinkle of salt. Stir. Cook, covered, on High for about 10 minutes until heated through.

4. Add coriander (cilantro). Stir. Makes about 2 L (8 cups).

250 mL (1 cup): 1055 Kilojoules (252 Calories); 3.0 g Total Fat; 467 mg Sodium; 17 g Protein; 40 g Carbohydrate

Salsa Veggie Chilli

This is an easy vegetarian chilli with delicious, crowd-pleasing results. Tasty with corn (nacho) chips or crusty bread for dipping.

Can of kidney beans, rinsed and drained	19 oz	540 g
Chunky salsa	2 cups	500 mL
Tomato sauce (ketchup)	2 cups	500 mL
Soy-based meat substitute (veggie ground round)	12 oz	340 g
Chilli powder	2 tsp	10 mL

Combine all 5 ingredients in 3.5 to 4 L (3 1/2 to 4 quart) slow cooker. Cook, covered, on Low for 7 to 8 hours or on High for 3 1/2 to 4 hours. Makes about 1.5 L (6 cups).

250 mL (1 cup): 770 Kilojoules (184 Calories); 0 g Total Fat; 1442 mg Sodium; 16 g Protein; 30 g Carbohydrate

Pumpkin and Lentil Curry

A thick, mildly spiced lentil and vegetable curry – a fusion of fantastic flavours. Serve with flatbread and crisp salad.

Liquid vegetable stock (prepared vegetable broth)	3 cups	750 mL
Chopped onion	1 1/2 cups	375 mL
Plain (all-purpose) flour	2 tbsp	30 mL
Curry paste	2 tbsp	30 mL
Garlic cloves, minced (or 2 mL, 1/2 tsp, powder)	2	2
Pepper	1/4 tsp	1 mL
Chopped butternut pumpkin (squash)	2 cups	500 mL
Dried green lentils, rinsed and drained	1 1/4 cups	300 mL
Chopped sweet potato (yam)	1 cup	250 mL

Fresh spinach, stems removed, lightly packed	3 cups	750 mL
Frozen peas	1 cup	250 mL
Plain yoghurt	1/3 cup	75 mL
Raw cashews, toasted	1/3 cup	75 mL
Salt, just a pinch		

1. Combine first 6 ingredients in 3.5 to 4 L (3 1/2 to 4 quart) slow cooker.

2. Add pumpkin (squash), lentils and sweet potato (yam). Stir well. Cover. Cook on Low for 7 to 8 hours or on High for 3 1/2 to 4 hours.

3. Add spinach and peas. Stir gently. Cover. Cook on High for 5 to 10 minutes until spinach is wilted and peas are heated through.

4. Add remaining 3 ingredients. Stir gently. Serves 6.

Pictured between pages 96 & 97.

1 serving: 1402 Kilojoules (334 Calories); 6.8 g Total Fat; 488 mg Sodium; 19 g Protein; 53 g Carbohydrate

Sweet and Spicy Beans

Sweet, smoky tomato sauce (ketchup) coats a tasty mix of beans and bacon. Serve with your favourite pasta salad and rolls.

Bacon slices, cooked almost crisp and chopped	8	8
Cans of baked beans in tomato sauce (398 g, 14 oz, each)	2	2
Can of chickpeas (garbanzo beans), rinsed and drained	19 oz	540 g
Can of red kidney beans, rinsed and drained	19 oz	540 g
Finely chopped onion	1 cup	250 mL
Tomato sauce (ketchup)	1 1/2 cups	375 mL
Water	1/2 cup	125 mL

Treacle (molasses)	1/4 cup	60 mL
White vinegar	1/4 cup	60 mL
Brown sugar, packed	2 tbsp	30 mL
Worcestershire sauce	1 1/2 tbsp	25 mL
Hot chilli (pepper) sauce	2–3 tsp	10–15 mL

1. Combine first 5 ingredients in 3.5 to 4 L (3 1/2 to 4 quart) slow cooker.

2. Add remaining 7 ingredients. Stir well. Cover. Cook on Low for 8 to 10 hours or on High for 4 to 5 hours. Serves 8.

1 serving: 1374 Kilojoules (327 Calories); 4.8 g Total Fat; 1284 mg Sodium; 14 g Protein; 64 g Carbohydrate

Boston Baked Beans

When served as a breakfast dish in Boston in years past, it contained diced salt pork.

Dried cannellini (navy) beans (or peas)	2 1/4 cups	560 mL
Chopped onion	1 1/2 cups	375 mL
Water	5 cups	1.25 L
Tomato sauce (ketchup)	1/2 cup	125 mL
Treacle (molasses)	1/3 cup	75 mL
Brown sugar, packed	1/3 cup	75 mL
Mustard powder	1 tsp	5 mL
Salt	1 tsp	5 mL
Pepper	1/4 tsp	1 mL

1. Combine beans, onion and water in 3.5 L (3 1/2 quart) slow cooker. Stir. Cover. Cook on Low for 8 to 10 hours or on High for 4 to 5 hours.

2. Add remaining 6 ingredients. Stir well. Cover. Cook on High for 2 to 3 hours or on Low for 4 to 6 hours to blend flavours. Makes 1.5 L (6 cups).

125 mL (1/2 cup): 816 Kilojoules (195 Calories); 0.6 g Total Fat; 380 mg Sodium; 9 g Protein; 40 g Carbohydrate

White Bean Vegetable Chilli

This hearty bean chilli is quick to put together, and can be used as a taco filling too! Add your favourite mixed veggies and serve with corn (nacho) chips or corn bread.

Cans of cannellini (navy) beans (540 g, 19 oz, each), rinsed and drained	2	2
Cans of stewed tomatoes (398 g, 14 oz, each), cut up	2	2
Liquid vegetable stock (prepared vegetable broth)	1 cup	250 mL
Packet of chilli seasoning mix	1 1/4 oz	35 g
Frozen mixed vegetables, thawed	3 cups	750 mL

1. Combine first 4 ingredients in 3.5 to 4 L (3 1/2 to 4 quart) slow cooker. Cook, covered, on Low for 6 to 8 hours or on High for 3 to 4 hours.

2. Add vegetables. Stir. Cook, covered, on High for about 30 minutes until vegetables are tender. Makes about 1.75 L (7 cups).

250 mL (1 cup): 862 Kilojoules (206 Calories); 4.2 g Total Fat; 630 mg Sodium; 10 g Protein; 34 g Carbohydrate

MEATY MAINS

MEATY MAINS

Pictured on reverse:

1. Lamb With Spinach, page 150
2. Moroccan Lamb Stew, page 142

Props Courtesy Of: Danesco Inc.

Fragrant Spiced Chicken

A colourful, attractive dish with Middle Eastern flair.
Serve with couscous and pita bread.

Cooking oil	1 tbsp	15 mL
Boneless, skinless chicken thighs (57–85 g, 2–3 oz, each)	8	8
Chopped onion	1 1/2 cups	375 mL
Garlic cloves, minced (or 5 mL, 1 tsp, powder)	4	4
Ground cinnamon	1/2 tsp	2 mL
Ground cumin	1/2 tsp	2 mL
Can of chickpeas (garbanzo beans), rinsed and drained	19 oz	540 g
Can of diced tomatoes (with juice)	28 oz	796 g
Dried oregano	1 tsp	5 mL
Salt	1/4 tsp	1 mL
Fresh spinach, stems removed, lightly packed	2 cups	500 mL
Instant potato flakes	2 tbsp	30 mL
Grated lemon zest	1/2 tsp	2 mL

1. Heat cooking oil in large frying pan (skillet) on Medium. Add chicken. Cook for 8 to 10 minutes, turning occasionally, until browned. Transfer to large plate. Cover to keep warm.

2. Add next 4 ingredients to same large frying pan. Heat and stir for about 1 minute until fragrant. Spread evenly in bottom of 4 to 5 L (4 to 5 quart) slow cooker. Arrange chicken over top.

3. Combine next 4 ingredients in large bowl. Pour over chicken. Do not stir. Cover. Cook on Low for 8 to 9 hours or on High for 4 to 4 1/2 hours.

4. Add spinach, potato flakes and lemon zest. Stir gently. Cover. Heat on High for 1 to 2 minutes until spinach is wilted. Serves 4.

1 serving: 1587 Kilojoules (379 Calories); 12 g Total Fat; 764 mg Sodium; 32 g Protein; 38 g Carbohydrate

Chilli Chicken

Spicy and sweet. Everyone will love this saucy stew.

Plain (all-purpose) flour	2 tbsp	30 mL
Boneless, skinless chicken thighs, halved	1 lb	454 g
Cooking oil	1 tbsp	15 mL
Can of diced tomatoes (with juice)	14 oz	398 g
Chopped red capsicum (pepper)	1 cup	250 mL
Frozen corn kernels	1 cup	250 mL
Chopped onion	2/3 cup	150 mL
Smoked jalapeño chilli (chipotle pepper), chopped	1	1
Salt	1/4 tsp	1 mL
Sour cream	3 tbsp	50 mL
Chopped fresh coriander (cilantro) or parsley (or 7 mL, 1 1/2 tsp, dried)	2 tbsp	30 mL

1. Measure flour into large resealable freezer bag. Add chicken. Seal bag. Toss until coated. Heat cooking oil in large frying pan (skillet) on Medium. Add chicken. Cook for 8 to 10 minutes, turning occasionally, until browned. Transfer to 1.5 L (1 1/2 quart) slow cooker.

2. Add next 6 ingredients. Stir well. Cover. Cook on Low for 8 to 10 hours or on High for 4 to 5 hours.

3. Add sour cream and coriander (cilantro). Stir well. Cover. Cook on High for about 5 minutes until heated through. Serves 4.

Pictured on back cover.

MAKE AHEAD: The night before, prepare tomato mixture. Chill overnight in covered bowl. Assemble and cook as directed.

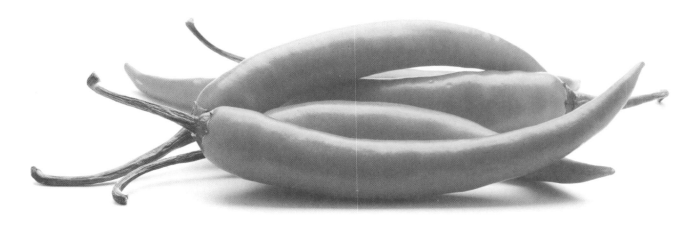

1 serving: 1235 Kilojoules (294 Calories); 11.9 g Total Fat; 322 mg Sodium; 26 g Protein; 23 g Carbohydrate

Country Chicken Stew

A 'thyme-ly' meal, ready when you are!
Serve this delicately seasoned, hearty stew in bread bowls
(round loaves of bread with the middle removed).

Chopped onion	1 cup	250 mL
Chopped potato (with skin)	2 cups	500 mL
Sliced carrot	2 cups	500 mL
Shredded green cabbage, lightly packed	2 cups	500 mL
Chopped celery	1/2 cup	125 mL
Boneless, skinless chicken thighs	3 1/2 lbs	1.6 kg
Liquid chicken stock (prepared chicken broth)	2 cups	500 mL
Can of condensed cream of mushroom soup	10 oz	284 g
Dried thyme	1 tsp	5 mL
Salt	1 1/2 tsp	7 mL
Pepper	1 1/2 tsp	7 mL
Bay leaves	2	2

Liquid chicken stock (prepared chicken broth)	1/4 cup	60 mL
Cornflour (cornstarch)	1/4 cup	60 mL
Frozen peas	1 cup	250 mL

1. Layer first 6 ingredients, in order given, in 5 to 7 L (5 to 7 quart) slow cooker.

2. Combine next 5 ingredients in medium bowl. Pour over chicken. Add bay leaves. Do not stir. Cover. Cook on Low for 9 to 10 hours or on High for 4 1/2 to 5 hours. Remove and discard bay leaves.

3. Stir second amount of stock (broth) into cornflour (cornstarch) in small cup until smooth. Add to chicken mixture. Stir. Add peas. Stir well. Cover. Cook on High for 15 to 20 minutes until peas are heated through and sauce is thickened. Serves 14.

Pictured between pages 144 & 145.

1 serving: 970 Kilojoules (231 Calories); 8.2 g Total Fat; 596 mg Sodium; 25 g Protein; 14 g Carbohydrate

Coq au Vin

Sounds fancy, tastes like it too, but it's easy to prepare this delicious French stew! 'Coq' is chicken, 'vin' is wine – dinner's ready – come, let's dine!

Bacon slices, diced	6	6
Plain (all-purpose) flour	1/4 cup	60 mL
Paprika	1/4 tsp	1 mL
Boneless, skinless chicken thighs (57–85 g, 2–3 oz, each)	12	12
Halved fresh white mushrooms	4 cups	1 L
Chopped onion	1 cup	250 mL
Garlic clove, minced (or 1 mL, 1/4 tsp, powder)	1	1
Can of condensed cream of mushroom soup	10 oz	284 g
Liquid chicken stock (prepared chicken broth)	1/2 cup	125 mL
Dry red (or alcohol-free) wine	1/2 cup	125 mL
Dried thyme	1/2 tsp	2 mL
Bay leaves	2	2
Chopped fresh parsley, for garnish	2 tbsp	30 mL

1. Cook bacon in large frying pan (skillet) on Medium until crisp. Remove to paper towels to drain. Remove and discard drippings, reserving 15 mL (1 tbsp) in pan. Set aside.

2. Combine flour and paprika in large resealable freezer bag. Add 1/2 of chicken. Seal bag. Toss until coated. Repeat with remaining chicken. Heat reserved drippings in same large frying pan on Medium. Add chicken in 2 batches. Cook for 8 to 10 minutes per batch, turning occasionally, until browned. Transfer to 3.5 to 4 L (3 1/2 to 4 quart) slow cooker.

3. Add mushrooms, onion and garlic to same large frying pan. Cook for about 2 minutes, stirring occasionally and scraping any brown bits from bottom of pan, until onion starts to soften.

4. Add bacon and next 5 ingredients. Heat and stir for about 2 minutes until mixture just starts to boil. Pour over chicken. Cover. Cook on Low for 7 to 8 hours or on High for 3 1/2 to 4 hours. Remove and discard bay leaves. Remove chicken mixture to large serving platter.

5. Garnish with parsley. Serves 6.

1 serving: 1335 Kilojoules (318 Calories); 15.7 g Total Fat; 580 mg Sodium; 27 g Protein; 13 g Carbohydrate

Creamy Chicken Dijon

A chicken stew, brimming with broccoli.

Chopped onion	1 1/2 cups	375 mL
Can of sliced mushrooms, drained	10 oz	284 g
Can of condensed cream of chicken soup	10 oz	284 g
Water	1/2 cup	125 mL
Dijon mustard	1/4 cup	60 mL
Dried crushed chillies	1/4 tsp	1 mL
Boneless, skinless chicken breast halves (113-170 g, 4-6 oz, each), each cut into 2 pieces	8	8
Can of evaporated milk	5 1/2 oz	160 mL
Bag of frozen cut broccoli, thawed, chopped smaller	26 oz	750 g

1. Combine first 6 ingredients in 4 to 5 L (4 to 5 quart) slow cooker.

2. Add chicken. Stir well. Cover. Cook on Low for 8 to 9 hours or on High for 4 to 4 1/2 hours.

3. Add evaporated milk. Stir. Add broccoli. Stir well. Cover. Cook on High for about 20 minutes until heated through and broccoli is tender but crisp. Serves 8.

1 serving: 995 Kilojoules (237 Calories); 6.7 g Total Fat; 525 mg Sodium; 32 g Protein; 14 g Carbohydrate

Turkey Goulash

A hearty goulash, rich with flavourful turkey and paprika. Serve over egg noodles or spaetzle and garnish with a dollop of sour cream and a sprinkle of chopped fresh dill.

Can of tomato paste	5 1/2 oz	156 g
Minute tapioca	3 tbsp	50 mL
Packet of onion soup mix	1 1/2 oz	42 g
Paprika	1 tbsp	15 mL
Boneless, skinless turkey thighs, cut into 2 cm (3/4 inch) pieces	2 lbs	900 g

1. Combine first 4 ingredients, 625 mL (2 1/2 cups) water and a sprinkle of salt and pepper in 4 to 5 L (4 to 5 quart) slow cooker.

2. Add turkey. Stir. Cook, covered, on Low for 6 to 7 hours or on High for 3 to 3 1/2 hours. Makes about 1.75 L (7 cups).

175 mL (3/4 cup): 682 Kilojoules (163 Calories); 4.5 g Total Fat; 554 mg Sodium; 2 g Protein; 10 g Carbohydrate

Parmesan Chicken

When you just want something deliciously messy for dinner,
serve this with fries and don't forget the napkins!

Plain yoghurt	3/4 cup	175 mL
Chicken drumettes (or whole chicken wings, split in half and tips discarded)	3 lbs	1.4 kg
Grated Parmesan cheese	1 1/2 cups	375 mL
Fine dry breadcrumbs	1/3 cup	75 mL
Parsley flakes	1 1/2 tsp	7 mL
Paprika	1 1/2 tsp	7 mL
Seasoned salt	1 1/2 tsp	7 mL

1. Measure yoghurt into extra-large bowl. Add chicken. Stir until coated.

2. Combine remaining 5 ingredients in large resealable freezer bag. Add 1/3 of chicken. Seal bag. Toss until coated. Repeat twice with remaining 2/3 of chicken. Put chicken into greased 3.5 to 4 L (3 1/2 to 4 quart) slow cooker. Cover. Cook on Low for 8 to 9 hours or on High for 4 to 4 1/2 hours. Remove chicken with slotted spoon to large serving platter. Discard liquid. Serves 4.

1 serving: 1634 Kilojoules (389 Calories); 17.2 g Total Fat; 1387 mg Sodium; 44 g Protein; 12 g Carbohydrate

Taco Beef Hash

A one-dish meal with Mexican flair! It makes a satisfying
brunch or lunch for the whole family.

Lean beef mince (ground beef)	1 lb	454 g
Diced cooked potato	4 cups	1 L
Taco seasoning mix, stir before measuring	2 tbsp	30 mL
Large eggs	6	6
Processed cheese spread (condensed Cheddar cheese or condensed cream of onion soup)	10 oz	285 g

1. Scramble-fry beef in large greased frying pan (skillet) on Medium-High for about 5 minutes until no longer pink. Transfer to large bowl.

2. Add potato, taco seasoning and a generous sprinkle of pepper. Stir well. Transfer to well-greased 3.5 to 4 L (3 1/2 to 4 quart) slow cooker.

3. Whisk eggs and cheese spread in medium bowl until smooth. Pour over beef mixture. Stir. Cook, covered, on High for about 2 hours until set. Serves 6.

VARIATION: To spice up this dish, replace taco seasoning with 10 mL (2 tsp) finely chopped jalapeño chillies and smoky barbecue sauce (chipotle peppers in adobo sauce) (see Tip, page 36). Add a generous sprinkle of salt to the potato mixture.

1 serving: 1449 Kilojoules (346 Calories); 14.7 g Total Fat; 1077 mg Sodium; 24 g Protein; 28 g Carbohydrate

Lemon Cream Chicken

Scrumptious served over buttered noodles.

Cooking oil	1 tbsp	15 mL
Boneless, skinless chicken thighs (about 12)	1 1/2 lbs	680 g
Chopped onion	1 cup	250 mL
Chopped carrot	2 cups	500 mL
Chopped celery	1 cup	250 mL
Sliced fresh white mushrooms	2 cups	500 mL
Liquid chicken stock (prepared chicken stock)	1 cup	250 mL
Italian seasoning	1 tsp	5 mL
Salt	1/4 tsp	1 mL
Pepper	1/4 tsp	1 mL
Water	1 tbsp	15 mL

Cornflour (cornstarch)	1 tbsp	15 mL
Sour cream	1/4 cup	60 mL
Lemon juice	1 tbsp	15 mL

1. Heat cooking oil in large frying pan (skillet) on Medium. Add chicken. Cook for 5 to 10 minutes, turning occasionally, until browned.

2. Layer next 4 ingredients, in order given, in 3.5 to 4 L (3 1/2 to 4 quart) slow cooker. Arrange chicken over vegetables. Combine next 4 ingredients in small bowl. Pour over chicken. Do not stir. Cover. Cook on Low for 8 to 10 hours or on High for 4 to 5 hours.

3. Stir water into cornflour (cornstarch) in small bowl until smooth. Add sour cream and lemon juice. Stir. Add to chicken mixture. Stir. Cover. Cook on High for about 5 minutes until sauce is thickened. Serves 6.

1 serving: 1083 Kilojoules (258 Calories); 11 g Total Fat; 361 mg Sodium; 27 g Protein; 13 g Carbohydrate

Spicy Peanut Chicken

A spicy blend of interesting flavours makes this
a great way to turn up the dial on dinner!

Cooking oil	1 tbsp	15 mL
Bone-in, skinless chicken thighs	4	4
Chicken drumsticks, skin removed	4	4
Thinly sliced onion	1 1/2 cups	375 mL
Garlic cloves, minced (or 2 mL, 1/2 tsp, powder)	2	2
Curry powder	2 tsp	10 mL
Dried crushed chillies	1 tsp	5 mL
Liquid chicken stock (prepared chicken broth)	1/2 cup	125 mL
Tomato paste	1/4 cup	60 mL
Salt	1/4 tsp	1 mL
Warm water	2 tbsp	30 mL
Smooth peanut butter	1/3 cup	75 mL
Chopped red capsicum (pepper)	3/4 cup	175 mL
Chopped, peeled cucumber	1/4 cup	60 mL
Coarsely chopped unsalted peanuts	2 tbsp	30 mL
Chopped fresh coriander (cilantro) or parsley (or 4 mL, 3/4 tsp, dried), optional	1 tbsp	15 mL

1. Heat cooking oil in large frying pan (skillet) on Medium. Add chicken thighs and drumsticks. Cook for 8 to 10 minutes, turning occasionally, until browned. Transfer to 3.5 to 4 L (3 1/2 to 4 quart) slow cooker.

2. Add onion to same large frying pan. Cook for 5 to 10 minutes, stirring often, until softened.

3. Add next 3 ingredients. Heat and stir for about 1 minute until fragrant.

4. Add stock (broth), tomato paste and salt. Stir well. Pour over chicken. Do not stir. Cover. Cook on Low for 8 to 9 hours or on High for 4 to 4 1/2 hours.

5. Stir warm water into peanut butter in small cup until smooth. Add to chicken mixture. Stir. Add red capsicum (pepper). Stir well. Cover. Cook on High for about 15 minutes until red capsicum is tender but crisp. Remove to large serving bowl.

6. Scatter cucumber, peanuts and coriander (cilantro) over top. Serves 4.

1 serving: 1713 Kilojoules (408 Calories); 24.3 g Total Fat; 378 mg Sodium; 33 g Protein; 18 g Carbohydrate

Thai Green Curry Chicken

This saucy curry has melt-in-your-mouth chicken, crisp colourful vegetables and an authentic coconut flavour. Serve with fragrant jasmine or basmati rice.

Boneless, skinless chicken thighs, halved	2 lbs	900 g
Thai green curry paste	2 tbsp	30 mL
Can of coconut milk	14 oz	398 mL
Cornflour (cornstarch)	2 tbsp	30 mL
Frozen Oriental mixed vegetables, thawed	4 1/2 cups	1.1 L

1. Heat large well-greased frying pan (skillet) on Medium-High. Cook chicken, in 2 batches, for about 3 minutes per side until browned. Transfer to 4 to 5 L (4 to 5 quart) slow cooker. Sprinkle with salt and pepper.

2. Add curry paste and 375 mL (1 1/2 cups) water to same frying pan. Heat and stir, scraping any brown bits from bottom of pan, until boiling. Add to slow cooker. Cook, covered, on Low for 6 to 7 hours or on High for 3 to 3 1/2 hours.

3. Stir coconut milk into cornflour (cornstarch) in medium bowl until smooth. Add to chicken mixture. Stir. Add vegetables. Stir. Cook, covered, on High for about 45 minutes until bubbling. Makes about 1.9 L (7 1/2 cups).

137

250 mL (1 cup): 1411 Kilojoules (337 Calories); 23.1 g Total Fat; 326 mg Sodium; 24 g Protein; 9 g Carbohydrate

Pork and Apples

Apples are a natural go-with. They taste great and aren't sweet when cooked. Some clear juice to pour over pork chops.

Pork loin chops, trimmed of fat, about 2.5 cm (1 inch) thick	4	4
Liquid gravy browner (optional)	1 tsp	5 mL
Salt, sprinkle		
Pepper, sprinkle		
Medium cooking apples, peeled, cored and sliced	2	2
White (granulated) sugar	1/2 tsp	2 mL

1. Brush both sides of pork chops with gravy browner. Arrange pork chops in 4.5 L (4 1/2 quart) slow cooker. If cooker isn't big enough to hold in 1 layer, make 2 layers. Sprinkle with salt and pepper. Cover with apple slices.

2. Sprinkle with sugar. Cover. Cook on Low for 8 to 10 hours or on High for 4 to 5 hours. Serves 4.

1 serving: 775 Kilojoules (185 Calories); 5.9 g Total Fat; 104 mg Sodium; 22 g Protein; 11 g Carbohydrate

Mild Turkey Chilli

Colourful dish, with a light flavour.
Serve with corn (nacho) chips or crusty bread.

Cooking oil	2 tsp	10 mL
Chopped onion	1 cup	250 mL
Chopped red capsicum (pepper)		
Chilli powder	1 tsp	5 mL
Paprika	1 tsp	5 mL
Ground cumin	1 tsp	5 mL
Salt	1/4 tsp	1 mL
Lean turkey mince (ground turkey)	1 1/2 lbs	680 g
Cans of red kidney beans (398 g, 14 oz, each), rinsed and drained	2	2
Can of diced tomatoes (with juice)	14 oz	398 g
Tomato paste	2 tbsp	30 mL
Diced jalapeño chilli (Chipotle pepper), seeds and ribs removed (cilantro)	1 tbsp	15 mL
Chopped fresh coriander or parsley (or 7 mL, 1 1/2 tsp, dried)	2 tbsp	30 mL

1. Heat cooking oil in large frying pan (skillet) on Medium. Add onion and red capsicum (pepper). Cook for 5 to 10 minutes, stirring often, until onion is softened.

2. Add next 4 ingredients. Heat and stir for about 1 minute until fragrant.

3. Add turkey mince (ground turkey). Scramble-fry on Medium-High for 5 to 10 minutes until turkey is no longer pink. Drain. Transfer to 3.5 to 4 L (3 1/2 to 4 quart) slow cooker.

4. Add next 4 ingredients. Stir well. Cover. Cook on Low for 10 to 11 hours or on High for 5 to 5 1/2 hours.

5. Add coriander (cilantro). Stir well. Serves 6.

Pictured on back cover.

MAKE AHEAD: The night before, chop vegetables and prepare kidney bean mixture. Chill overnight in separate covered bowls. Scramble-fry turkey mince until no longer pink. Drain. Chill overnight in separate covered bowl. Assemble and cook as directed.

1 serving: 1335 Kilojoules (318 Calories); 11.8 g Total Fat; 504 mg Sodium; 28 g Protein; 26 g Carbohydrate

Pork and Mushroom Ragoût

Simple to prepare, with sophisticated flavour – white wine and tomato-cream sauce coats tender pork and mushrooms. Serve over egg noodles.

Plain (all-purpose) flour	3 tbsp	50 mL
Boneless pork shoulder roast or steaks, trimmed of fat and cut into 2 cm (3/4 inch) pieces	2 lbs	900 g
Cooking oil	1 tbsp	15 mL
Cooking oil	1 tbsp	15 mL
Sliced fresh white mushrooms	2 1/2 cups	625 mL
Large leek (white part only), thinly sliced	1	1
Liquid chicken stock (prepared chicken broth)	1 1/4 cups	300 mL
Dry white (or alcohol-free) wine	1 cup	250 mL
Tomato paste	2 tbsp	30 mL
Salt	1/4 tsp	1 mL
Pepper	1/2 tsp	2 mL
Sour cream	1/4 cup	60 mL

1. Measure flour into large resealable freezer bag. Add 1/2 of pork. Seal bag. Toss until coated. Repeat with remaining pork. Heat first amount of cooking oil in large frying pan (skillet) on Medium-High. Add pork in 2 batches. Cook for 8 to 10 minutes per batch, stirring occasionally, until browned. Transfer to 3.5 to 4 L (3 1/2 to 4 quart) slow cooker.

2. Heat second amount of cooking oil in same large frying pan on Medium. Add mushrooms and leek. Cook for about 5 minutes, stirring often, until leek is softened.

3. Slowly add stock (broth), stirring constantly and scraping any brown bits from bottom of pan. Add next 4 ingredients. Heat and stir for about 2 minutes until boiling. Pour over pork. Do not stir. Cover. Cook on Low for 8 to 10 hours or on High for 4 to 5 hours.

4. Add sour cream. Stir well. Serves 8.

1 serving: 1125 Kilojoules (268 Calories); 12.4 g Total Fat; 293 mg Sodium; 26 g Protein; 7 g Carbohydrate

Hoisin Honey Ribs

These sweet, saucy and very tender pork ribs have an Asian flavour that goes well with basmati rice and stir-fried vegetables.

Hoisin sauce	1/2 cup	125 mL
Liquid honey	1/2 cup	125 mL
Soy sauce	1/3 cup	75 mL
Garlic cloves, minced (or 2 mL, 1/2 tsp, powder)	2	2
Pork side ribs, trimmed of fat and cut into 3-bone portions	3 lbs	1.4 kg

1. Combine first 4 ingredients in large bowl. Reserve 75 mL (1/3 cup).

2. Add ribs. Stir until coated. Transfer to 3.5 to 4 L (3 1/2 to 4 quart) slow cooker. Cook, covered, on Low for 8 to 9 hours or on High for 4 to 4 1/2 hours. Transfer ribs to serving platter. Brush with reserved hoisin mixture. Makes ten 3-bone portions.

1 portion: 2336 Kilojoules (558 Calories); 40.3 g Total Fat; 1270 mg Sodium; 34 g Protein; 22 g Carbohydrate

Bratwurst Stew

Sausage makes a unique substitute for beef in this stew, and adds richness to the sauce. A filling and hearty meal!

Baby potatoes, larger ones cut in half	2 lbs	900 g
Baby carrots	3 cups	750 mL
Uncooked bratwurst sausage, cut into 5 cm (2 inch) pieces	2 lbs	900 g
Can of condensed onion soup	10 oz	284 g
Sour cream	1/4 cup	60 mL

1. Layer first 3 ingredients, in order given, in 4 to 5 L (4 to 5 quart) slow cooker. Sprinkle generously with pepper.

2. Pour soup over top. Cook, covered, on Low for 8 to 10 hours or on High for 4 to 5 hours. Transfer sausage, potato and carrot with slotted spoon to large serving platter. Cover to keep warm. Skim and discard fat from cooking liquid.

3. Add sour cream. Stir until combined. Pour sauce over sausage and vegetables. Serves 8.

1 serving: 2018 Kilojoules (482 Calories); 31.6 g Total Fat; 1443 mg Sodium; 18 g Protein; 29 g Carbohydrate

Fruity Pork Roast

Cooked on Low, this tender pork roast with a rich, sweet fruit sauce is sure to delight! Serve with roasted baby potatoes.

Bacon slices, diced	4	4
Boneless pork shoulder roast, trimmed of fat	3 lbs	1.4 kg
Chopped onion	1 cup	250 mL
Garlic clove, minced (or 1 mL, 1/4 tsp, powder)	1	1
Plain (all-purpose) flour	1/4 cup	60 mL
Orange juice	1 1/2 cups	375 mL
Medium bananas, mashed	2	2
Dried apricots, halved	1/2 cup	125 mL
Dried pitted prunes, halved	1/2 cup	125 mL
Bay leaf	1	1
Ground allspice	1/4 tsp	1 mL
Ground cinnamon	1/4 tsp	1 mL
Dried crushed chillies	1/4 tsp	1 mL
Grated orange zest	1/2–1 tsp	2–5 mL

1. Cook bacon in large frying pan (skillet) on Medium until crisp. Remove to paper towels to drain. Set aside. Remove and discard drippings, reserving 15 mL (1 tbsp) in pan.

2. Heat reserved drippings in same large frying pan on Medium. Add roast. Cook for about 10 minutes, turning occasionally, until browned on all sides. Transfer to 3.5 to 4 L (3 1/2 to 4 quart) slow cooker.

3. Add onion and garlic to same large frying pan. Cook for about 2 minutes, stirring often, until starting to brown.

4. Add flour. Heat and stir for 1 minute. Slowly add orange juice, stirring constantly, until boiling and thickened.

5. Add bacon and next 7 ingredients. Stir well. Pour over roast. Cover. Cook on Low for 8 to 10 hours. Remove roast to large serving platter. Cover to keep warm. Skim and discard any fat from surface of liquid in slow cooker. Remove and discard bay leaf.

6. Add orange zest to liquid in slow cooker. Stir well. Makes about 1.1 L (4 1/2 cups) sauce. Cut roast into thin slices. Serve with sauce. Makes 12 servings (57 to 85 g, 2 to 3 oz, each, cooked weight).

1 serving: 1146 Kilojoules (273 Calories); 9.9 g Total Fat; 116 mg Sodium; 26 g Protein; 20 g Carbohydrate

Moroccan Lamb Stew

Thick and rich, this warmly spiced stew
is best served over couscous or steamed rice.

Medium carrots, cut into 2.5 cm (1 inch) pieces	4	4
Cooking oil	2 tbsp	30 mL
Lamb stewing meat	2 lbs	900 g
Cooking oil	1 tbsp	15 mL
Thinly sliced onion	2 cups	500 mL
Garlic cloves, minced (or 5 mL, 1 tsp, powder)	4	4
Ground cumin	2 tsp	10 mL
Ground coriander (cilantro)	1 tsp	5 mL
Ground ginger	1 tsp	5 mL
Ground cinnamon	1/2 tsp	2 mL
Dried crushed chillies	1/2 tsp	2 mL
Dry white (or alcohol-free) wine	1/2 cup	125 mL
Orange juice	1/2 cup	125 mL
Brown sugar, packed	1 tbsp	15 mL
Salt	1/4 tsp	1 mL
Large pitted green olives, halved (optional)	12	12
Honey	1 tbsp	15 mL
Grated orange zest	1/2 tsp	2 mL
Water	1 tbsp	15 mL
Cornflour (cornstarch)	1 tbsp	15 mL

1. Put carrot into 3.5 to 4 L (3 1/2 to 4 quart) slow cooker.

2. Heat first amount of cooking oil in large frying pan (skillet) on Medium-High. Add lamb in 2 batches. Cook for 8 to 10 minutes per batch, stirring occasionally, until browned. Arrange on top of carrot.

3. Heat second amount of cooking oil in same large frying pan on Medium. Add onion. Cook for 5 to 10 minutes, stirring often, until softened.

4. Add next 6 ingredients. Heat and stir for about 1 minute until fragrant. Scatter over lamb mixture.

5. Combine next 4 ingredients in 500 mL (2 cups) measuring jug. Pour over lamb mixture. Do not stir. Cover. Cook on Low for 8 to 10 hours or on High for 4 to 5 hours.

6. Add olives, honey and orange zest. Stir.

7. Stir water into cornflour (cornflour) in small cup until smooth. Add to lamb mixture. Stir well. Cover. Cook on High for 5 to 10 minutes until sauce is slightly thickened. Serves 8.

Pictured between pages 128 & 129.

1 serving: 1146 Kilojoules (273 Calories); 11.5 g Total Fat; 167 mg Sodium; 24 g Protein; 16 g Carbohydrate

Chilli Rhubarb Pork

This lean and moist pork roast has a sweet fruity sauce with a hint of spicy heat – just the thing to jazz up your next Sunday dinner.

Boneless pork loin roast	3 lbs	1.4 kg
Frozen rhubarb, thawed	1 cup	250 mL
Tomato sauce (ketchup)	1/2 cup	125 mL
Brown sugar, packed	1/4 cup	60 mL
Chilli paste (sambal oelek)	2 tsp	10 mL

1. Sprinkle roast with salt and pepper. Cook in large greased frying pan (skillet) on Medium-High for about 8 minutes, turning occasionally, until browned on all sides. Transfer to 4 to 5 L (4 to 5 quart) slow cooker.

2. Process remaining 4 ingredients and 250 mL (1 cup) water in blender or food processor until smooth. Pour over roast. Cook, covered, on Low for 8 to 9 hours or on High for 4 to 4 1/2 hours. Transfer roast to cutting board. Cover with foil. Let stand for 10 minutes. Skim and discard fat from cooking liquid. Carefully process liquid in blender until smooth (see Safety Tip). Makes about 625 mL (2 1/2 cups) sauce. Cut roast into thin slices. Serve with sauce. Serves 10.

SAFETY TIP: Follow blender manufacturer's instructions for processing hot liquids.

1 serving 60 mL (1/4 cup) sauce: 1390 Kilojoules (332 Calories); 13.6 g Total Fat; 249 mg Sodium ; 39 g Protein; 12 g Carbohydrate

Sausage Cabbage Stew

This hearty stew has a colourful mix of meat and vegetables and a peppery kick to keep you cosy on a cold winter's day.

Hot Italian sausage, casing removed	1 1/2 lbs	680 g
Chopped onion	1 1/2 cups	375 mL
Diced peeled potato	3 cups	750 mL
Cans of stewed tomatoes (398 g, 14 oz, each)	2	2
Shredded cabbage	4 cups	1 L

1. Scramble-fry sausage and onion in large greased frying pan (skillet) on Medium-High for about 12 minutes until sausage is no longer pink. Drain. Transfer to 3.5 to 4 L (3 1/2 to 4 quart) slow cooker.

2. Add potato, tomatoes, 250 mL (1 cup) of water and a sprinkle of salt and pepper. Stir. Cook, covered, on Low for 6 to 7 hours or on High for 3 to 3 1/2 hours.

3. Add cabbage. Stir. Cook, covered, on High for about 1 hour until cabbage is tender. Makes about 2.2 L (8 3/4 cups).

250 mL (1 cup): 1587 Kilojoules (379 Calories); 21.9 g Total Fat; 1404 mg Sodium; 18 g Protein; 28 g Carbohydrate

French Lamb Casserole

This rich, comforting dish was inspired by the classic French cassoulet (ka-soo-LAY). Make it a meal with a fresh baguette, steamed green beans and a bottle of wine.

Lamb shank, trimmed of fat, meat cut into 2 cm (3/4 inch) pieces, bone reserved	1 lb	454 g
Can of diced tomatoes (with juice)	28 oz	796 mL
Cans of black-eyed peas (540 mL 19 oz, each), rinsed and drained	2	2
Smoked ham sausage, cut into 6 mm (1/4 inch) slices	4 oz	113 g
Onion soup mix, stir before measuring	3 tbsp	50 mL

1. Heat medium greased frying pan on Medium-High. Add lamb. Cook for about 8 minutes, stirring occasionally, until browned. Transfer to 4 to 5 L (4 to 5 quart) slow cooker.

2. Add remaining 4 ingredients and reserved bone. Stir. Cook, covered, on Low for 8 to 10 hours or on High for 4 to 5 hours. Remove and discard bone. Makes about 1.5 L (6 cups).

Pictured on back cover.

VARIATION: Lamb shoulder may be substituted, but the addition of the lamb bone provides extra richness.

1. Country Chicken Stew, page 131
2. Ginger Beef Stew, page 158

Props Courtesy Of: Danesco Inc
The Bay

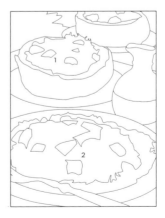

Rosemary Lamb

Hearty lamb shanks in a rustic red wine and rosemary sauce.
Serve with garlic mashed potatoes and spinach.

Coarsely chopped carrot	2 cups	500 mL
Thinly sliced onion	1 cup	250 mL
Plain (all-purpose) flour	1/4 cup	60 mL
Salt	1/2 tsp	2 mL
Pepper	1/2 tsp	2 mL
Lamb shanks (340 g, 3/4 lb, each)	4	4
Cooking oil	1 tbsp	15 mL
Dry red (or alcohol-free) wine	2/3 cup	150 mL
Tomato paste	2 tbsp	30 mL
Chopped fresh rosemary leaves (or 6 mL, 1 1/4 tsp, dried, crushed)	1 1/2 tbsp	25 mL

1. Put carrot and onion into 5 to 7 L (5 to 7 quart) slow cooker.

2. Combine next 3 ingredients in large resealable freezer bag. Add 1/2 of lamb shanks. Seal bag. Toss until coated. Repeat with remaining lamb. Heat cooking oil in large frying pan (skillet) on Medium-High. Add lamb in 2 batches, reserving any remaining flour mixture. Cook for 5 to 7 minutes per batch, turning occasionally, until browned. Arrange on top of vegetables. Sprinkle with remaining flour mixture.

3. Combine remaining 3 ingredients in 500 mL (2 cups) measuring jug. Pour over lamb. Cover. Cook on Low for 8 to 10 hours or on High for 4 to 5 hours. Remove lamb to large serving platter. Cover to keep warm. Skim and discard any fat from surface of liquid in slow cooker. Drizzle liquid from slow cooker over individual servings. Serves 4.

Corned Beef Dinner, page 153

Props Courtesy Of: Cherison Enterprises Inc
Danesco Inc

1 serving: 2020 Kilojoules (481 Calories); 25.7 g Total Fat; 478 mg Sodium; 34 g Protein; 21 g Carbohydrate

Easy Lamb Ragoût

Juicy pieces of lamb and tender vegetables seasoned with fragrant herbs – a delicious meal that's quick and easy to prepare. Serve with a crisp salad.

Medium carrots, cut into 12 mm (1/2 inch) slices	4	4
Red baby potatoes, quartered	1 lb	454 g
Fennel bulb (white part only), halved and thinly sliced	1	1
Plain (all-purpose) flour	1/4 cup	60 mL
Lamb stewing meat	1 1/2 lbs	680 g
Liquid beef stock (prepared beef broth)	1 cup	250 mL
Dry white (or alcohol-free) wine	1/2 cup	125 mL
Garlic clove, minced (or 1 mL, 1/4 tsp, powder)	1	1

Dill leaf tips (dill weed)	1/2 tsp	2 mL
Dried marjoram	1/2 tsp	2 mL
Salt	1/2 tsp	2 mL
Pepper	1/4 tsp	1 mL

1. Layer first 3 ingredients, in order given, in 4 to 5 L (4 to 5 quart) slow cooker.

2. Measure flour into large resealable freezer bag. Add lamb. Seal bag. Toss until coated. Scatter lamb evenly over fennel. Sprinkle with any remaining flour.

3. Combine remaining 7 ingredients in small bowl. Pour over lamb. Do not stir. Cover. Cook on Low for 8 to 10 hours or on High for 4 to 5 hours. Serves 6.

1 serving: 1184 Kilojoules (282 Calories); 6.4 g Total Fat; 455 mg Sodium; 27 g Protein; 26 g Carbohydrate

Leg of Lamb

A complete meal awaits! Tender lamb and herb-crusted vegetables cooked to perfection in a sensational pesto and wine sauce.

Medium onions, chopped	3	3
Garlic cloves, minced (or 4 mL, 3/4 tsp, powder)	3	3
Whole leg of lamb roast, trimmed of fat	3 3/4–4 lbs	1.7–1.8 kg
Baby potatoes, larger ones cut in half	2 lbs	900 g
Baby carrots	2 lbs	900 g
Dry red (or alcohol-free) wine	1 1/2 cups	375 mL
Water	1 1/2 cups	375 mL
Jar of sun-dried tomato pesto	9 1/2 oz	270 g
Parsley flakes	1 tbsp	15 mL
Dried rosemary, crushed	2 tsp	10 mL
Dried oregano	2 tsp	10 mL
Pepper	1 tsp	5 mL

Water	2 tbsp	30 mL
Cornflour (cornstarch)	4 tsp	20 mL

1. Put onion and garlic into 7 L (7 quart) slow cooker. Place roast on top.

2. Arrange potatoes and carrots around roast.

3. Combine next 7 ingredients in large bowl. Pour over roast. Cover. Cook on Low for 8 to 10 hours or on High for 4 to 5 hours. Remove roast to large serving platter. Cover to keep warm. Remove vegetables with slotted spoon to large serving bowl. Cover to keep warm. Skim and discard any fat from surface of liquid in slow cooker.

4. Stir water into cornflour (cornstarch) in small cup until smooth. Add to liquid in slow cooker. Stir well. Cover. Cook on High for 15 to 20 minutes until slightly thickened. Makes about 1 L (4 cups) sauce. Cut roast into thin slices. Makes 10 servings of meat (57 to 85 g, 2 to 3 oz, each, cooked weight). Serve with sauce and vegetables. Serves 10.

1 serving: 1340 Kilojoules (319 Calories); 7.1 g Total Fat; 143 mg Sodium; 27 g Protein; 32 g Carbohydrate

Sweet Lamb Curry

A rich, Middle Eastern–flavoured dish. Serve over rice or couscous.

Cooking oil	2 tbsp	30 mL
Lamb stewing meat	2 lbs	900 g
Thinly sliced onion	2 cups	500 mL
Cinnamon stick (10 cm, 4 inches)	1	1
Garlic cloves, minced (or 5 mL, 1 tsp, powder)	4	4
Whole green cardamom, bruised (see Tip, page 184)	6	6
Finely grated, peeled fresh ginger (gingeroot) (or 2 mL, 1/2 tsp, ground ginger)	2 tsp	10 mL
Ground cumin	1 tsp	5 mL
Ground coriander (cilantro)	1 tsp	5 mL
Dried crushed chillies	1 tsp	5 mL
Salt	1/4 tsp	1 mL
Liquid chicken stock (prepared chicken broth)	2/3 cup	150 mL
Tart medium cooking apples (such as Granny Smith), peeled and cores removed, diced	3	3
Can of coconut milk	14 oz	398 mL
Cornflour (cornstarch)	4 tsp	20 mL
Raisins	1/2 cup	125 mL

1. Heat cooking oil in large frying pan (skillet) on Medium. Add lamb in 2 batches. Cook for 5 to 10 minutes per batch, stirring occasionally, until browned. Transfer with slotted spoon to 3.5 to 4 L (3 1/2 to 4 quart) slow cooker.

2. Add onion to same large frying pan. Cook for 5 to 10 minutes, stirring often, until softened. Add next 8 ingredients. Heat and stir for 1 to 2 minutes until fragrant.

3. Slowly add stock (broth), stirring constantly and scraping any brown bits from bottom of pan. Pour over lamb.

4. Add apple. Stir well. Cover. Cook on Low for 8 to 9 hours or on High for 4 to 4 1/2 hours. Remove and discard cinnamon stick and cardamom.

5. Stir coconut milk into cornflour (cornstarch) in small bowl until smooth. Add to lamb mixture. Stir. Add raisins. Stir well. Cover. Cook on High for about 20 minutes until slightly thickened. Serves 8.

1 serving: 1541 Kilojoules (367 Calories); 20.1 g Total Fat; 155 mg Sodium; 25 g Protein; 24 g Carbohydrate

Shoulder of Lamb

A small, economical cut of lamb.

Lamb shoulder roast (bone in)	2 1/2 lbs	1.1 kg
Liquid gravy browner (optional)	2 tsp	10 mL
Salt, sprinkle		
Pepper, sprinkle		
GRAVY		
Plain (all-purpose) flour	2 tbsp	30 mL
Salt	1/4 tsp	1 mL
Pepper	1/16 tsp	0.5 mL

Meat juice or liquid, strained if needed, fat removed, plus water to make	1 cup	250 mL
Beef stock (bouillon) powder	1 tsp	5 mL
Liquid gravy browner, enough to make a pleasing colour (optional)		

1. Brush roast with gravy browner. Place in 3.5 L (3 1/2 quart) slow cooker. Sprinkle with salt and pepper. Cover. Cook on Low for 8 to 9 hours or on High for 4 to 4 1/2 hours.

2. Skim off any fat from remaining juice. Make gravy.

3. **GRAVY:** Combine flour, salt and pepper in saucepan. Stir.

4. Gradually whisk in meat juice and water until no lumps remain. Heat and stir until boiling and thickened.

5. Taste, adding stock powder for more flavour if needed. Stir in gravy browner to colour. Add more salt and pepper if needed. Makes 250 mL (1 cup).

1 serving (with gravy): 1386 Kilojoules (331 Calories); 17.6 g Total Fat; 490 mg Sodium; 36 g Protein; 4 g Carbohydrate

Lamb Loaf

A moist firm loaf that cuts well. Serve very hot or very cold, as all lamb should be served.

Large eggs, fork-beaten	2	2
Minced onion	1/2 cup	125 mL
Beef stock (bouillon) powder	2 tsp	10 mL
Quick-cooking rolled oats (not instant)	1 cup	250 mL
Lean lamb mince (ground lamb)	2 lbs	900 g

Tomato sauce (ketchup) (optional)	2 tbsp	30 mL

1. Combine eggs, onion, stock (bouillon) powder and rolled oats in bowl. Stir.

2. Add lamb mince (ground lamb). Mix. Shape into round loaf and place in 3.5 L (3 1/2 quart) slow cooker, not touching sides.

3. Spread tomato sauce (ketchup) over top. Cover. Cook on Low for 7 to 9 hours or on High for 3 1/2 to 4 1/2 hours. Cuts into 8 wedges.

1 wedge: 909 Kilojoules (217 Calories); 7.9 g Total Fat; 239 mg Sodium; 26 g Protein; 8 g Carbohydrate

Lamb with Spinach

Vibrant green spinach and red, juicy tomatoes add wonderful colour to delicately seasoned lamb. Serve with couscous.

Cooking oil	1 tbsp	15 mL
Lamb stewing meat	2 lbs	900 g
Sliced fresh white mushrooms	2 cups	500 mL
Chopped onion	1 cup	250 mL
Chopped red capsicum (pepper)	1 cup	250 mL
Can of diced tomatoes (with juice)	14 oz	398 g
Liquid chicken stock (prepared chicken broth)	1 cup	250 mL
Chopped fresh thyme leaves (or 2 mL, 1/2 tsp, dried)	2 tsp	10 mL
White (granulated) sugar	1/2 tsp	2 mL
Salt	1/4 tsp	1 mL
Pepper	1/4 tsp	1 mL
Water	1 tbsp	15 mL
Cornflour (cornstarch)	1 tbsp	15 mL
Fresh spinach, stems removed, lightly packed	2 cups	500 mL
Chopped fresh basil (see Note)	2 tbsp	30 mL

1. Heat cooking oil in large frying pan (skillet) on Medium-High. Add lamb in 2 batches. Cook for 8 to 10 minutes per batch, stirring occasionally, until browned. Transfer to 3.5 to 4 L (3 1/2 to 4 quart) slow cooker.

2. Add mushrooms, onion and red capsicum (pepper) to same large frying pan. Cook on Medium for 5 to 10 minutes, stirring often, until onion is softened. Add to lamb. Stir.

3. Combine next 6 ingredients in medium bowl. Pour over lamb mixture. Stir well. Cover. Cook on Low for 8 to 10 hours or on High for 4 to 5 hours.

4. Stir water into cornflour (cornstarch) in small cup until smooth. Add to lamb mixture. Stir well. Cover. Cook on High for 5 to 10 minutes until sauce is thickened.

5. Add spinach and basil. Stir well. Serves 8.

NOTE: Omit fresh basil. Add 7 mL (1 1/2 tsp) dried basil to tomato mixture before cooking.

Pictured between pages 128 & 129.

1 serving: 873 Kilojoules (208 Calories); 8.2 g Total Fat; 346 mg Sodium; 25 g Protein; 8 g Carbohydrate

Sun-Dried Tomato Lamb

A distinct sun-dried tomato flavour makes this stew a delightful meal
to serve with mashed potatoes or couscous.

Plain (all-purpose) flour	3 tbsp	50 mL
Lamb stewing meat	2 lbs	900 g
Medium onions, each cut into 8 wedges	2	2
Medium carrot, chopped	1	1
Liquid chicken stock (prepared chicken broth)	1 1/2 cups	375 mL
Sun-dried tomatoes in oil, drained and sliced	1/2 cup	125 mL
Honey	2 tbsp	30 mL
Salt	1/4 tsp	1 mL
Chopped fresh parsley (or 7 mL, 1 1/2 tsp, flakes)	2 tbsp	30 mL

1. Measure flour into large resealable freezer bag. Add 1/2 of lamb. Seal bag. Toss until coated. Repeat with remaining lamb. Put lamb into 3.5 to 4 L (3 1/2 to 4 quart) slow cooker. Sprinkle with any remaining flour.

2. Add next 6 ingredients. Stir well. Cover. Cook on Low for 8 to 10 hours or on High for 4 to 5 hours. Skim and discard any fat from surface of liquid in slow cooker.

3. Add parsley. Stir well. Serves 8.

1 serving: 907 Kilojoules (216 Calories); 7.3 g Total Fat; 326 mg Sodium; 25 g Protein; 12 g Carbohydrate

Beef and Apricot Braise

Cumin, coriander (cilantro) and apricot add a subtly sweet, exotic flavour to tender beef. Serve with oven-roasted potatoes and steamed vegetables.

Chopped carrot	1 cup	250 mL
Plain (all-purpose) flour	3 tbsp	50 mL
Beef stewing meat	2 lbs	900 g
Cooking oil	2 tbsp	30 mL
Cooking oil	2 tsp	10 mL
Chopped onion	1 1/2 cups	375 mL
Garlic cloves, minced (or 2 mL, 1/2 tsp, powder)	2	2
Ground cumin	1/2 tsp	2 mL
Ground coriander (cilantro)	1/2 tsp	2 mL
Chopped dried apricots	1 cup	250 mL
Liquid beef stock (prepared beef broth)	1 cup	250 mL
Dry sherry (or apple juice)	1/2 cup	125 mL
Bay leaf	1	1
Salt	1/4 tsp	1 mL
Pepper	1/4 tsp	1 mL
Chopped fresh (or frozen, thawed) green beans	1 cup	250 mL

1. Scatter carrot in bottom of 3.5 to 4 L (3 1/2 to 4 quart) slow cooker.

2. Measure flour into large resealable freezer bag. Add 1/2 of beef. Seal bag. Toss until coated. Repeat with remaining beef. Heat first amount of cooking oil in large frying pan (skillet) on Medium. Add beef in 2 batches. Cook for 5 to 10 minutes per batch, stirring occasionally, until browned. Layer on top of carrot.

3. Heat second amount of cooking oil in same large frying pan on Medium. Add onion. Cook for 5 to 10 minutes, stirring often and scraping any brown bits from bottom of pan, until softened.

4. Add next 3 ingredients. Heat and stir for about 1 minute until fragrant. Spread on top of beef.

5. Combine next 6 ingredients in medium bowl. Pour over beef mixture. Do not stir. Cover. Cook on Low for 8 to 10 hours or on High for 4 to 5 hours.

6. Add green beans. Stir well. Cover. Cook on High for 10 to 15 minutes until beans are tender but crisp. Remove and discard bay leaf. Serves 8.

1 serving: 1323 Kilojoules (315 Calories); 13.5 g Total Fat; 262 mg Sodium; 27 g Protein; 20 g Carbohydrate

Corned Beef Dinner

Tender corned beef and winter vegetables make a comforting meal.
Strain and save the broth to use in your favourite soup recipe.

Baby carrots	1 lb	454 g
Red baby potatoes, larger ones cut in half	1 lb	454 g
Medium swede (yellow turnip), cut into 2.5 cm (1 inch) cubes	1	1
Chopped onion	2 cups	500 mL
Corned beef brisket	2 lbs	900 g
Water	4 cups	1 L
Bay leaves	2	2
Whole black peppercorns	1 tbsp	15 mL

1. Layer first 4 ingredients, in order given, in 5 to 7 L (5 to 7 quart) slow cooker. Place corned beef brisket on top, fat-side up.

2. Add water, bay leaves and peppercorns. Do not stir. Cover. Cook on Low for 8 to 10 hours or on High for 4 to 5 hours. Remove and discard bay leaves. Remove corned beef to large serving platter. Cut into thin slices. Makes 8 servings of meat (57 to 85 g, 2 to 3 oz, each, cooked weight). Remove vegetables from slow cooker with slotted spoon to large serving bowl. Serve with corned beef. Serves 8.

Pictured between pages 144 & 145 and on front cover.

1 serving: 1054 Kilojoules (251 Calories); 11.5 g Total Fat; 1757 mg Sodium; 18 g Protein; 20 g Carbohydrate

Hungarian Goulash

Super good dish. Beef cubes cook in a medium-thick gravy.

Beef stewing meat (or round steak), cut into 2 cm (3/4 inch) cubes	1 1/2 lbs	680 g	Canned tomatoes, with liquid	14 oz	398 g	
Chopped onion	1 1/2 cups	375 mL	Liquid gravy browner (optional)	1/2 tsp	2 mL	
Garlic clove, minced (or 1/4 tsp, 1 mL, garlic powder)	1	1	Beef stock (bouillon) powder	2 tsp	10 mL	
Plain (all-purpose) flour	2 tbsp	30 mL	White (granulated) sugar	1 tsp	5 mL	
Paprika	2 tsp	10 mL	Sour cream	1/2–1 cup	125–250 mL	
Salt	1 tsp	5 mL				
Pepper	1/4 tsp	1 mL				

1. Combine first 7 ingredients in 3.5 L (3 1/2 quart) slow cooker. Stir well to coat beef and onion with flour.

2. Stir tomato, gravy browner, stock (bouillon) powder and sugar together in bowl. Pour over beef mixture. Stir. Cover. Cook on Low for 8 to 10 hours or on High for 4 to 5 hours.

3. Spoon off a few spoonfuls of juice into bowl. Add sour cream. Stir. Pour back into slow cooker. Stir before serving. Serves 6.

1 serving: 1139 Kilojoules (272 Calories); 13.1 g Total Fat; 851 mg Sodium; 27 g Protein; 11 g Carbohydrate

Luau Meatballs

These sweet-and-sour meatballs are smothered in a tasty pineapple and green capsicum (pepper) sauce. Serve with steamed rice.

Cooked meatballs (box of frozen cooked meatballs, thawed)	2 lbs	900 g	Cornflour (cornstarch)	3 tbsp	50 mL
Cans of crushed pineapple (with juice), 398 g, 14 oz, each	2	2	Diced green capsicum (pepper)	1 1/2 cups	375 mL
Thick teriyaki basting sauce	2/3 cup	150 mL			

1. Put meatballs into 4 to 5 L (4 to 5 quart) slow cooker.

2. Combine pineapple, teriyaki sauce, 75 mL (1/3 cup) water and a sprinkle of pepper in medium bowl. Pour over meatballs. Cook, covered, on Low for 6 to 8 hours or on High for 3 to 4 hours.

3. Stir 75 mL (1/3 cup) water into cornflour (cornstarch) in small bowl until smooth. Pour over meatballs. Add green capsicum (pepper). Stir well. Cook, covered, on High for about 20 minutes until boiling and thickened. Makes about 2.25 L (9 cups).

250 mL (1 cup): 1750 Kilojoules (418 Calories); 23.8 g Total Fat; 1370 mg Sodium; 6 g Protein; 33 g Carbohydrate

Beef Stew Diane

A less peppery cousin of Hungarian goulash, with a unique brandy accent.
Serve over egg noodles with a salad on the side.

Plain (all-purpose) flour	3 tbsp	50 mL
Pepper	1/2 tsp	2 mL
Beef stewing meat	2 lbs	900 g
Cooking oil	2 tbsp	30 mL
Cooking oil	2 tsp	10 mL
Chopped onion	1 1/2 cups	375 mL
Can of diced tomatoes (with juice)	14 oz	398 g
Liquid beef stock (prepared beef broth)	1 cup	250 mL
Worcestershire sauce	2 tbsp	30 mL
Sour cream	1/4 cup	60 mL
Brandy (or apple juice)	2–3 tbsp	30–50 mL
Chopped fresh parsley (or 7 mL, 1 1/2 tsp, dried)	2 tbsp	30 mL

1. Combine flour and pepper in large resealable freezer bag. Add half of beef. Seal bag. Toss until coated. Repeat with remaining beef. Heat first amount of cooking oil in large frying pan (skillet) on Medium. Add beef in 2 batches. Cook for 5 to 10 minutes per batch, stirring occasionally, until browned. Transfer to 3.5 to 4 L (3 1/2 to 4 quart) slow cooker.

2. Heat second amount of cooking oil in same large frying pan on Medium. Add onion. Cook for 5 to 10 minutes, stirring often, until softened. Add to beef. Stir.

3. Add next 3 ingredients to beef mixture. Stir well. Cover. Cook on Low for 8 to 9 hours or on High for 4 to 4 1/2 hours.

4. Add remaining 3 ingredients. Stir well. Serves 8.

1 serving: 1218 Kilojoules (290 Calories); 15.6 g Total Fat; 303 mg Sodium; 26 g Protein; 8 g Carbohydrate

Steak and Mushrooms

Ready and waiting in its own gravy.

156

Beef round steak (about 2.5 cm, 1 inch, thick), cut into cubes	1 lb	454 g
Salt, sprinkle		
Pepper, sprinkle		
Condensed cream of mushroom soup	10 oz	284 g
Canned mushroom pieces, drained (optional)	10 oz	284 g
Liquid gravy browner (optional)	1/4 tsp	1 mL

1. Place beef cubes in 3.5 L (3 1/2 quart) slow cooker. Sprinkle with salt and pepper.

2. Combine soup and mushroom pieces in bowl. Add gravy browner. Stir well. Spoon over steak. Cover. Cook on Low for 7 to 9 hours or on High for 3 1/2 to 4 1/2 hours. Serves 4.

1 serving: 1110 Kilojoules (265 Calories); 13.4 g Total Fat; 685 mg Sodium; 29 g Protein; 6 g Carbohydrate

BBQ Beef Ribs

Awesome flavour and so tender.

Cooking oil	2 tbsp	30 mL
Beef short ribs, trimmed of fat	3 lbs	1.4 kg
Barbecue sauce	1 cup	250 mL
Treacle (molasses)	2 tbsp	30 mL
White vinegar	2 tbsp	30 mL
Salt	1 1/2 tsp	7 mL
Pepper	1/2 tsp	2 mL
Soy sauce	1 tbsp	15 mL
Chopped onion	1/2 cup	125 mL

1. Heat cooking oil in frying pan (skillet). Add ribs. Brown all sides. Drain. Place ribs in 5 L (5 quart) slow cooker.

2. Mix next 6 ingredients well in bowl.

3. Stir in onion. Pour over short ribs. Cover. Cook on Low for 8 to 10 hours or on High for 4 to 5 hours. Serves 6.

1 serving: 1298 Kilojoules (310 Calories); 15.9 g Total Fat; 1415 mg Sodium; 27 g Protein; 13 g Carbohydrate

Tomato Olive Beef

Rich flavours abound in this mildly spiced dish. Serve with rice.

Can of diced tomatoes (with juice)	28 oz	796 g
Thinly sliced red onion	1 1/2 cups	375 mL
Fresh chillies, seeds and ribs removed, chopped	2	2
Tomato paste	1/3 cup	75 mL
Dry red (or alcohol-free) wine	1/4 cup	60 mL
Chilli powder	1 tbsp	15 mL
Salt	1/4 tsp	1 mL
Pepper	1/4 tsp	1 mL
Beef stewing meat	2 lbs	900 g
Bacon slices, cooked crisp and crumbled	6	6
Chopped fresh basil (see Note)	1/4 cup	60 mL
Kalamata olives, pitted and chopped	6	6
Pine nuts, toasted for garnish (optional)	1/4 cup	60 mL

1. .Combine first 8 ingredients in 3.5 to 4 L (3 1/2 to 4 quart) slow cooker. Add beef and bacon. Stir well. Cover. Cook on Low for 8 to 10 hours or on High for 4 to 5 hours.

2. Add basil. Stir well. Remove to large serving bowl. Scatter olives and pine nuts over top. Serves 8.

NOTE: Omit fresh basil. Add 15 mL (1 tbsp) dried basil to first 10 ingredients.

1 serving: 1172 Kilojoules (279 Calories); 13 g Total Fat; 456 mg Sodium; 28 g Protein; 11 g Carbohydrate

Tomato Paprikash

Tender, bite-sized beef pairs well with tomatoes and paprika in this rich, saucy dish. It can be served with boiled potatoes or spooned over egg noodles.

Chopped onion	1 1/2 cups	375 mL
Boneless beef blade steak, trimmed of fat, cut into 2.5 cm (1 inch) cubes	3 lbs	1.4 kg
Can of diced tomatoes (with juice)	14 oz	398 g
Can of tomato paste	5 1/2 oz	156 g
Paprika	2 tbsp	30 mL

1. Put onion into 4 to 5 L (4 to 5 quart) slow cooker. Arrange beef over top. Sprinkle generously with salt and pepper.

2. Combine remaining 3 ingredients, 125 mL (1/2 cup) water and a generous sprinkle of salt and pepper in medium bowl. Pour over beef. Cook, covered, on Low for 8 to 10 hours or on High for 4 to 5 hours. Makes about 2 L (8 cups).

175 mL (3/4 cup): 1097 Kilojoules (262 Calories); 13.8 g Total Fat; 433 mg Sodium 26 g Protein; 8 g Carbohydrate

Ginger Beef Stew

A taste of the Far East. Thick ginger sauce coats tender beef,
water chestnuts and snow peas (mange tout). Great served over rice noodles.

Medium onions, cut into wedges	2	2
Medium carrot, sliced diagonally	1	1
Can of sliced water chestnuts, drained	8 oz	227 g
Roasted red capsicum (pimento), drained and blotted dry, cut into strips	1 cup	250 mL
Cooking oil	1 tbsp	15 mL
Round steak, trimmed of fat and cut into 12 mm (1/2 inch) pieces	1 1/2 lbs	680 g
Finely grated, peeled fresh ginger (gingeroot) (or 7 mL, 1 1/2 tsp, ground ginger)	2 tbsp	30 mL
Garlic cloves, minced (or 2 mL, 1/2 tsp, powder)	2	2
Water	2/3 cup	150 mL
Dry sherry (or liquid beef stock/prepared beef broth)	1/4 cup	60 mL
Brown sugar, packed	1 tbsp	15 mL
Soy sauce	3 tbsp	50 mL
Cornflour (cornstarch)	1 tbsp	15 mL
Snow peas, (mange tout) trimmed	1 cup	250 mL

1. Layer first 4 ingredients, in order given, in 3.5 to 4 L (3 1/2 to 4 quart) slow cooker.

2. Heat cooking oil in large frying pan (skillet) on Medium. Add beef. Cook for 8 to 10 minutes, stirring occasionally, until browned.

3. Add ginger and garlic. Heat and stir for about 1 minute until fragrant.

4. Add water, sherry and brown sugar. Stir. Bring to a boil. Pour over vegetables. Do not stir. Cover. Cook on Low for 8 to 9 hours or on High for 4 to 4 1/2 hours.

5. Stir soy sauce into cornflour (cornstarch) in small cup until smooth. Add to beef mixture. Stir. Add snow peas (mange tout). Stir well. Cover. Cook on High for about 10 minutes until snow peas are tender but crisp and sauce is thickened. Serves 6.

Pictured between pages 144 & 145.

1 serving: 1117 Kilojoules (266 Calories); 8.4 g Total Fat; 603 mg Sodium; 28 g Protein; 17 g Carbohydrate

Beef in Wine

Just the right amount of wine flavour. Meat is tender with a delicate blend of flavours. Serve over rice or noodles.

Boneless beef blade steak, cut into 5 cm (2 inch) cubes	2 1/8 lbs	1 kg
Hot water	1/2 cup	125 mL
Beef stock (bouillon) powder	2 tsp	10 mL
Condensed cream of mushroom soup	10 oz	284 g
Canned mushroom pieces, drained	10 oz	284 g
Onion soup mix	1 1/2 oz	42 g
Red (or alcohol-free) wine	1/2 cup	125 mL

1. Place beef cubes in 6 L (6 quart) slow cooker.

2. Stir hot water and stock (bouillon) powder together in medium bowl.

3. Add soup, mushroom pieces, soup mix and wine. Stir. Pour over beef cubes. Cover. Cook on Low for 7 to 9 hours or on High for 3 1/2 to 4 1/2 hours. Makes 1.65 L (6 2/3 cups). Serves 6 to 8.

1/6 recipe: 1980 Kilojoules (473 Calories); 32.9 g Total Fat; 982 mg Sodium; 31 g Protein; 9 g Carbohydrate

Italian-Style Roast

Topped with red sauce, this is very tender.

Beef sirloin (tip) roast	3 lbs	1.4 kg
Canned mushroom pieces, drained	10 oz	284 g
Chopped onion	1 cup	250 mL
Pasta sauce	1 cup	250 mL
Garlic salt	1/2 tsp	2 mL
Gravy, page 149		

1. Place roast in 3.5 L (3 1/2 quart) slow cooker. Add mushroom pieces and onion.

2. Stir pasta sauce and garlic salt together in bowl. Pour over all. Cover. Cook on Low for 8 to 10 hours or on High for 4 to 5 hours.

3. Make gravy with remaining liquid. Serves 6 to 8.

1 serving: 1704 Kilojoules (407 Calories); 14.4 g Total Fat; 797 mg Sodium; 54 g Protein; 13 g Carbohydrate

Oriental Beef

Snow peas (mange tout) and bean sprouts are added 30 minutes before serving. They add great flavour.

Beef steak, cut across the grain into thin slices	1 1/2 lbs	680 g
Beef stock (bouillon) powder	1 tbsp	15 mL
Hot water	2 cups	500 mL
Liquid gravy browner (optional)	1/2 tsp	2 mL
Soy sauce	3 tbsp	50 mL
Ground ginger	1/4 tsp	1 mL
Garlic powder	1/4 tsp	1 mL

Cornflour (cornstarch)	2 tbsp	30 mL
Water	2 tbsp	30 mL
Snow peas (mange tout)	6 oz	170 g
Bean sprouts, handful	1	1

1. Place steak strips in 5 L (5 quart) slow cooker.

2. Stir next 6 ingredients together in bowl. Pour over top. Cover. Cook on Low for 8 to 10 hours or on High for 4 to 5 hours.

3. Mix cornflour (cornstarch) and second amount of water in small cup. Add to slow cooker. Stir. Stir in snow peas (mange tout) and bean sprouts. Cover. Cook on High for about 20 minutes until thickened and tender. Serves 6 to 8.

1/6 recipe: 925 Kilojoules (221 Calories); 8.7 g Total Fat; 907 mg Sodium; 27 g Protein; 7 g Carbohydrate

Sweet Chilli Chicken

Tender, sweet chicken with a hint of chilli will be a hit with the kids! Make it a meal with rice and steamed vegetables.

Boneless, skinless chicken thighs	2 lbs	900 g
Liquid chicken stock (prepared chicken broth)	2/3 cup	150 mL
Sweet chilli sauce	1/2 cup	125 mL
Minute tapioca	3 tbsp	50 mL
Soy sauce	1 tbsp	15 mL

1. Heat large greased frying pan (skillet) on Medium-High. Add chicken. Sprinkle with salt and pepper. Cook for about 3 minutes per side until browned. Transfer to 3.5 to 4 L (3 1/2 to 4 quart) slow cooker.

2. Combine stock (broth), 60 mL (1/4 cup) chilli sauce, tapioca and soy sauce in small bowl. Pour over chicken. Cook, covered, on Low for 6 to 7 hours or on High for 3 to 3 1/2 hours. Add remaining chilli sauce. Stir. Serves 8.

1 serving: 892 Kilojoules (213 Calories); 9.2 g Total Fat; 571 mg Sodium; 21 g Protein; 10 g Carbohydrate

DESSERTS & DRINKS

DESSERTS & DRINKS

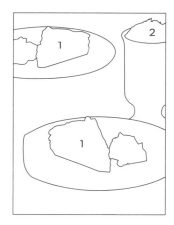

Pictured on reverse:

1. Chocolate PB Brownies, page 171
2. Chocolate Peanut Delight, page 183

Danish Rice Pudding

This creamy pudding with tangy raspberry sauce is traditionally served at Christmas in Denmark. It's customary to hide a whole blanched almond in the pudding. Whoever finds the almond in their serving wins a prize.

Can of sweetened condensed milk	11 oz	300 g
Arborio rice, rinsed and drained	1 cup	250 mL
Slivered almonds, toasted (see Tip, below)	3/4 cup	175 mL
Thickened (whipping) cream, divided	2 cups	500 mL
Container of frozen raspberries in syrup, thawed	15 oz	425 g

1. Combine condensed milk, rice and 550 mL (2 1/4 cups) water in well-greased 3.5 to 4 L (3 1/2 to 4 quart) slow cooker. Cook, covered, on Low for 4 hours or on High for 2 hours. Transfer rice mixture to large bowl. Let stand, uncovered, for 15 minutes.

2. Add almonds and 60 mL (1/4 cup) thickened (whipping) cream. Stir. Chill, covered, for about 45 minutes, stirring occasionally, until cooled completely. Beat remaining cream in medium bowl until stiff peaks form. Fold into rice mixture.

3. Put raspberries and syrup into medium saucepan. Cook, uncovered, on Medium for about 10 minutes, stirring occasionally, until slightly reduced. Spoon over individual servings. Serves 8.

Pictured between pages 176 & 177 and on front cover.

TIP: When toasting nuts, seeds or coconut, cooking times will vary for each type of nut – so never toast them together. For small amounts, place ingredient in an ungreased shallow frying pan. Heat on Medium for 3 to 5 minutes, stirring often, until golden. For larger amounts, spread ingredient evenly in an ungreased shallow pan. Bake in a 175ºC (350ºF) oven for 5 to 10 minutes, stirring or shaking often, until golden.

1 serving: 2190 Kilojoules (523 Calories); 30.2 g Total Fat; 82 mg Sodium; 8 g Protein; 57 g Carbohydrate

Maple Orange Pears

These tender, golden pears make an elegant yet simple dessert when drizzled with their delicate buttery sauce. Serve with vanilla ice-cream for a dinner party.

Maple syrup	1/2 cup	125 mL
Butter (or hard margarine), melted	2 tbsp	30 mL
Medium peeled pears	6	6
Orange juice	2 tbsp	30 mL
Cornflour (cornstarch)	2 tsp	10 mL

1. Combine maple syrup, melted butter and 30 mL (2 tbsp) water in 4 to 5 L (4 to 5 quart) slow cooker.

2. Carefully remove cores from bottom of pears using apple corer, leaving stems intact. Set upright in maple syrup mixture. Cook, covered, on High for 2 hours. Transfer pears with slotted spoon to serving plate.

3. Stir orange juice into cornflour (cornstarch) in small cup until smooth. Add to cooking liquid.

Stir. Cook, covered, on High for about 20 minutes until thickened. Pour over pears. Serves 6.

Pictured between pages 176 & 177 and on front cover.

1 serving: 858 Kilojoules (205 Calories); 4.1 g Total Fat; 31 mg Sodium; 1 g Protein; 45 g Carbohydrate

Buttery Ginger Pineapple

This light dessert is simple yet exotic, with tangy bites of pineapple, buttery sauce with spicy ginger, and a sprinkling of toasted coconut.

Fresh (or frozen, thawed) pineapple chunks (3.8 cm, 1 1/2 inch, pieces)	6 cups	1.5 L
Ginger marmalade	1/4 cup	60 mL
Butter	3 tbsp	50 mL
Cornflour (cornstarch)	1 tbsp	15 mL
Flaked coconut, toasted (see Tip, page 161)	1/2 cup	125 mL

1. Put pineapple into 3.5 to 4 L (3 1/2 to 4 quart) slow cooker.

2. Combine marmalade and butter in small saucepan on Medium-Low. Heat and stir until butter is melted. Pour over pineapple. Stir until coated. Cook, covered, on Low for 3 to 4 hours or on High for 1 1/2 to 2 hours.

3. Stir 15 mL (1 tbsp) water into cornflour (cornstarch) in small cup until smooth. Add to pineapple. Stir. Cook, covered, on High

for 15 minutes until boiling and thickened.

4. Sprinkle individual servings with coconut. Makes about 1 L (4 cups).

125 mL (1/2 cup): 605 Kilojoules (144 Calories); 5.9 g Total Fat; 49 mg Sodium; 1 g Protein; 24 g Carbohydrate

Chocolate Hazelnut Cheesecake

This chocolatey cheesecake has rich flavour but a light texture – delicious!
Top each slice with whipped cream and garnish with fresh berries.

Cream-filled chocolate cookies	10	10
Blocks of cream cheese (250 g, 8 oz, each), softened	2	2
Chocolate hazelnut spread, divided	1 1/3 cups	325 mL
Large eggs, fork-beaten	3	3
Sour cream	1 cup	250 mL

1. Process cookies in food processor until coarse crumbs form. Press firmly in parchment paper–lined, greased 20 cm (8 inch) springform pan. Let stand in freezer for 10 minutes.

2. Beat cream cheese and 250 mL (1 cup) chocolate hazelnut spread in large bowl, scraping down sides as necessary, until smooth.

3. Add eggs and sour cream. Beat well. Spread evenly over cookie crumbs. Put an even layer (5 to 7.5 cm, 2 to 3 inches, thick) of crumpled foil into bottom of 5 to 7 L (5 to 7 quart) slow cooker (See Tip, below). Pour 500 mL (2 cups) boiling water into slow cooker. Place pan on foil, pushing down gently to settle evenly. Lay double layer of tea towel over slow cooker liner. Cover with lid. Cook on High for 1 1/2 hours. Transfer pan to wire rack. Cool completely. Chill, covered, for at least 6 hours or overnight. Remove from pan. Spread remaining chocolate hazelnut spread over top and sides of cheesecake. Cuts into 12 wedges.

Pictured between pages 176 & 177 and on front cover.

TIP: Instead of using crumpled foil to elevate pans and other items, you can use canning jar lids or a roasting rack that fits your slow cooker if you have one.

1 wedge: 1511 Kilojoules (361 Calories); 26.3 g Total Fat; 185 mg Sodium; 6 g Protein; 24 g Carbohydrate

Steamed Pumpkin Carrot Cake

This spicy snack cake is really easy to prepare. If desired, ice with prepared cream cheese frosting, drizzle with caramel sauce or dust with icing sugar.

Carrot cake (muffin) mix	2 cups	500 mL
Mixed spices	1 tsp	5 mL
Mashed pumpkin	1 cup	250 mL
Large eggs	2	2
Raisins	1/2 cup	125 mL

1. Combine cake (muffin) mix and spices in large bowl. Make a well in centre.

2. Whisk pumpkin, eggs and 150 mL (2/3 cup) water in medium bowl until smooth. Add raisins. Stir. Add to well. Stir until just moistened. Pour into greased 20 cm (8 inch) springform pan. Put an even layer (5 to 7.5 mL, 2 to 3 inches, thick) of crumpled foil into bottom of 5 to 7 L (5 to 7 quart) slow cooker (see Tip, page 163). Place pan on foil, pushing down gently to settle evenly. Lay double layer of tea towel over slow cooker liner. Cover with lid. Cook on High for about 2 1/2 hours until wooden pick inserted in centre comes out clean. Transfer pan to wire rack. Cool completely. Cuts into 12 wedges.

1 wedge: 682 Kilojoules (163 Calories); 6.7 g Total Fat; 536 mg Sodium; 7 g Protein; 29 g Carbohydrate

Café au Lait Custard

Rich, coffee-flavoured baked custard is a smooth, sweet ending to a meal. Whether you serve it warm or chilled, a dollop of whipped cream is the perfect garnish.

Large eggs	3	3
White (granulated) sugar	1/2 cup	125 mL
Vanilla extract	1 tsp	5 mL
Can of evaporated milk	13 1/2 oz	385 mL
Instant coffee granules	1 1/2 tbsp	25 mL

1. Whisk first 3 ingredients and a sprinkle of salt in medium heatproof bowl until smooth.

2. Combine milk and coffee granules in medium saucepan on Medium. Heat for about 5 minutes, stirring often, until coffee granules are dissolved and bubbles form around edge of saucepan. Slowly add to egg mixture, stirring constantly, until sugar is dissolved. Strain mixture through sieve back into pan. Pour mixture into 4 greased 175 mL (3/4 cup) ovenproof ramekins. Put an even layer (5 to 7.5 cm, 2 to 3 inches, thick) of crumpled foil into bottom of 5 to 7 L (5 to 7 quart) slow cooker (see Tip, page 163). Place ramekins on foil, pushing down gently to settle evenly. Pour hot water into slow cooker until halfway up side of ramekins. Lay double layer of tea towel over slow cooker liner. Cover with lid. Cook on High for about 1 1/2 hours until custard is set. Serves 4.

Pictued on back cover.

1 serving: 1156 Kilojoules (276 Calories); 9.5 g Total Fat; 286 mg Sodium; 11 g Protein; 35 g Carbohydrate

Marbled Cheesecake

A perfect dessert to make when your oven is already in use.

BISCUIT CRUST

Hard margarine (or butter)	4 tsp	20 mL
Shredded wheatmeal biscuit crumbs	1/3 cup	75 mL
White (granulated) sugar	1 tsp	5 mL

FILLING

Semisweet chocolate baking squares, cut up	3	84 g
Light cream cheese, softened	12 oz	375 g
White (granulated) sugar	3/4 cup	175 mL
Non-fat plain yoghurt	1/3 cup	75 mL
Vanilla essence	1 tsp	5 mL
Large eggs	4	4
Plain (all-purpose) flour	1/2 cup	125 mL

1. BISCUIT CRUST: Melt margarine in saucepan. Stir in biscuit crumbs and sugar. Press in ungreased 20 cm (8 inch) springform tin.

2. FILLING: Melt chocolate in saucepan over Low, stirring often.

3. Beat cream cheese, sugar, yoghurt and vanilla together in large bowl until smooth. Beat in eggs, 1 at a time. Add flour. Mix. Reserve 425 mL (1 3/4 cups) of cheese mixture. Pour remaining cheese mixture over bottom crust.

4. Stir melted chocolate into reserved 425 mL (1 3/4 cups) of cheese mixture. Stir. Drizzle over top of white layer. Cut through in a zig-zag motion to get a marbled look.

5. Tear off a 40 cm (16 inch) long piece of foil to make a foil strap. Fold lengthwise to make a strip 40 cm (16 inches) long and 10 cm (4 inches) wide. Set cake pan on centre of foil strap. Put wire trivet in bottom of 5 L (5 quart) round slow cooker.

6. Using foil strap, carefully lower pan into slow cooker, leaving foil strap in the slow cooker to use to remove pan when baking is complete. Place 5 paper towels between top of slow cooker and lid. Cook on High for 3 hours. Remove pan. Cool. Refrigerate for several hours or overnight. Cuts into 12 wedges.

1 wedge: 946 Kilojoules (226 Calories); 11 g Total Fat; 362 mg Sodium; 7 g Protein; 26 g Carbohydrate

Apple Cake

A handy cake mix and apple sauce combine to make this spicy cake.

Yellow cake mix (2 layer size)	1	1
Instant vanilla pudding (4 serving size)	1	1
Ground cinnamon	1/2 tsp	2 mL
Ground nutmeg	1/4 tsp	1 mL
Ground allspice	1/4 tsp	1 mL
Large eggs, fork-beaten	4	4
Canned apple sauce	14 oz	398 g
Readymade icing		

1. Place first 7 ingredients in bowl. Beat on Low to moisten. Beat on Medium for 2 minutes until smooth. Line greased 5 L (5 quart) round slow cooker with foil. Pour batter over foil. Place 5 paper towels between top of slow cooker and lid. Put wooden match or an object 3 mm (1/8 inch) thick between paper towels and edge of slow cooker to allow a bit of steam to escape. Do not lift lid for at least 2 hours. Cook on High for 2 1/2 hours until wooden pick inserted in centre comes out clean. Remove slow cooker liner to rack or turn slow cooker off. Let stand for 20 minutes. Loosen sides of cake with knife, taking care not to scratch the slow cooker's liner. Invert cake onto plate, foil side up, then onto rack, foil side down, to cool. Remove foil before serving.

2. Cut cake into 2 layers if desired. Ice. Cuts into 12 wedges.

1 wedge: 1943 Kilojoules (464 Calories); 13.1 g Total Fat; 296 mg Sodium; 4 g Protein; 85 g Carbohydrate

Stewed Pears

Wonderful pear flavour. Cloves add just a bit of zip. Great for brunch or dessert.

Apple juice	1 1/2 cups	375 mL
White (granulated) sugar	1/2 cup	125 mL
Lemon juice	1 tbsp	15 mL
Whole cloves	2	2
Fresh pears, peeled, cored and thinly sliced (see Note)	4	4

1. Stir apple juice, sugar, lemon juice and cloves together in 3.5 L (3 1/2 quart) slow cooker.

2. Add pears. Cover. Cook on Low for 6 to 7 hours or on High for 3 to 3 1/2 hours. Makes 925 mL (3 3/4 cups).

NOTE: If using canned pears, check if cooked sooner as they soften quickly. Double cloves for shorter stewing time.

125 mL (1/2 cup): 435 Kilojoules (104 Calories); 0.1 g Total Fat; 4 mg Sodium; trace Protein; 27 g Carbohydrate

Stewed Prunes

Worry-free. Juice doesn't have a chance of boiling away as it does on a burner.

Dried pitted prunes	1 lb	454 g
Water	3 cups	750 mL

Combine prunes and water in 3.5 L (3 1/2 quart) slow cooker. Cover. Cook on Low for 4 to 5 hours or on High for 2 to 2 1/2 hours. Stir. Makes 1 L (4 1/4 cups).

125 mL (1/2 cup): 607 Kilojoules (145 Calories); 0.3 g Total Fat; 2 mg Sodium; 2 g Protein; 38 g Carbohydrate

Chocolate Fudge Pudding

No need to heat up the kitchen to enjoy this yummy dessert.
Good chocolate flavour with lots of sauce.

Plain (all-purpose) flour	1 cup	250 mL
Brown sugar	3/4 cup	175 mL
Cocoa	2 tbsp	30 mL
Baking powder	2 tsp	10 mL
Salt	1/4 tsp	1 mL
Milk	1/2 cup	125 mL
Cooking oil	2 tbsp	30 mL
Vanilla essence	1/2 tsp	2 mL
Brown sugar	3/4 cup	175 mL

Cocoa	2 tbsp	30 mL
Hot water	1 3/4 cups	425 mL

1. Place first 5 ingredients in bowl. Stir.

2. Add milk, cooking oil and vanilla. Stir well. Turn into 3.5 L (3 1/2 quart) slow cooker.

3. Stir second amount of brown sugar and second amount of cocoa together well in bowl. Add hot water. Mix.

Pour carefully over batter in slow cooker. Do not stir. Cover. Cook on High for about 2 hours until wooden pick inserted in centre comes out clean. Serves 6.

1 serving: 1499 Kilojoules (358 Calories); 5.4 g Total Fat; 148 mg Sodium; 4 g Protein; 77 g Carbohydrate

Strawberries and Dumplings

Tender dumplings top scrumptious strawberries, all with a hint of lemon – like strawberry shortcake with a twist. Drizzle each serving with some cream.

Small lemon	1	1
Frozen whole strawberries, thawed	4 cups	1 L
White (granulated) sugar, divided	1/2 cup	125 mL
Muffin (biscuit) mix	1 cup	250 mL
Milk	1/3 cup	75 mL

1. Grate 5 mL (1 tsp) lemon zest into small bowl. Set aside. Squeeze 5 mL (1 tsp) lemon juice into 3.5 to 4 L (3 1/2 to 4 quart) slow cooker.

2. Add strawberries and 100 mL (6 tbsp) sugar to slow cooker. Stir. Cook, covered, on Low for 4 to 5 hours or on High for 2 to 2 1/2 hours until boiling.

3. Add muffin (biscuit) mix and remaining sugar to reserved zest. Stir. Add milk. Stir until just moistened. Drop evenly over strawberry mixture in 6 mounds. Cook, covered, on High for about 30 minutes until wooden pick inserted in centre comes out clean. Serves 6.

1 serving: 1181 Kilojoules (282 Calories); 2.7 g Total Fat; 277 mg Sodium; 3 g Protein; 66 g Carbohydrate

Toffee Pudding Cake

This is a soft, sponge-textured butterscotch cake with a tasty toffee layer on the bottom. Serve each slice with vanilla ice cream.

Large eggs	2	2
Package of white cake mix (1 layer size)	1	1
Box of instant butterscotch pudding powder (4-serving size)	1	1
Cooking oil	1/3 cup	75 mL
Toffee bits	1/2 cup	125 mL

1. Beat first 4 ingredients and 125 mL (1/2 cup) water on High in medium bowl for about 3 minutes until smooth. Pour into greased 20 cm (8 inch) springform pan. Put an even layer (5 to 7.5 cm, 2 to 3 inches, thick) of crumpled foil into bottom of 5 to 7 L (5 to 7 quart) slow cooker (see Tip, page 163). Pour 500 mL (2 cups) boiling water into slow cooker. Place pan on foil, pushing down gently to settle evenly.

2. Sprinkle toffee bits over top. Lay double layer of tea towel over slow cooker liner. Cover with lid. Cook on High for 2 hours until wooden pick inserted in centre comes out clean. Transfer pan to wire rack. Let stand for 15 minutes. Cuts into 12 wedges.

1 wedge: 1360 Kilojoules (325 Calories); 14.7 g Total Fat; 461 mg Sodium; 3 g Protein; 46 g Carbohydrate

Tropical Fruit Cobbler

A traditional dessert with a mango twist! Coconut-sprinkled, fluffy cake tops a sweet, fruity sauce. Brown sugar gives the cake a nice colour.

Frozen mango pieces, thawed	6 cups	1.5 L
Can of peaches (peach pie filling)	19 oz	540 g
Muffin (biscuit) mix	2 cups	500 mL
Brown sugar, packed	1/3 cup	75 mL
Medium sweetened coconut, toasted, divided (see Tip, page 161)	1 cup	250 mL

1. Combine mango and peaches (peach pie filling) in 3.5 to 4 L (3 1/2 to 4 quart) slow cooker. Cook, covered, on Low for 6 to 8 hours or on High for 3 to 4 hours. Stir.

2. Combine muffin (biscuit) mix, brown sugar and 175 mL (3/4 cup) coconut in medium bowl. Make a well in centre. Add 150 mL (2/3 cup) water. Mix until just combined. Drop batter onto fruit mixture, using about 60 mL (1/4 cup) for each mound. Sprinkle with remaining coconut. Cook, covered, on High for about 1 hour until wooden pick inserted in centre comes out clean. Serves 12.

1 serving: 984 Kilojoules (235 Calories); 4.5 g Total Fat; 295 mg Sodium; 3 g Protein; 49 g Carbohydrate

Brown Betty

Serve this delicious baked fruit dessert warm.

Medium cooking apples, peeled, cored and sliced	4	4
Brown sugar	3/4 cup	175 mL
Quick-cooking rolled oats (not instant)	1/3 cup	75 mL
Plain (all-purpose) flour	1/2 cup	125 mL
Salt	1/4 tsp	1 mL
Hard margarine (or butter), softened	1/3 cup	75 mL

1. Place apple slices in 3.5 L (3 1/2 quart) slow cooker.

2. Mix remaining 5 ingredients in bowl until crumbly. Sprinkle over apple. Place 5 paper towels between top of slow cooker and lid. Put wooden match or an object 3mm (1/8 inch) thick between paper towels and edge of slow cooker to allow a bit of steam to escape. Cook on High for 1 1/2 to 2 hours. Serves 4.

250 mL (1 cup): 1959 Kilojoules (468 Calories); 17.2 g Total Fat; 374 mg Sodium; 3 g Protein; 79 g Carbohydrate

Winter's Day Compote

A warm compote is lovely alongside plain cheesecake or vanilla ice-cream. If you have any leftovers, it makes a delicious addition to granola or oatmeal for breakfast.

Sliced peeled cooking apple	3 cups	750 mL
Sliced peeled tart apple (such as Granny Smith)	3 cups	750 mL
Chopped dried apricot	1 cup	250 mL
Brown sugar, packed	1/3 cup	75 mL
Mixed dried fruit (raisin pie filling)	19 oz	540 mL

1. Combine first 4 ingredients and 250 mL (1 cup) water in 3.5 to 4 L (3 1/2 to 4 quart) slow cooker.

2. Spoon dried fruit (raisin pie filling) over top. Do not stir. Cook, covered, on Low for 5 to 6 hours or on High for 2 1/2 to 3 hours. Stir. Makes about 1.6 L (6 1/2 cups).

125 mL (1/2 cup): 481 Kilojoules (115 Calories); 0.1 g Total Fat; 46 mg Sodium; trace Protein; 29 g Carbohydrate

Chocolate PB Brownies

Pour yourself a nice cold glass of milk to go with these delicious chocolate brownies. They would look especially appetising served with a scoop of vanilla ice-cream, drizzled with chocolate sauce and sprinkled with peanuts.

Semi-sweet cooking chocolate squares (28 g, 1 oz, each), chopped	5	5
Sweetened condensed milk (see Note)	2/3 cup	150 mL
Crunchy peanut butter	1/2 cup	125 mL
Large egg, fork-beaten	1	1
Muffin (biscuit) mix	3/4 cup	175 mL

1. Heat chocolate in medium heavy saucepan on lowest heat, stirring often, until chocolate is almost melted. Remove from heat. Stir until smooth. Transfer to medium bowl.

2. Add condensed milk. Stir until smooth. Add peanut butter and egg. Stir until combined.

3. Add muffin (biscuit) mix. Stir until no dry mix remains. Spread evenly in parchment paper-lined greased 20 cm (8 inch) round cake pan. Put an even layer (5 to 7.5 cm, 2 to 3 inches, thick) of crumpled foil into bottom of 5 to 7 L (5 to 7 quart) slow cooker. Pour 500 mL (2 cups) boiling water into slow cooker. Place pan on foil, pushing down gently to settle evenly. Lay double layer of tea towel over slow cooker liner. Cover with lid. Cook on High for 1 1/2 hours. Transfer pan to wire rack. Let stand for 10 minutes. Cuts into 12 wedges.

Pictured between pages 160 & 161.

NOTE: Store remaining sweetened condensed milk in the fridge and use it as a decadent addition to your morning coffee.

1 wedge: 867 Kilojoules (207 Calories); 9.8 g Total Fat; 170 mg Sodium; 6 g Protein; 26 g Carbohydrate

Coconut Rice Pudding

Creamy and comforting, sweet coconut rice contrasts with the vibrant colour of fresh mango. This is an easy dessert to accompany a Thai or Vietnamese dinner.

Short-grain white rice	2 cups	500 mL
White (granulated) sugar	1 cup	250 mL
Can of coconut milk	14 oz	398 mL
Chopped ripe (or frozen, thawed) mango	1 1/2 cups	375 mL
Medium sweetened coconut, toasted	1/2 cup	125 mL

1. Put rice into large bowl. Add water until rice is covered. Let stand for at least 6 hours or overnight. Drain.

2. Combine sugar and 750 mL (3 cups) water in 3.5 to 4 L (3 1/2 to 4 quart) slow cooker. Add rice and a light sprinkle of salt. Stir. Cook, covered, on Low for 4 hours or on High for 2 hours.

3. Add coconut milk and mango. Stir.

4. Sprinkle coconut over individual servings. Makes about 1.75 L (7 cups).

125 mL (1/2 cup): 879 Kilojoules (210 Calories); 7.1 g Total Fat; 32 mg Sodium; 2 g Protein; 36 g Carbohydrate

Oatmeal Cookie Crisp

Choose your favourite fruit to cook up in this easy dessert. Serve it warm with whipped cream or vanilla ice-cream.

Fresh (or frozen, thawed) mixed berries	4 cups	1 L
Minute tapioca	3 tbsp	50 mL
Crushed crisp oatmeal cookies (about 12)	1 1/2 cups	375 mL
Chopped pecans	1/2 cup	125 mL
Butter (or hard margarine), melted	2 tbsp	30 mL

1. Combine berries and tapioca in greased 3.5 to 4 L (3 1/2 to 4 quart) slow cooker. Cook, covered, on Low for 3 hours or on High for 1 1/2 hours.

2. Combine remaining 3 ingredients in small bowl. Spoon over berry mixture. Do not stir. Lay double layer of tea towel over slow cooker liner. Cover with lid. Cook on High for about 30 minutes until browned and crisp. Makes about 1 L (4 cups).

125 mL (1/2 cup): 1076 Kilojoules (257 Calories); 14.6 g Total Fat; 150 mg Sodium; 3 g Protein; 30 g Carbohydrate

Orange Tapioca Pudding

This citrus-scented tapioca makes for rich and creamy comfort food
when served warm, but it can be served up chilled as well.

Seed tapioca (sago)	1/2 cup	125 mL
Homogenised milk	3 cups	750 mL
Medium orange	1	1
Large egg	1	1
White (granulated) sugar	1/3 cup	75 mL

1. Combine tapioca (sago) and 500 mL (2 cups) cold water in medium bowl. Stir. Let stand, covered, for 1 hour. Drain. Transfer to 3.5 to 4 L (3 1/2 to 4 quart) slow cooker.

2. Add milk and a sprinkle of salt. Stir. Cook, covered, on Low for 4 hours or on High for 2 hours, stirring once at halftime.

3. Grate 2 mL (1/2 tsp) orange zest into small bowl. Set aside. Squeeze 75 mL (1/3 cup) orange juice into separate medium bowl.

4. Add egg and sugar to orange juice. Whisk until smooth. Slowly add about 250 mL (1 cup) hot tapioca mixture, whisking constantly until combined. Slowly add mixture back to slow cooker, stirring constantly. Cook, covered, on High for 15 minutes. Add orange zest. Stir. Makes about 875 mL (3 1/2 cups).

125 mL (1/2 cup): 649 Kilojoules (155 Calories); 4.1 g Total Fat; 146 mg Sodium; 4 g Protein; 26 g Carbohydrate

Pineapple Cherry Cobbler

This easy cobbler has sweet cherry and pineapple flavours underneath
a cake-like layer. Add a scoop of ice cream to each bowlful.

Can of pitted cherries (cherry pie filling)	19 oz	540 g
Can of crushed pineapple (with juice)	19 oz	540 g
Muffin (biscuit) mix	1 1/2 cups	375 mL
Large egg, fork-beaten	1	1
Buttermilk (or soured milk, see Note)	1 cup	250 mL

1. Combine cherries (cherry pie filling) and pineapple in greased 3.5 to 4 L (3 1/2 to 4 quart) slow cooker.

2. Measure muffin (biscuit) mix into medium bowl. Make a well in centre.

3. Add egg and buttermilk to well. Stir until just moistened. Spoon evenly over pineapple mixture. Cook, covered, on High for 2 1/2 to 3 hours until wooden pick inserted in centre comes out clean. Serves 8.

NOTE: To make soured milk, measure 15 mL (1 tbsp) white vinegar or lemon juice into a 250 mL (1 cup) liquid measure. Add enough milk to make 250 mL (1 cup). Stir. Let stand for 1 minute.

1 serving: 976 Kilojoules (233 Calories); 3.9 g Total Fat; 354 mg Sodium; 5 g Protein; 45 g Carbohydrate

Chunky Spiced Apple Sauce

This fragrant apple sauce is delicious whether served hot or cold, and can be paired with gingerbread or sponge cake.

Chopped peeled tart apples (such as Granny Smith)	16 cups	4 L
White (granulated) sugar	1 cup	250 mL
Ground cinnamon	1 1/2 tsp	7 mL
Ground nutmeg	1/2 tsp	2 mL
Dark raisins (optional)	1/2 cup	125 mL

1. Combine first 4 ingredients in 5 to 7 L (5 to 7 quart) slow cooker. Pour 250 mL (1 cup) water over top. Cook, covered, on Low for 4 hours or on High for 2 hours.

2. Add raisins. Stir. Cook, covered, on High for about 1 hour. Stir to break up apples. Makes about 2 L (8 cups).

125 mL (1/2 cup): 544 Kilojoules (131 Calories); 0.2 g Total Fat; 3 mg Sodium; trace Protein; 34 g Carbohydrate

Rhuberry Sauce

This thick, delicious rhubarb and strawberry sauce would be wonderful spooned over cakes, ice-cream or even pancakes and waffles.

Chopped fresh (or frozen, thawed) rhubarb	6 cups	1.5 L
Container of frozen strawberries in light syrup, thawed	15 oz	425 g
White (granulated) sugar	1 cup	250 mL
Minute tapioca	1 tbsp	15 mL
Cinnamon stick (10 cm, 4 inches)	1	1

1. Combine all 5 ingredients in 3.5 to 4 L (3 1/2 to 4 quart) slow cooker. Cook, covered, on Low for 5 to 6 hours or on High for 2 1/2 to 3 hours. Remove and discard cinnamon stick. Makes about 1.25 L (5 cups).

125 mL (1/2 cup): 544 Kilojoules (130 Calories); 0.2 g Total Fat; 3 mg Sodium; 1 g Protein; 33 g Carbohydrate

Saucy Brandied Apples

A great choice for a winter dessert when your oven is occupied! Serve with a scoop of vanilla ice-cream or a dollop of whipped cream.

Brandy	1/2 cup	125 mL
Dried cranberries	1/2 cup	125 mL
Mixed dried fruit (raisin pie filling)	1 cup	250 mL
Peeled tart apples (such as Granny Smith)	6	6
Chopped pecans, toasted (see Tip, page 161)	1/4 cup	60 mL

1. Combine brandy and cranberries in small bowl. Let stand for 15 minutes.

2. Add dried fruit (raisin pie filling). Stir. Transfer to 5 to 7 L (5 to 7 quart) slow cooker.

3. Cut apples in half. Remove cores (see Note). Arrange apples, cut-side up, in slow cooker. Cook, covered, on Low for 6 to 7 hours or on High for 3 to 3 1/2 hours. Transfer fruit to large serving plate with slotted spoon. Makes about 250 mL (1 cup) sauce.

4. Sprinkle apples with pecans. Serve with sauce. Serves 12.

NOTE: A melon baller is a very handy tool for coring an apple that is already peeled and halved.

1 serving with 15 mL (1 tbsp) sauce: 465 Kilojoules (111 Calories); 1.9 g Total Fat; 17 mg Sodium; trace Protein; 18 g Carbohydrate

Peaches à la Mode

This combination of sweet, syrupy peaches with sponge cake and ice-cream makes enough to please a crowd – no oven space required!

Cans of sliced peaches (796 g, 28 oz, each), drained and juice reserved	2	2
Minute tapioca	2 tbsp	30 mL
Ground cinnamon	1/2 tsp	2 mL
Sponge cake	10 1/2 oz	298 g
Butterscotch ripple ice cream	2 1/2 cups	625 mL

1. Combine first 3 ingredients and 125 mL (1/2 cup) reserved peach juice in 3.5 to 4 L (3 1/2 to 4 quart) slow cooker. Cook, covered, on Low for 3 to 4 hours or on High for 1 1/2 to 2 hours.

2. Slice cake into 10 slices, about 2 cm (3/4 inch) thick. Top each slice with ice cream. Spoon peach mixture over top. Serves 10.

1 serving: 1352 Kilojoules (323 Calories); 11.2 g Total Fat; 184 mg Sodium; 4 g Protein; 52 g Carbohydrate

Steamed Fruit Pudding

Serve with your favourite pudding sauce. A carefree
method for cooking a fruit pudding.

Hard margarine (or butter), softened	3/4 cup	175 mL
White (granulated) sugar	3/4 cup	175 mL
Large eggs	2	2
Orange (or apple) juice	1/2 cup	125 mL
Raisins	2 cups	500 mL
Cut mixed glazed fruit	1 1/2 cups	375 mL
Fine dry breadcrumbs	1 cup	250 mL
Ground cinnamon	1 tsp	5 mL
Ground allspice	1/2 tsp	2 mL
Baking powder	3/4 tsp	4 mL

Bicarbonate soda (baking soda)	1/2 tsp	2 mL
Salt	1 tsp	5 mL
Plain (all-purpose) flour	1 cup	250 mL

1. Cream margarine and sugar together in bowl. Beat in eggs, 1 at a time. Add orange juice. Beat.

2. Combine remaining 9 ingredients in separate large bowl. Stir together well. Pour orange juice mixture into dry ingredients. Stir until moistened. Turn into greased 2 L (8 cup) pudding pan. Cover with greased foil, tying sides down with string. Place on wire trivet in 5 L (5 quart) slow cooker. Pour boiling water into slow cooker to reach halfway up sides of pudding pan. Cover. Cook on High for 5 hours. Serves 16.

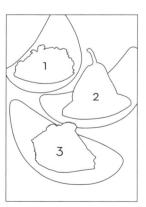

1. Danish Rice Pudding, page 161
2. Maple Orange Pears, page 162
3. Chocolate Hazelnut Cheesecake, page 163

1 serving: 1302 Kilojoules (311 Calories); 10.4 g Total Fat; 397 mg Sodium; 3 g Protein; 54 g Carbohydrate

Lemon-Sauced Pudding

A yummy lemon flavour. A cake-like top with lemon sauce to spoon over. Serve with ice-cream.

Plain (all-purpose) flour	1 cup	250 mL
White (granulated) sugar	1/2 cup	125 mL
Baking powder	2 tsp	10 mL
Grated lemon peel	2 tsp	10 mL
Salt	1/8 tsp	0.5 mL
Milk	1/2 cup	125 mL
Cooking oil	2 tbsp	30 mL
Hot water	1 3/4 cups	425 mL
Lemon juice	1/4 cup	60 mL
White (granulated) sugar	3/4 cup	175 mL

1. Measure first 7 ingredients into bowl. Mix well. Turn into greased 3.5 L (3 1/2 quart) slow cooker.

2. Stir hot water, lemon juice and second amount of sugar together in separate bowl. Pour carefully over batter. Do not stir. Place 5 paper towels between top of slow cooker and lid. Cook on High for about 2 hours until wooden pick inserted in centre comes out clean. Makes 6 small servings.

1. Mulled Blackcurrant Sipper, page 179
2. Warm and Fuzzy Navel, page 179
3. Hot Fruit Punch, page 180

1 serving: 1273 Kilojoules (304 Calories); 5.1 g Total Fat; 76 mg Sodium; 3 g Protein; 63 g Carbohydrate

Chocolate Cake

The crowning glory is the pink raspberry icing.

Chocolate cake mix (2 layer size), see Note	1	1
FILLING		
Raspberry (or strawberry) jam	1 cup	250 mL
RASPBERRY ICING		
Hard margarine (or butter), softened	6 tbsp	100 mL
Raspberry cordial	1 tsp	5 mL
Icing (confectioner's) sugar	1 1/2 cups	375 mL
Water	1/4 cup	60 mL
Icing (confectioner's) sugar	1 1/2 cups	375 mL

1. Prepare cake mix as directed on package. Line bottom of 5 L (5 quart) round slow cooker with foil. Pour batter over foil. Place 5 paper towels between top of slow cooker and lid. Put wooden match or an object 3 mm (1/8 inch) thick between paper towels and edge of slow cooker to allow a bit of steam to escape. Do not lift lid for at least 2 hours. Cook on High for about 2 1/2 hours until wooden pick inserted in centre comes out clean. Remove slow cooker liner to rack or turn slow cooker off. Let stand, uncovered, for 20 minutes. Loosen sides of cake with knife, taking care not to scratch the slow cooker's liner. Invert cake onto plate, foil side up, then onto rack, foil side down, to cool. Remove foil before serving.

2. FILLING: Cut cake into 2 layers. Spread bottom layer with jam. Place second layer on top.

3. RASPBERRY ICING: Measure first 4 ingredients into bowl. Beat until creamy.

4. Add second amount of icing (confectioner's) sugar. Beat well. Add more water or icing sugar if needed to make proper spreading consistency. Makes 500 mL (2 cups). Ice top and sides of cake. Cuts into 12 wedges.

NOTE: Testing showed that white or yellow cake mixes could not be substituted.

'SCRATCH' CHOCOLATE CAKE: Combine 1 chocolate cake mix, 1 chocolate or vanilla instant pudding (4 serving size), 4 eggs, 125 mL (1/2 cup) cooking oil and 250 mL (1 cup) water. Mix and cook as for Chocolate Cake, above.

1 wedge: 1775 Kilojoules (424 Calories); 10.5 g Total Fat; 309 mg Sodium; 2 g Protein; 84 g Carbohydrate

Mulled Blackcurrant Sipper

While cinnamon, cloves and allspice are typically used for mulling, aniseed and star anise impart a lovely hint of licorice that pairs well with blackcurrant.

Cranberry juice	10 cups	2.5 L
Blackcurrant cordial (concentrated blackcurrant nectar)	2 cups	500 mL
Aniseed	1 tbsp	15 mL
Star anise	2	2
Brown sugar, packed (optional)	1 tbsp	15 mL

1. Combine juice and cordial (nectar) in 4 to 5 L (4 to 5 quart) slow cooker.

2. Put aniseed and star anise onto 12.5 cm (5 inch) square piece of cheesecloth. Draw up corners and tie with butcher's string. Submerge in cranberry juice mixture. Cook, covered, on Low for 6 to 8 hours or on High for 3 to 4 hours. Remove and discard cheesecloth bag.

3. Add brown sugar. Stir. Makes about 3 L (12 cups).

Pictured between pages 176 & 177 and on back cover.

250 mL (1 cup): 481 Kilojoules (115 Calories); 0 g Total Fat; 15 mg Sodium; trace Protein; 27 g Carbohydrate

Warm and Fuzzy Navel

Serve this in a punchbowl for a cosy winter brunch, or hand it out as a welcoming cocktail for a party.

Apricot fruit juice	6 cups	1.5 L
Orange juice	6 cups	1.5 L
Grenadine syrup (optional)	1 tbsp	15 mL
Orange liqueur	3/4 cup	175 mL
Peach schnapps	3/4 cup	175 mL

1. Combine first 3 ingredients in 3.5 to 4 L (3 1/2 to 4 quart) slow cooker. Cook, covered, on Low for 2 to 4 hours or on High for 1 to 2 hours.

2. Add liqueur and schnapps. Stir. Makes about 3.4 L (13 1/2 cups).

Pictured between pages 176 & 177 and on back cover.

250 mL (1 cup): 766 Kilojoules (183 Calories); 0.3 g Total Fat; 9 mg Sodium; 1 g Protein; 35 g Carbohydrate

Hot Fruit Punch

Treat the kids to a mug of this warming winter beverage.

Apple juice	4 cups	1 L
Cranberry juice	4 cups	1 L
Pineapple juice	4 cups	1 L
Cinnamon stick (10 cm, 4 inches), broken up	1	1
Whole allspice	1 tsp	5 mL

1. Combine first 3 ingredients in 3.5 to 4 L (3 1/2 to 4 quart) slow cooker.

2. Put cinnamon stick pieces and allspice onto 15 cm (6 inch) square piece of cheesecloth. Draw up corners and tie with butcher's string. Submerge in juice mixture. Cook, covered, on Low for 4 to 6 hours or on High for 2 to 3 hours. Remove and discard cheesecloth bag. Makes about 3 L (12 cups).

Pictured between pages 176 & 177 and on back cover.

250 mL (1 cup): 532 Kilojoules (127 Calories); 0 g Total Fat; 2 mg Sodium; 0 g Protein; 32 g Carbohydrate

Cranberry Warmer

Mild with a hint of tang. A pick-me-up rosy drink.

Cranberry juice	4 cups	1 L
Pineapple juice	4 cups	1 L
Orange juice	2 cups	500 mL
Brown sugar, packed	1/2 cup	125 mL
Whole cloves	20	20
Cinnamon sticks (10 cm, 4 inches, each in length), broken up and crushed in plastic bag	4	4

1. Combine first 4 ingredients in 3.5 L (3 1/2 quart) slow cooker. Stir.

2. Tie cloves and cinnamon in double layer of cheesecloth. Add to slow cooker. Cover. Cook on Low for at least 3 hours until quite warm. Discard spice bag. Makes 2.5 L (10 cups).

VARIATION: Wine or gin may be added if desired. Use about 500 mL (2 cups) wine or about 375 mL (1 1/2 cups) gin.

250 mL (1 cup): 787 Kilojoules (188 Calories); 0.2 g Total Fat; 9 mg Sodium; 1 g Protein; 47 g Carbohydrate

Ginger Citrus Tonic

This works wonders on a cold. Mint tea also works well in place of Rooibos. Remove the solids, and keep a batch hot on Low for up to 12 hours.

Lemon slices (6 mm, 1/4 inch, thick)	1 cup	250 mL
Orange slices (6 mm, 1/4 inch, thick)	1 cup	250 mL
Liquid honey	1/3 cup	75 mL
Sliced ginger root (6 mm, 1/4 inch, thick)	1/4 cup	60 mL
Vanilla rooibos teabags	4	4

1. Combine all 5 ingredients in 3.5 to 4 L (3 1/2 to 4 quart) slow cooker. Add 2 L (8 cups) of water. Cook, covered, on Low for 5 to 6 hours or on High for 2 1/2 to 3 hours. Remove and discard solids with slotted spoon. Makes about 2 L (8 cups).

250 mL (1 cup): 188 Kilojoules (45 Calories); 0 g Total Fat; 0 mg Sodium; 0 g Protein; 11 g Carbohydrate

Apple Punch

Cinnamon-apple flavour makes a great cold-day sipper.

Apple juice	4 1/3 cups	1 L
Brown sugar	1 tbsp	15 mL
Lemon juice	1/2 tsp	2 mL
Cinnamon stick (5 cm, 2 inches, in length), broken up and crushed in plastic bag	1	1
Whole cloves	15	15
Orange pekoe tea bag (or 15 mL, 1 tbsp, loose tea)	1	1

1. Combine apple juice, brown sugar and lemon juice in 3.5 L (3 1/2 quart) slow cooker. Stir.

2. Tie cinnamon, cloves and tea bag in double layer of cheesecloth. Add to slow cooker. Cover. Heat on Low for at least 3 hours until quite warm. Discard spice bag. Makes 1 L (4 cups).

250 mL (1 cup): 628 Kilojoules (150 Calories); 0.3 g Total Fat; 17 mg Sodium; trace Protein; 38 g Carbohydrate

Peppermint Hot Chocolate

Creamy chocolate and peppermint make a deliciously sweet pair!

Milk	6 cups	1.5 L
Chocolate-covered peppermint patties, chopped	2 cups	500 mL
Chocolate milk	2 cups	500 mL
Whipped cream (or whipped topping)	1 cup	250 mL
Finely crushed candy cane	2 tbsp	30 mL

1. Combine first 3 ingredients in 3.5 to 4 L (3 1/2 to 4 quart) slow cooker. Cook, covered, on Low for 4 to 5 hours or on High for 2 to 2 1/2 hours. Stir. Makes about 2 L (8 cups).

2. Pour into 8 mugs. Spoon whipped cream over top. Sprinkle with crushed candy cane. Serves 8.

1 serving: 1984 Kilojoules (474 Calories); 18.3 g Total Fat; 197 mg Sodium; 11 g Protein; 68 g Carbohydrate

Mocha Hot Spot

Triple the flavour with coffee, chocolate and liqueur.

Prepared coffee, warm or cold	8 cups	2 L
Sweetened chocolate drink powder	1/2 cup	125 mL
Powdered coffee whitener	1/4 cup	60 mL
Kahlua (or Tia Maria) liqueur	1/2 cup	125 mL
Whipped cream (optional)		
Grated chocolate, sprinkle (optional)		

1. Combine first 4 ingredients in 3.5 L (3 1/2 quart) slow cooker. Stir. Cover. Cook on Low for at least 3 hours until hot.

2. Pour into mugs. Top with a dollop of whipped cream. Sprinkle with chocolate. Makes 2.1 L (8 1/2 cups).

250 mL (1 cup): 461 Kilojoules (110 Calories); 1.4 g Total Fat; 33 mg Sodium; 1 g Protein; 17 g Carbohydrate

Glögg

To make this Swedish-style drink more authentic, add a
few raisins and whole almonds to each mug

Cardamom seeds, crushed in plastic bag	20	20
Whole cloves	25	25
Cinnamon sticks (10 cm, 4 inches, each in length), broken up and crushed in plastic bag	4	4
Red wine (or alcohol-free wine)	6 cups	1.5 L
Orange juice	1 cup	250 mL
Lemon juice	1/4 cup	60 mL
White (granulated) sugar	1/2 cup	125 mL

1. Tie cardamom, cloves and cinnamon in double layer of cheesecloth. Add to 3.5 L (3 1/2 quart) slow cooker.

2. Add remaining 4 ingredients. Stir. Cover. Cook on Low for at least 3 hours until quite warm. Discard spice bag. Makes 1.8 L (7 1/3 cups).

250 mL (1 cup): 921 Kilojoules (220 Calories); trace Total Fat; 11 mg Sodium; 1 g Protein; 22 g Carbohydrate

Chocolate Peanut Delight

This hot-chocolatey drink is topped with whipped cream and peanuts, for all
the chocolate-with-peanut-butter lovers out there – kids will love it too!

Chocolate milk powder	1 cup	250 mL
Smooth peanut butter	1/2 cup	125 mL
Milk	8 cups	2 L
Whipped cream (or whipped topping)	1 cup	250 mL
Finely chopped unsalted peanuts	2 tsp	10 mL

1. Stir first 3 ingredients in 3.5 to 4 L (3 1/2 to 4 quart) slow cooker until milk powder is dissolved. Cook, covered, on Low for 4 to 5 hours or on High for 2 to 2 1/2 hours until heated through and peanut butter is melted. Whisk until combined. Makes about 2.4 L (9 1/2 cups).

2. Pour into 8 mugs. Spoon whipped cream over top. Sprinkle with peanuts. Serves 8.

Pictured between pages 160 & 161.

1 serving: 1746 Kilojoules (417 Calories); 22.8 g Total Fat; 289 mg Sodium; 16 g Protein; 41 g Carbohydrate

Mulled Wine

A very convenient potful, ready for company.

Dry red (or alcohol-free) wine	8 cups	2 L	Medium orange, sliced	1	1
Glucose (corn) syrup	2/3 cup	150 mL	Lemon juice	1 tsp	5 mL
Cinnamon sticks (10 cm, 4 inches, each in length), broken up and crushed in plastic bag	3	3	Orange juice (or cranberry juice)	2 cups	500 mL
Whole allspice	1 tsp	5 mL			
Whole cloves	1 tsp	5 mL			

1. Combine wine and syrup in 3.5 L (3 1/2 quart) slow cooker. Stir.

2. Tie cinnamon, allspice and cloves in double layer of cheesecloth. Add to slow cooker.

3. Add remaining 3 ingredients. Cover. Cook on Low for at least 3 hours. Discard spice bag. Discard orange slices if desired. Makes 2.25 L (9 cups).

250 mL (1 cup): 1118 Kilojoules (267 Calories); 0.1 g Total Fat; 29 mg Sodium; 1 g Protein; 31 g Carbohydrate

Vanilla Chai Temptation

A smooth and creamy treat. Turn your slow cooker to the Low or Warm setting to maintain serving temperature.

Chai tea bags	10	10
Vanilla bean	1	1
Whole green cardamom, bruised (see Tip, right)	12	12
Canned evaporated milk	3 cups	750 mL
Honey	1/4 cup	60 mL

1. Pour 6 cups (1.5 L) of water into 3.5 to 4 L (3 1/2 to 4 quart) slow cooker. Put first 3 ingredients onto 25 cm (12 inch) square piece of cheesecloth. Draw up corners and tie with butcher's string. Submerge in water. Cook, covered, on Low for 4 to 5 hours or on High for 2 to 2 1/2 hours. Remove and discard cheesecloth bag.

2. Add evaporated milk and honey. Stir. Cook, covered, on High for 30 minutes until heated through. Makes about 2.25 L (9 cups).

TIP: To bruise cardamom, pound pods with mallet or press with flat side of wide knife to 'bruise', or crack them open slightly.

250 mL (1 cup): 574 Kilojoules (137 Calories); 5.3 g Total Fat; 80 mg Sodium; 5 g Protein; 16 g Carbohydrate

General Slow Cooking Tips

Each recipe in this book offers directions for preparing a specific dish. However, here are some general tips to keep in mind when using a slow cooker:

- Fill slow cooker at least half full with food so the heat will be distributed more evenly.

- Layer food so root vegetables (such as carrots, swedes/yellow turnips, potatoes) are on bottom, followed by meat, seasoning, then non-root vegetables (such as peas, corn, mushrooms). This keeps food moist and ensures more even cooking.

- With a lower cooking temperature, liquids don't evaporate as much so vegetables and meat are less likely to dry out. You may have to add more herbs or spices because the flavour will be diluted, or you may reduce amount of liquid used. When following the recipes in this book, these adjustments have been made for cooking on Low.

- Use dried herbs or spices during longer cooking times and add fresh herbs or spices when cooking is almost complete.

- Dairy products should be added close to end of cooking time as they can separate and look curdled when cooked for too long.

- If you miss the scheduled end of your cooking time on Low, an extra hour or so won't hurt. Be careful of extra time when cooking on High or when cooking pasta, as pasta has a tendency to become overcooked. We prefer to cook pasta separately so it maintains its shape and flavour.

- To prevent white meat from drying out, keep skin on to lock in moisture then remove before serving. Darker meat, such as thighs and legs, cooks slower than white meat so it may help to keep near bottom of slow cooker.

- As an economical alternative for those recipes calling for boneless, skinless chicken, substitute same number of bone-in, skinless chicken pieces. After slow cooking, the meat may be falling off the bones so be careful when serving, as small bones may not be visible in the sauce.

- Meat should be well trimmed of fat before adding to slow cooker to reduce fat.

- Pre-browning meat is recommended. It adds flavour and colour to the dish. But if time won't allow, meat (except mince/ground meat) can be added without pre-browning.

- Make slow cooker meals delectable by sprinkling chopped fresh herbs, tomato, spring (green) onion, grated cheese or crumbs on top before serving.

Nutrition Information Guidelines

Each recipe is analysed using the most current version of the Canadian Nutrient File from Health Canada, which is based on the United States Department of Agriculture (USDA) Nutrient Database.

- If more than one ingredient is listed (such as 'butter or hard margarine'), or if a range is given (1–2 tsp, 5–10 mL), only the first ingredient or first amount is analysed.

- For meat, poultry and fish, the serving size per person is based on the recommended 113 g (4 oz) uncooked weight (without bone), which is 57–85 g (2–3 oz) cooked weight (without bone) – approximately the size of a deck of playing cards.

- Milk used is 1% M.F. (milk fat), unless otherwise stated.

- Cooking oil used is canola oil, unless otherwise stated.

- Ingredients indicating 'sprinkle', 'optional', or 'for garnish' are not included in the nutrition information.

- The fat in recipes and combination foods can vary greatly depending on the sources and types of fats used in each specific ingredient. For these reasons, the amount of saturated, monounsaturated and polyunsaturated fats may not add up to the total fat content.

Vera C. Mazurak, Ph.D.
Nutritionist

Handy Hints

BEVERAGES: Slow cookers make an excellent warmer for any hot drink. As a general rule, always heat beverages on Low. When ready, simply leave your slow cooker on, ready to serve hot drinks to your guests.

BREADS & CAKES: Slow cookers will successfully cook yeast breads and scratch cakes, but you should expect slightly different results in appearance. For instance, they may or may not dome slightly in the centre. Also, because moisture is retained in a slow cooker, both breads and cakes will appear more porous with larger air holes and a slightly coarser texture.

If you would like to warm dinner rolls in your slow cooker, wrap them securely first in foil. Cover and heat on Low for 2 to 3 hours, or on High for 1 to 1 1/2 hours.

DESSERTS: As a general rule of thumb, most desserts (such as puddings and cakes) are cooked on High. Also, because some dessert recipes call for a pan or dish to be set inside the slow cooker, make sure everything fits before you begin.

MEATS: Less tender cuts of meat work well in a slow cooker. Increased moisture and longer cooking times break down tougher cuts, producing a more tender result. There is also less shrinkage of meat because of the low heat and long cooking duration. A meat thermometer, especially an instant one, is a big help in determining if the meat is ready – but avoid checking it too often, and do it as quickly as you can to prevent loss of heat and moisture. Meat should be defrosted before cooking; however, for safety reasons we do not recommend that you use your slow cooker to defrost.

PREPARATION: As a convenience to avoiding rushed mornings, most ingredients can be prepared, measured and put into a slow cooker the night before. Note that rice and pasta are an exception to this, and should only be added just before cooking begins. If meat, milk or eggs are included in the recipe, be sure to place your assembled ingredients in the refrigerator overnight.

RICE: The best form of rice to use in a slow cooker is converted (or parboiled) rice, because it is less likely to become too sticky or mushy.

SETTINGS: Most slow cookers use only two settings – Low and High. It is virtually impossible to overcook foods on Low, but overcooking may become a problem on High. For best results, you should develop a 'feel' for your slow cooker by keeping track of cooking times that produce the results you want. When cooking on Low, try to avoid removing the lid too often since it takes a long time to build up lost heat and moisture.

SIZES: Regular slow cookers range in size from 3.5 litres (3 1/2 quarts) to 6 litres (6 quarts), and may or may not have a removable liner. In addition, you may find smaller sizes on the market, about 0.5 L (0.5 quart). These are primarily used for making dips and sauces, and are an ideal size for serving chocolate or cheese fondue.

TIMING: The cooking time of a recipe will depend on the type of food, the starting temperature of the food and the size, or various sizes, the food is cut into.

VEGETABLES: Because fresh, raw vegetables take longer to cook than meats, they should be thinly sliced or cut into small pieces and then placed on the bottom of the slow cooker. Frozen or canned vegetables may be added to the top if desired.

Measurement Tables

Throughout this book measurements are given in imperial and metric measure. To compensate for differences between the two measurements due to rounding, a full metric measure is not always used. The cup used is the standard 8 fluid ounce. Temperature is given in degrees Fahrenheit and Celsius. Baking pan measurements are in inches and centimetres as well as quarts and litres. An exact metric conversion is given below as well as the working equivalent (Metric Standard Measure).

Spoons

Imperial Measure	Metric Exact Conversion Millilitre (mL)	Metric Standard Measure Millilitre (mL)
1/8 teaspoon (tsp)	0.6 mL	0.5 mL
1/4 teaspoon (tsp)	1.2 mL	1 mL
1/2 teaspoon (tsp)	2.4 mL	2 mL
1 teaspoon (tsp)	4.7 mL	5 mL
2 teaspoons (tsp)	9.4 mL	10 mL
1 tablespoon (tbsp)	14.2 mL	15 mL

Oven Temperatures

Fahrenheit (°F)	Celsius (°C)
175°	80°
200°	95°
225°	110°
250°	120°
275°	140°
300°	150°
325°	160°
350°	175°
375°	190°
400°	205°
425°	220°
450°	230°
475°	240°
500°	260°

Cups

Imperial Measure	Metric Exact Conversion Millilitre (mL)	Metric Standard Measure Millilitre (mL)
1/4 cup (4 tbsp)	56.8 mL	60 mL
1/3 cup (5 1/3 tbsp)	75.6 mL	75 mL
1/2 cup (8 tbsp)	113.7 mL	125 mL
2/3 cup (10 2/3 tbsp)	151.2 mL	150 mL
3/4 cup (12 tbsp)	170.5 mL	175 mL
1 cup (16 tbsp)	227.3 mL	250 mL
4 1/2 cups	1022.9 mL	1000 mL (1 L)

Pans

Imperial Inches	Metric Centimetres
8 x 8 inch	20 x 20 cm
9 x 9 inch	22 x 22 cm
9 x 13 inch	22 x 33 cm
10 x 15 inch	25 x 38 cm
11 x 17 inch	28 x 43 cm
8 x 2 inch round	20 x 5 cm
9 x 2 inch round	22 x 5 cm
10 x 4 1/2 inch tube	25 x 11 cm
8 x 4 x 3 inch loaf	20 x 10 x 7.5 cm
9 x 5 x 3 inch loaf	22 x 12.5 x 7.5 cm

Dry Measurements

Imperial Measure Ounces (oz)	Metric Exact Conversion Grams (g)	Metric Standard Measure Grams (g)
1 oz	28.3 g	28 g
2 oz	56.7 g	57 g
3 oz	85.0 g	85 g
4 oz	113.4 g	125 g
5 oz	141.7 g	140 g
6 oz	170.1 g	170 g
7 oz	198.4 g	200 g
8 oz	226.8 g	250 g
16 oz	453.6 g	500 g
32 oz	907.2 g	1000 g (1 kg)

index

Front Cover

 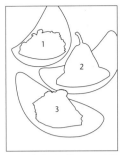 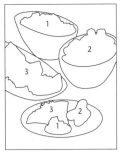 

1. Tomato Chickpea Pasta, page 72
2. Bacon Chicken Pasta, page 71
3. Meatballs In Sauce, page 77

Props courtesy of: Cherison Enterprises Inc.
Danesco Inc.
Out of the Fire Studio

1. Danish Rice Pudding, page 161
2. Maple Orange Pears, page 162
3. Chocolate Hazelnut Cheesecake, page 163

1. Red-Peppered Chorizo, page 23
2. Smokin' Smokies, page 27
3. Pork and Guacamole Tostadas, page 26

Corned Beef Dinner, page 153

Props courtesy of: Cherison Enterprises Inc.
Danesco Inc.

Back Cover

  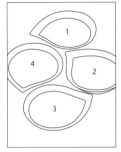

1. Mulled Blackcurrant Sipper, page 179
2. Warm and Fuzzy Navel, page 179
3. Hot Fruit Punch, page 180

1. Mild Turkey Chilli, page 138
2. Chilli Chicken, page 130
3. Chilli Black Beans, page 102

Props courtesy of: Cherison Enterprises Inc

1. Ruby Beetroot Soup, page 39
2. Orange Sweet Potato Soup, page 48
3. Easy Tomato Soup, page 53
4. Butternut Cream Soup, page 33

1. Café au Lait Custard, page 164
2. French Lamb Casserole, page 144

We gratefully acknowledge the following suppliers for their generous support of our Test and Photography Kitchens:

Broil King Barbecues
Corelle®

Hamilton Beach® Canada
Lagostina®

Proctor Silex® Canada
Tupperware®

5-Ingredient Slow Cooker Recipes, Slow Cooker Dinners and Slow Cooker Recipes

Copyright © Company's Coming Publishing Limited

All rights reserved worldwide. No part of this book may be reproduced, stored in a retrieval system or transmitted in any form by any means without written permission in advance from the publisher.

Everyday Slow Cooking

Published by Hinkler Books Pty Ltd
45–55 Fairchild Street
Heatherton Victoria 3202 Australia
www.hinklerbooks.com

Cover design: Imagine Graphic Design
Internal design: Mandi Cole
Prepress: Graphic Print Group
Typesetting: Midland Typesetters Australia

All rights reserved. No part of this publication may be reproduced, stored in a retrieval system, or transmitted in any way or by any means, electronic, mechanical, photocopying, recording or otherwise, without the prior written permission of Hinkler Books Pty Ltd.

ISBN: 978 1 7418 5403 9

Printed and bound in China

Originally published as 5-Ingredient Slow Cooker Recipes, Slow Cooker Dinners and Slow Cooker Recipes by
Company's Coming Publishing Limited
2311–96 Street
Edmonton, Alberta, Canada T6N 1G3
Tel: 780-450-6223   Fax: 780-450-1857
www.companyscoming.com

Company's Coming is a registered trademark owned by Company's Coming Publishing Limited